# THE
# POPE
# OF
# ANTISEMITISM

## The Career and Legacy of Edouard-Adolphe Drumont

## Frederick Busi

UNIVERSITY
PRESS OF
AMERICA

LANHAM • NEW YORK • LONDON

iii

To my father, Albert
and my mother, Josephine

Other books by the author

L'Esthétique d'André Suarès 1969

The Transformations of Godot 1980

vi

This book has been published with the
asistance of the Louis and Minna Epstein
Fund of the American Academy for Jewish
Research.

## Acknowledgements

This present study is not a general history of antisemitism in France. It does consider the scope and significance of the social and historical factors which led to the rise of modern political antisemitism in that land. In order to achieve this goal I have attempted to write a critical study of Edouard Drumont who was known to his contemporaries as "the Pope of Antisemitism" and was mainly responsible for the popularization of this movement in the last two decades of the nineteenth century.

This book had its inception in an essay "The Legacy of Edouard Drumont as an écrivain de combat," which was published in *Nineteenth Century French Studies* in 1976. This piece and other articles on aspects of this subject ultimately led to the formulation of the present book which was initially supported with the help of a grant from the American Philosophical Society and further sustained by various stipends from the Graduate Research Council of the University of Massachusetts, Amherst. My study was aided by sabbatical leaves which made it possible for me to spend parts of 1975 and 1980 conducting research in Paris.

In a book of this kind one is indebted to many colleagues, and I have benefited particularly from the studies on the history of French antisemitism by Robert Byrnes, Nelly Wilson, and Steven Wilson. I am grateful to various individuals and institutions which have assisted me in the preparation of this book. First, I wish to express my gratitude for valuable suggestions to Professors Phyllis Albert Cohen, Salo Baron, Erik Beekman, Bernhard Blumenkranz, Robert Byrnes, Stanley Hoffmann, Michael Marrus, George Mosse, Henri Peyre, Jules Piccus, Pierre Pierrard, Emile Poulat, Pierre Sorlin, Eugen Weber, Roger Williams, Michel Winock, and Robert Wistrich. And I must express my indebtedness to the late Emmanuel Beau de Loménie, Henry Coston, and Jacques Ploncard d'Assac for their intimate knowledge and personal experience regarding fascist and antisemitic movements in France. I am also grateful to Joel Carmichael, Amos Elon, Léon Poliakov, and the late Zosa Szajkowski for various helpful suggestions.

I wish to thank the officers and staffs of the Bibliothèque Nationale, Paris, particularly the former director of its manuscript division, Marcel Thomas, the Bibliothèque Historique de la Ville de Paris and its former director, Patrice Boussel, the Bibliothèque du Centre de Documentation Juive Contemporaine where Sarah Halpérine and Olga Imbert were particularly helpful, the Bibliothèque de l'Arsenal, Paris, where I was assisted by Marie-Odette Bullion-Barthouil, the Bibliothèque de L'Alliance Israélite Universelle, the Wiener Library, London, Houghton and Widener Libraries of Harvard, Sterling Library of Yale, the New York Public Library at 42nd St., the Library of the YIVO Institute for Jewish

Research, New York, and not least I would like to thank the staff at the library of the University of Massachusetts, Amherst, Massachusetts.

Finally, I wish to thank Patrick Gregory for reading, correcting and editing the complete manuscript, and Renée Lajeunesse and my wife Esta, who have had to share me with Edouard Drumont for one decade.

Northampton, Massachusetts                                   Frederick Busi

x

Read again *La France juive* of Drumont; that book of a "high French morality" is a collection of ignoble or obscene stories. Nothing reflects better the complex nature of the anti-Semite.

--Jean-Paul Sartre

*Anti-Semite and Jew*

xiii

## Table of Contents

## Introduction

There are few complete studies devoted to the phenomenon of antisemitism in nineteenth century France. As a movement it has been credited with being a major cause in provoking the Dreyfus affair and on a wider scale it has also been seen as a protest against the advance of secularism as embodied in the Third Republic, as a particular form of Christian socialism, as a counterforce to modernization and as a precursor of fascism in that country. This particular tradition to which so many consequences have been attributed deserves a careful, scholarly investigation. More than one volume would be needed to do this theme justice. The aspect which I have tried to examine here centers on the influence of Edouard Drumont. The book that follows is a critical account of his career and posthumous legacy. It is not a personal but rather an intellectual biography, a narrative history, of the man, the newspaper, and the racist tradition which he exploited so effectively.

I have chosen this path of investigation because Drumont's public life was far more important than his private life. Throughout this study I have consistently tried to avoid what historian W. B. Gallie terms "the self-righteousness of vulgar hindsight." In order to appreciate Drumont's legacy he must be studied in the context of his era. And before the impact of this figure, who is considered to be France's most famous antisemite, can be assessed, a brief survey of the origins of modern antisemitism is first in order in this introduction.

In its most conspicuous manifestation antisemitism initially signified a form of modern hatred of Jews and was chiefly operative in the arena of politics. Before the Franco-Prussian war of 1870 most antipathy towards Jews in modern Europe had its origins in the traditional *odium theologicum* of the Christian churches. This belief was tenacious enough to be appreciated even in certain political trends estranged from established Christianity. From this classical anti-Judaism there emerged antisemitism which was based on various pseudo-scientific currents common to contemporary thought. Chapters two and three of this study are devoted to Drumont's experiences during this period of ideological transition.

Traditional religious anti-Judaism and modern antisemitism could often coexist although among advocates of the latter a certain secular spirit and independence from Christianity could also be discernible. While antisemitism was often thought to be found on the Right, traces of anti-Jewish sentiment were not known in various progressive quarters. As Professor Robert Byrnes observes: "Most antisemitism in France before 1880 or 1885 came from the Left and not the Right.' [1] One decade later the Dreyfus affair came to stand as the watershed for the divergence of these political tendencies with regard to what was then termed the Jewish question. After the sensational trials and events which convulsed France from 1894 to 1899 anti-Jewish hostility seemed to become the exclusive purview of the political Right. Drumont's influence was a major factor in realizing this transformation.

The importance of France in the development of antisemitism is especially significant. In general it could be stated that the growth of modern political conservatism in Europe was a reaction to the liberal and radical ideals promulgated by the French revolution. When the Napoleonic sphere of influence was destroyed, reactionary, traditionalist forms of government attempted to reassert themselves. The emancipation of the Jews had been spread by Napoleon's armies and was among the various progressive measures which were repealed in many of those lands opposed to French hegemony.

With this view of emancipation and reaction in mind the growth of anti-Jewish measures becomes comprehensible in the political evolution of nineteenth century Europe. What is not so easily understandable is the development of this same hostility in France itself. Students of this period have not been surprised through hindsight by antisemitic manifestations in Germany, Austria, Russia, Romania and in other lands unsympathetic to those ideals embodied by the French revolution, lands which had a past of violent anti-Jewish hostility and relatively sizeable Jewish populations. But how does one account for the rise of this same movement in France itself?

By the middle of the nineteenth century the number of Jews in western Europe was quite low. In France they accounted for roughly one fourth of one percent of the total population. During the Middle Ages Jews had been expelled from the kingdom of France. Their later presence in the country was largely due to French conquests of peripheral areas that contained Jewish settlements. At the time of the Revolution and after some struggle they were formally accorded equal civil rights in 1791. Once freed from medieval constraints, many though by no means the majority of these Jews began to participate in the expansion of the middle class. Their rapid assimilation into various strata of the middle classes and national life was resented by various factions all along the political spectrum. [2] To certain socialists Jews represented the essence of capitalism and to many conservatives their civic equality was construed as a threat to the traditional Christian order of things. It was Drumont's genius to be able to fuse these two sources of hostility.

It would be misleading to attribute exclusively the rise of antisemitism in France to mere imitation of a foreign ideology. Antisemitism as a modern social phenomenon and ideology did first arise in Germany after the war of 1870 and was rapidly welcomed in Russia, and it is also undeniable that certain conservative circles in France were in part inspired by these political developments. Like other countries in Europe, France had elements which long harbored grievances against Jews and the principles of its own revolutionary traditions. Compared with most European countries, however, France under the early Third Republic was thought to be by many a model for progressive social policy. And yet antisemitism gained a foothold there as well.

In spite of the difference between France and these European countries what they had in common was a shared Christian perception of Jews during a period of rapidly changing social, political, and intellectual conditions. The importance of French antisemitism goes beyond the subject of the internal politics of the Third Republic. While the anti-Jewish movement made extensive use of traditional anti-Judaic theological arguments, it also relied upon contemporary ideologies to bolster its program for activism. As an organized social force it was resolutely modern. It could at times hark back to the past for inspiration, but more importantly it cast an eye toward the future as well in order to implement its political goals. For this reason the main body of early French antisemites in the period of the Dreyfus affair could at time refer to themselves as "national socialists." They were nationalists through their belief in France's special destiny and they were socialists of a sort in their radical will to change the foundations of their society by destroying the enemy and confiscating its property.

The individual whose name will always be associated with French antisemitism is Edouard-Adolphe Drumont. There were precursors such as Toussenel and Gougenot des Mousseaux and there were various figures at both ends of the political spectrum like Proudhon and de Maistre who occasionally had recourse to anti-Judaism as part of their respective ideologies. On the Jewish question it is Drumont who is chiefly remembered for his success as an *écrivain de combat,* the French equivalent of a committed muckraker, for his journalistic talents and energy in propagating the anti-Jewish world view in his native land. Before Drumont it is fair to state that the majority of Frenchmen probably harbored only the vaguest animosity, if any at all, toward the tiny Jewish minority living among them. After Drumont and the Dreyfus affair it could be observed that in many quarters the vague uneasiness had increased and in some cases given way to a deeper enmity. It should be stated in all fairness that even regarding the latter most Frenchmen probably did not share the virulent hatred promulgated by Drumont and his followers. But Drumont's importance resides in the fact that he had created a change of consciousness in the minds of many of his countrymen, one that would outlive him and have a disastrous effect on the fate of Jews in France.

Drumont did not invent antisemitism in France. What he did was to exploit it on a mass scale. What forms the heart of this book is the study of Drumont's ability to create a small core of antisemitic militants and to arouse varying degrees of anti-Jewish sentiment among large numbers of Frenchmen.

During his long career Drumont was denounced by some as a lackey of clerical factions, a harbinger of intolerance, a talented though unscrupulous purveyor of hatred and racism. To many others he was a stout patriot, devout Catholic, Christian socialist, a paladin in the struggle against those liberal forces which were believed to be corrosive to traditional social and religious values, and an intellectual analyst of contemporary society. To his enemies he was known as "the pope of antisemitism." By all sides he was hailed as something of a major force in the newspaper world for his ability to express brilliantly his social views.

Drumont was an intensely private man and has left behind little record of his personal life. He cherished his reclusiveness as a means to devote all his energies to his books and journalism. Although he was elected to the Chamber of Deputies as the leader of the antisemitic block, he was temperamentally unsuited to parliamentary procedures and felt himself uncomfortable in the Chamber. This aspect of his career is scarcely reflected in his memoirs. Drumont preferred direct action, even if it led to violence, and he mainly saw himself as a tribune appealing to the people over the heads of their elected representatives. He also demonstrated a difficult character to his colleagues and followers. Vilification and vitriol were his hallmarks. To his friends and enemies he was a flamboyant, fanatical advocate of racist politics.

Stated in the most summary form, Drumont was a highly complex, energetic personality who exerted considerable influence over his and succeeding generations in France. He lived at a time when France after the traumatic defeat of 1870 was struggling to adjust itself to its relatively diminished status in European and international affairs. This study will examine the rise of Drumont's popularity as an outgrowth of the status deprivation suffered by France in general and by the Catholic church in particular in that land. Many sensitive Frenchmen held differing views on the nature and cause of what they perceived to be a decline in national prestige and purpose. For Drumont the answer was the Jews and the solution was antisemitism.

Antisemitism in France can be examined and comprehended through an understanding of the ideas an career of Edouard Drumont. He was its principal and most eloquent advocate and was responsible in his time for popularizing this doctrine on a wide scale. His most famous book, *La France juive,* published in 1886, he came the largest bestseller in the France of that period and ultimately surpassed 200 editions. His newspaper, *La Libre Parole,* founded in 1892, became one of France's leading and best written journals. It achieved extensive authority and credibility during the Panama scandals and many historians credit it with being responsible for helping to create the climate of public opinion which ultimately led to the Dreyfus affair.[3] Although the Panama and Dreyfus affairs have often been studied. no extensive attention has been paid to

Drumont's important roles in these events. These major scandals were important in the development of modern antisemitism because, in the words of Hannah Arendt, they were a "kind of dress rehearsal for the performance of our own time." [4]

Drumont was the first anti-Jewish agitator in France to attract a wide following and sympathy. His influence over figures as diverse as Barrès, Bernanos, Céline, Herzl, and Proust was profound. Drumont and his followers early called themselves national socialists with all the connotations which the term was later to acquire in Germany. Although he died in 1917, his journal on a vastly reduced scale continued to appear until 1939 when it was suppressed on the eve of the Second World War. Some of his disciples were active in the rise of fascism in France and during the collaboration period under the German occupation. After that conflict some of his direct successors went on to become prominent spokesmen for political causes on the extreme Right. The durability of this ideological lineage bears testimony to the influence which Drumont was able to exert on his and successive generations.

Few studies on the herald of French antisemitism have until now been published. Almost all of the works devoted to his career have been written by biased supporters or detractors. Israel Schapira published in 1927 a brief, informative monograph mainly dealing with those influences which largely determined his intellectual formation. William C. McCully composed a doctoral dissertation in 1973 which examined almost exclusively Drumont's role during the Dreyfus affair.[5] The present study attempts to investigate all the pertinent factors involved in his controversial and significant career, his successes and failures, which left their imprint on the consciousness of France.

This study is divided into two major parts. With an eye to the last three decades of the nineteenth century the first section presents a detailed examination of Drumont's career through the Panama and Dreyfus scandals. Because Drumont scored his greatest triumphs while he was a newspaper man, a careful consideration of his role in the history of Parisian journalism is pertinent to understand the social and professional world that shaped Drumont. The second section briefly examines Drumont's decline and concentrates on his posthumous influence. These concluding chapters follow Drumont's legacy, particularly among those of his successors who were active in the rise of French fascism in the 1920s and 1930s, collaborationism during the occupation years, and antisemitic activities in both postwar periods.

Interpretations of the origins of antisemitism are controversial because conditions affecting Jews and Gentiles were not the same throughout the western world. The most widespread explanation of antisemitism is commonly known as the scapegoat theory. Hannah Arendt specifically rejects this particular interpretation. Instead she prefers to explain its origins by the status of Jews as pariahs in Western society. This view does not necessarily exclude the scapegoat theory. Indeed it may constitute one of its variants. I would like to suggest that modern antisemitism also can be traced to the perception of the Jews as traitors. In Christian mythology and theology this view is millenial and central, and in an age of rampant nationalisms treason became the supreme crime against the nation-state. In this view the Jews came to be regarded as the archetypal betrayer of both God and country.

These negative images of Jews would not by themselves have been able to produce the particularly virulent strain of modern antisemitism if social and cultural conditions had not encouraged them. Displacement of anger onto Jews intensified when segments of society or at times entire countries underwent the traumatic experience of status deprivation. The combination of these two distinct factors provides the impetus and circumstances in which antisemitism arose.

Drumont made a special appeal to the lower middle class. Marx observed that the *petite bourgeoisie* was a highly unstable class. He did not, notice that this class was also growing along with the proletariat. Their collision provides the background for the mighty confrontation between fascism and communism in our century. The lower middle class felt especially threatened by the advance of big capital and later by the strength of Marxism. Drumont claimed they were both controlled by Jews. He managed to combine elements of nationalism and a certain species of socialism, and in doing so he, like his counterparts in Germany and elsewhere, was helping to lay the foundations for the emergence of fascism in the following generation.

Because Drumont's ideology and politics can be considered proto-fascist and in his own words "national socialist" I have chosen to examine his activities in relation to some of the social and cultural developments in modern France. Scholars recognize that the concept of status deprivation is a major factor contributing to the rise of fascism. This study attempts to demonstrate this hypothesis by showing how Drumont's ideology exploited successive political crises in France. Whenever antisemitism appears in France Drumont's influence is always present in one way or another. Antisemitism is a variety of racism. Drumont preached that Jews were a physically alien race bent on destroying France.

I have written this book neither to analyze the entire history of French antisemitism nor to chronicle its extensive role during the rise and fall of the Third Republic.[7] Neither have I written a sociological interpretation of modern French history. In the main what I have written can be termed an intellectual biography. If I have explored some subjects in detail, for example Drumont's early career and posthumous influence, I do not claim to have investigated in depth each and every facet of his personal life

Drumont was reticent about discussing his private life and left little material of autobiographical interest. The public personality is much more important and this aspect has received most of my attention. With the aid of sympathetic archivists and librarians I have concluded that the paucity of archival material must lead me to write an intellectual and not a personal study of Drumont.

Although this book does not strive to be exhaustive, it does attempt to be comprehensive, to examine Drumont's thought, experiences, social and professional contemporaries, and the ways by which they influenced his attempts to understand and change politics and society. A number of informative studies by scholars, for example, Steven Wilson's recent work *Ideology and Experience,* have examined aspects of French antisemitism and touched in passing on Drumont's significance, but their broad scope only emphasizes the call for a more thorough critical and detailed examination of the founder and leader of antisemitism in France. This study is designed to fill that gap. This is therefore a book that covers a long period of time because it has to relate and analyze a long story, one which has not stopped evolving in France over the past century.

8

[1] Robert Byrnes, *Antisemitism in Modern France* (New Brunswick: Rutgers University Press, 1950), vol. I, p. 114.

[2] On these developments see Michael Marrus, *The Politics of Assimilation: A Study of the French Jewish Community at the Time of the Dreyfus Affair* (Oxford: Oxford University Press, 1971).

[3] See my "The Balzacian Imagination in the Dreyfus Affair: Edouard Drumont as a Reader of Balzac," *Nineteenth Century French Studies,* vol. VI, nos. 3 & 4 (Spring-Summer 1978), 174-188.

[4] Hannah Arendt, *The Origins of Totalitarianism* (New York: Meridan Books, 1958), p. 10. See also Hannah Arendt, *The Jew as Pariah* (New York: Grove Press, 1978).

[5] See also Michel Winock, *Edouard Drumont et Cie: antisémitisme et fascisme en France* (Paris: Seuil, 1982).

[6] See Arendt, *The Origins of Totalitarianism*, pp. 5-10.

[7] For a general study of antisemitism in this period, see Leon Poliakov, *L'Histoire de l'antisémitisme: l'Europe suicidaire 1870-1933.* Paris: Calmann-Levy, 1977), vol. 4, and Jacob Katz *From Prejudice to Destruction: Antisemitism, 1700-1933* (Cambridge, Mass. Harvard University Press, 1980) See also Steven Wilson, *Ideology and Experience* (Rutherford, N.J. Fairleigh Dickinson University Press, 1982).

1
# The Priesthood of the Press

*Paris, the workshop of
all progressive, but also of
all retrograde associations.*
*--Heinrich Heine*

Edouard Drumont was born, lived, worked and died in Paris. The city was the center of his life and career. Paris, writes Walter Benjamin, was "the capital of the nineteenth century." [1] Other cities, for example, London and Berlin, eventually surpassed it as centers of greater political, financial and military power, but Paris did not lag too far behind in these fields and it remained the model city for artists and intellectuals, the capital of luxury and fashion of every description. According to Benjamin it was still the city of ideas that dominated the century. Those fortunate enough to be natives of the city were witnesses to some of the more momentous events of the age. This chapter is concerned with the earliest years of Drumont's life, his apprenticeship in the world of journalism, particularly the clerical press, and his activities during the war of 1870 and the Paris Commune. From these experiences Drumont profited immensely and subsequently rededicated himself to the church into which he had been born and shortly thereafter he became an antisemite.

Edouard-Adolphe Drumont was born in Paris on 3 May 1844 and he came to reside with his family at number 10, rue du 29 juillet. He was the son of Adolphe-Amand-Joseph Drumont, born in Lille in 1811 and of Anne-Honorine Buchon. From the beginning till almost the end of his exceptional career Drumont was often accused of being a renegade Jew, of belonging to that caste of converted Jews who were frequently among the more vociferous in denouncing their origins. An examination of his genealogical records, however, reveals that he sprang from a thoroughly Gentile background. [2]

His father was a low-level clerk employed at the Hôtel de Ville in Paris. There he was the office mate of Henri Rochefort, the future "prince of the gutter press," whose career would be an inspiration and source of annoyance to his son. [3] According to his memoirs it would seem that Edouard Drumont was deeply marked by the contrasting political attitudes of his parents. His father was a mildly anticlerical republican and no supporter of the Second Empire whereas his mother quietly supported the claims of the Catholic church. In later life Drumont would attempt to fuse these two traditions of French national and political life. A curious form of Catholic anticlericalism would add to his unique appeal in the arena of French politics.

At the Lycée Charlemagne he pursued his studies with mixed feelings towards the academic life. A certain amount of bookish learning he found appealing although he occasionally experienced difficulty associating with some fellow students. After leaving school because of his father's poor health, Drumont independently pursued his education and his love of books increased.

In 1861 at the age of seventeen Drumont found himself with the responsibility to help provide for the small family. He was well liked enough to be offered a position at his father's place of employment. The period 1861 to 1865 was, according to his memoirs, a dark chapter in his life. At the same time the decade in which he began to work molded and directed him along the path of journalism.

Drumont rapidly tired of his clerk's position. Although he was bookish and solitary by nature, his interrupted formal education prevented him from contemplating a career in the academic life. The only other field that would interest him was journalism. What universities would become for writers in the twentieth century newspapers were to those in the nineteenth, a refuge and source of income to those of modest talent as well as to those of eminent standing.

It was not surprising that Drumont entered the world of journalism when he did. Despite the fact that most journalists earned very little, the press was then in the throes of accelerated expansion. In Paris alone there were five hundred newspapers. Many were products of the *presse champignon,* the ephemeral sheets that sprouted during the course of various crises and scandals. It was Drumont's luck to make the acquaintance of a young neighbor named Alfred d'Aunay who founded a small journal, *Le Moniteur du Bâtiment.* Drumont recalled his first reaction: "I inhaled with delight the smell of printer's ink. I respectfully gazed upon the characters which allowed one's thoughts to be communicated to others."[4] It would not be an exaggeration to state that journalism became and remained his first and last love for the rest of his life.

During this phase of his life Drumont busied himself with odd jobs on the fringes of the press world where he occasionally managed to find a bit of hack work to see him through. In 1865 his first article was printed in *L'Illustration* and was a sentimental evocation of a part of Paris which was in the process of disappearing. The heart of this initial piece dealt with a catastrophe befalling rich Parisians in 1596 who were the victims of a collapsed bridge. Drumont did not express regret over their fate because they "were made rich from usury and pillaging." Even in this first article one could not fail to notice Drumont's inclination toward populist indignation, a trait which he would carefully cultivate throughout the rest of his career.

The various contacts which Drumont made in journalistic circles served him as models in his own professional development. They deserve to be briefly considered in order to appreciate the evolution of his career. The first important figure to take notice of him was a popular Catholic journalist of considerable talent. Drumont recalls: "Meeting Henri Lasserre had a serious influence on my future and opened to me a whole range of ideas of which I was still only vaguely aware.".[5] Lasserre was a successful although controversial Catholic writer who was largely responsible for popularizing the legend of the shrine of Lourdes. He had sworn to convert the young Drumont, who, deeply impressed, "understood better the social role of the church and the inept attacks directed against her. I was already a cerebral Catholic, but from there to be a real Christian was a great distance." It should be remembered that although his father harbored republican sympathies Drumont's mother was partial to the viewpoint of the church. This confession of a budding religious sentiment suggests an inclination toward his mother's outlook. Drumont was attracted to Lasserre for other aspects of journalism.

Lasserre had been so popular with the Catholic masses that Léon Bloy dubbed him "a travelling salesman of piety." On the other hand no less a Catholic spokesman than the novelist Huysmans, disgusted by his vulgarity, branded him a "cacographer."[6] Drumont came to appreciate both these talents. In Lasserre's journal Drumont wrote articles in the clerical vein which attacked those liberals who were branded public enemies of the church. From this newspaper experience Drumont graduated to write occasional pieces for *La Revue du Monde Catholique*, and in a piece dated 10 October 1865 he stoutly defended the philosophy of the celebrated conservative thinker Joseph de Maistre. Drumont's appreciation then for conservative politics antedated his dislike of Jews.

Drumont learned much from Lasserre but the journalist to whom he is often compared was Louis Veuillot. The latter combined Lasserre's popular appeal with his own style of vigorous, vitriolic prose which earned him the title of "the Catholic Voltaire." Veuillot became so influential that he was regarded as the true head of the church in French. Bishops and the government itself paid heed before his enthusiastic support of the papacy in its struggle against republican forces in Italy.[7] Veuillot, in his influential journal, *L'Univers,* occasionally wrote forceful articles denouncing the Jews. Because Drumont is often compared to him and thought to be his successor it is important to recognize the differences between them: Veuillot was a Catholic who happened to be a Judeophobe whereas Drumont was to become an antisemite who happened to be a Catholic.[8]

Under the influence of the Catholic press Drumont published his first anti-Jewish piece in the *Revue du Monde Catholique* in 1867. The occasion was his review of *Le Temple de Jérusalem* by the distinguished archeologist, Charles-Jean Melchior, the Marquis de Vogüé. Neither in this book nor in an earlier work, *Notes sur le temple de Jérusalem* (1863) is there any reference to Jews that could be considered defamatory or denigrating. Drumont in his review, however, commenting on the ancient temple itself, writes: "The sacred edifice saw the treachery of the disobedient people, which the most severe punishments and the warnings of murdered prophets could not convert." It is evident that at this early stage of his career Drumont took advantage of a pretext to vent his own growing anti-Jewish sentiment.

Feeling himself sufficiently prepared in clerical press circles, Drumont tried to curry favor with the formidable Villemessant, editor of *Le Figaro,* through the good graces of Veuillot. In a letter dated 28 March 1867 the latter wrote Villemessant and described Drumont as "rather well read, has a lively mind and an eloquent hand: he also has a very large appetite...he is an odd bird..." In a stroke of prophecy Veuillot suggested that Villemessant make Drumont "serve only wearing a mask until the reasonable age of a man of letters, around forty years of age." [9] In fact this was exactly the strategy Drumont would adopt until the publication of *La France juive* almost two decades later.

Drumont was unable to obtain the position he sought on the staff of Villemessant's prestigious journal. His resentment caused him to become involved in a major press scandal which was in part directed against the editor of *Le Figaro.* The entire affair is too complex to be examined here in detail but insofar as it sheds some light on Drumont's character it deserved some comment.

Somewhere in *Les Illusions Perdues* Balzac observes that "journalism is a hell, a sink of iniquity, of lies and betrayals..." Drumont had chosen this field of endeavor and he began to achieve some modest recognition. Of his work Roger Giron, for example, wrote in *L'Illustration* of 16 April 1868: "He finds his public in the middle class, le petit peuple catholique." But Drumont wished to achieve wider acclaim and he was quite disappointed when his overtures to Villemessant were spurned. Bitterness and a desire for revenge caused him to be implicated in a scheme to tarnish the reputation of the famous editor.

Drumont's role in what became known as the *Inflexible* affair was not immediately recognized. But the notoriety he was to bring upon himself was the result of his decision to become the accomplice of Charles Marchal de Bussy, one of the more unscrupulous and eccentric writers in Paris. Drumont's name was briefly cited as his associate in court records, pamphlets and newspapers.

What led to this scandal in 1868 was the extraordinary and controversial success of Henri Rochefort in his notorious campaign of satire against the government of Napoleon III. In short, Rochefort's editor, Villemessant, had been warned of his subversive activities by the imperial police. To avoid direct involvement, responsibility, and prosecution,

Villemessant allowed Rochefort to establish his own publication, *La Lanterne*, in order to continue his activities. Rochefort's new satirical publication became an instant success.

The entire country, including the police, took notice of Rochefort's sensationalist writings. In reaction it would appear that someone in official circles decided to counter-attack in print by engaging the services of an equally scurrilous writer like Charles Marchal. It is impossible to determine exactly how this campaign was launched because the special coded files on secret government operations were destroyed at the Prefecture of police during the Paris Commune of 1871. But the testimony of contemporaries, court records, and press accounts suggest that the government solicited the services of Charles Marchal de Bussy to denigrate Rochefort's reputation. In this task he engaged the help of Drumont.

Charles Marchal de Bussy was the personification of Ratapoil, the Bonapartist agent immortalized by Daumier. His life was a chronicle of the sordid side of that genre known as *littérature de combat.* [10] It is not impossible to tell exactly when Drumont took notice of his writings. He did recall, however, one book of de Bussy, one of those which "he had written against the Jews, a *Vie de Judas,* in particular which has some very vibrant pages." [11]

In collaboration with a young Polish nobleman, Alexandre de Stamir, de Bussy launched one of those ephemeral rags that abounded in Paris, dubbed it *L'Inflexible*, and began to attack Rochefort in extremely foul terms. Like Drumont, de Bussy had a grudge against Villemessant and his associates. For de Bussy the issue was a clear conflict between good and evil: "I'm an honorable man, you're all scum--I'm loyal, you're all crooks--I'm Catholic, you're pagans!" This was typical of his style.

The press duel might have run its course were it not for the violent impetuosity of Rochefort. He retaliated by going to the shop that printed *L'Inflexible* and assaulted the printer. This was the height of the scandal that shocked Paris. Francisque Sarcey in *Le Gaulois* commented:
"Behold these degenerates who write...I don't know what to call it all. Like dogs they snap at each other right and left." [12] Paris was then treated to the double spectacle of Rochefort and de Bussy attacking one another in the courts. On 31 July Rochefort won his case against de Bussy but on 5 August he was found guilty of assault and battery and he decided to flee the country by accepting Victor Hugo's invitation to share exile in Brussels.

At this point in the scandal Drumont's role became known. As they left the court he and de Bussy were pursued and threatened by a mob of Rochefort's supporters. In self-defense they drew pistols and a sword-cane and were arrested for illegal use of arms. For his recidivism de Bussy spent six days in jail and for his part Drumont was fined 25 francs.

For the first time in his life Drumont received a small measure of public notoriety. Villemessant was pleased by the turn of events. He instructed one of his correspondents, Albert Wolff, to publicize the matter, and in the 13 August 1868 issue of *Le Figaro* he reported that "one of Louis Veuillot's protégés, a Monsieur D"...had been implicated in the *Inflexible* affair. Veuillot vehemently repudiated any alleged encouragement to Drumont. Understandably, Drumont was upset by this publicity and he denounced the Jewish journalist for his revelations. Albert Wolff, because of his foreign birth, was known to his adversaries as "the Prussian hermaphrodite," and because he was Jewish Drumont bore him a long grudge.

As a result of the scandal Drumont became estranged from de Bussy. [13] His former mentor publicly and scurrilously denounced him in a series of newspaper articles. With regard to Drumont's development the question of the *Inflexible* affair was significant for various reasons. It demonstrated the sort of company the young journalist was willing to keep and the depths of his ire which in this case was directed against Rochefort and Villemessant. The affair also put Drumont in an unfavorable light before the public, but he did not seem to suffer very much as a result probably because of the relatively minor role which he played. [14]

Drumont immediately regained his equilibrium and sought a position on the staff of one of Paris' leading journals, *La Liberté*. This newspaper was directed by Emile de Girardin who was known as the "Napoleon of the press." On 6 May 1869 Drumont wrote a flattering article about him in *La Chronique Illustrée* that was calculated to attract his attention. Two things are remarkable in Drumont's decision to seek employment on his staff. The 1869 article stands in vivid contrast to what he had written in 1865 about this influential editor: "Parasites tell him in a chorus that he is the greatest man of modern times..." It is evident that in order to secure a position Drumont put himself in this category in 1869 when he wrote: "Girardin will remain one of the great and original figures of the nineteenth century." The other ironic factor in his choice of employer was the fact that *La Liberté* was owned at that time by the celebrated Jewish family Pereire, and it was at this journal that Drumont was to remain until just before the publication of *La France juive* in 1886. [15]

In his monumental cultural and social history of France Theodore Zeldin perceptibly entitled one of his chapters "Newspapers and Corruption." The venality of the press during this period was legendary and Drumont, through his involvement in the *Inflexible* affair, showed himself inclined in this direction. He learned much from his early years in newspaper circles. The clerical press of Veuillot and Lasserre taught him the virtues of populist appeal and the politics of Catholicism in France. His brief association with de Bussy demonstrated that Drumont was not above collaborating with members of the gutter press. Finally, his initiation to the staff of *La Liberté* taught him the benefits of working on a major influential newspaper.

In 1869 Drumont published his first book. It was not in itself a significant piece of work, but because of the circumstances surrounding its appearance and the fact that its author was Drumont a brief review of its message will illuminate how he handled controversial material. The subject of the book was Richard Wagner. For the most part this short work was not very different from many similar contemporary pieces with emphasis devoted to the flamboyant side of Wagner's career.

The occasion for this particular flood of writing on Wagner was the performance of his opera *Rienzi* scheduled to be produced in Paris that same year. Coincidental with its production was the appearance of a French translation of Wagner's antisemitic diatribe and renewed controversy surrounding the composer's Francophobia also caused a spate of works to be published on his life and work. Wagner hated Paris, the center of European art and culture, and he claimed that it was dominated by Jews. For the German composer "Judaism was the evil conscience of our civilization" and Paris was its capital. [16] Wagner claimed that his anti-Jewish pieces were republished to explain why newspapers in France were supposedly hostile to his work. He asserted that the press was controlled by Jews and that anything unflattering written about his return to Paris would be caused by their intrigues.

Drumont's book on Wagner is marked by a certain ambivalence. He is not so much concerned with music as with anecdotes about Wagner's adventures in Paris. The piece is of the order of hack work one would expect from journalists. [17] While Drumont briefly touched upon the philosophical aspects of the Wagnerian cult, he was also preoccupied with contemporary politics. Most students of Wagner's career attribute his decision to stage *Tannhäuser* in Paris to Princess Metternich of Austria. But Drumont in his little book offered another explanation and attributed this decision to the influence of French Marshal Bernard-Pierre Magnan. In asserting that Magnan's contacts at the French imperial court were responsible for Wagner's entry to Paris Drumont seemed to suggest that foreign influence through Magnan was operative at the highest level of decision making in France. [18]

Scholars familiar with this episode do not corroborate this version reported by Drumont. Why, then, would he attack Marshal Magnan? This venerable was hero had been appointed in 1862 by the emperor to be the grand master of the leading French masonic order, the *Grand Orient*. As the leader of French freemasonry this controversial high official was considered by many to be an enemy of the Catholic church. [19] In his later books Freemasons stood second to Jews as Drumont's favorite bugbears. The inclusion of Magnan's name in this first book of Drumont implies that the author's designs were in part political and not exclusively musicological. He had some reason to be concerned over foreign influence at this date because war with Germany was not far off. The outcome of this war was to have a determining impact on Drumont's way of viewing the world and politics.

Drumont was to owe in part his extraordinary success to the politics of revanchism which developed in France after the war of 1870. What made Drumont one of the precursors of fascist ideology in France was his ability to exploit his nation's sense of status deprivation in the wake of military defeat. Scholars agree that perceived status loss plays a major role in the development of rightist ideology during times of upheaval. [20] The Franco-Prussian war in 1870 and the Paris commune in 1871 had a deep effect on his social ideas and as such his reaction to them deserves to be examined in the last part of this chapter.

Not only did Drumont contemplate the consequences of the war and the Commune he also personally experienced them during his stay in the capital. His journalistic articles of the period provide valuable insight into his early thoughts on the nature of society in a state of acute crisis. By the end of August 1870 it had become apparent that France was losing the war it had sought with Germany. A review of the press of this period reveals that immediate explanations were demanded to account for the reverses incurred on the field of battle. Because France had expected confident victory a natural response was instead to blame shortcomings on the domestic scene of which the most heinous was treason and then its stepchild, espionage. At the height of his career Drumont liked to boast that all his articles, when laid end to end, would stretch for fifty kilometers. Of all these writings the one which appeared in the 16 August 1870 issue of *La Liberté* would remain the most pregnant indication of his character, his perception, and the direction of his thoughts.

In that piece Drumont observed: "Yesterday they arrested at the Porte de Pantin an individual suspected of spying (only suspected, but that's enough at this time). Arrested by some residents. It should be noted that the police took no part in the arrest." Here in 1870 Drumont crystallized the very reflex in all its ramifications that would one quarter century later lead directly to the Dreyfus affair. As in the case of Captain Dreyfus the figure mentioned in 1870 was merely suspected of the crime, but in Drumont's estimation that was proof enough. More revealing, as Drumont put it, was the fact that the official representatives of the government were incapable or unwilling to make the discovery: only the people were up to the patriotic task of vigilance on this occasion. When he finally acquired his own journal in 1892 the image he chiefly cultivated was that of the honest, indignant tribune who looked out for the public's welfare and chided the government for its alleged lack of concern.

By the end of 1870 Drumont expressed other causes for alarm. After the armistice terms were announced publicly political factions within

Paris rapidly polarized. Throughout the war and siege he had worked on the staff of *La Liberté*. Continuous political upheavals spawned an unprecedented number of fresh newspapers. [21] One of the new sheets *Le Bien Public*, was established by his fellow journalist, Charles Vrignault. Its general editorial policy reflected the opinion of the liberal bourgeoisie. It also became one of the more outspoken voices opposed to the Commune. [22] Drumont's association with this journal was especially significant for it was here that he first met Alphonse Daudet, who one decade later helped catapult him to fame.

Journals which were opposed to the establishment of the Commune in March 1871 accused the radical government of ruining France's ability to conclude an honorable peace treaty. From this perspective the radicals were charged with serving, however unwittingly, the imperialist designs of Germany. In later years Drumont took pride in the knowledge that he had remained in opposition in the capital during the brief life of the leftist regime. "I fought the Commune, not in Versailles, like so many others, but in Paris; I attacked it violently in the articles which I published, when it was mistress of the city." [23]

Like many journalists in Paris Drumont fulminated against the treaty conditions. He was also indignant at the spectacle of the triumphal entry into Paris of the Prussian army. [24] The bulk of his wrath was directed against the conduct of the war within the capital. He had become in effect a prisoner within the city for almost five months. Deprived of any real outside information journalists had recourse to turn inward in their search for answers to explain the military defeats. This was Drumont's assessment on 8 March 1871 in *Le Bien Public* of a very tense situation caused by those groups who were accused of causing and profiting from national disgrace and defeat:

> It was a Freemasonry of treachery from the top down to the last rung of the social ladder...What we have to do is to defend ourselves against these Iscariots, who, not happy like Judas, to guide toward their masters, the soldiers of treason, take the sword from their shameful hands and demand their place among the executioners. We don't have to say to these fine folks who've spied on us for so long and still wish to spy on us: Damn you! We have to say to them: Go hang yourselves somewhere else...

This is an important passage in the understanding of Drumont's use of polemical language. While Freemasons would also figure later as high on his list of France's enemies, it is not clear how he intended to use the terms in this article. It is possible that he intended them figuratively. The "Freemasonry of treachery" may or may not have reference to real masonic organizations just as "Iscariots" may or may not refer to Jewish bankers in particular. Considering Drumont's antipathy toward these groups it would not be unreasonable to assume, however, his use of the terms was literal. [25]

After the proclamation of the Paris Commune in March 1871 Vrignault increased attacks in his journal against the radical regime and it was consequently forbidden to be printed. Drumont found his work on that staff interrupted for the duration but his articles resumed after the bloody supression of the Commune in May. Vrignault singled out Marx's International Working Man's Association as responsible for the revolt. Drumont always expressed ambivalence about the nature of the Paris uprising but by 25 July he came to share his editor's viewpoint and he denounced most of those arrested as being "Bohemian good-for-nothings."

A survey of Drumont's early writings on the Commune reveals that his strongest prose was directed against foreign bankers. Here is a sample of Drumont at his sarcastic and vitriolic best on 29 June 1871:

> The expelled bankers have returned: it's all over, the fickle, forgetful people, the people without malice or memories, have quietly allowed spies to reoccupy their place in our land, but when the time comes and we take our revenge, we will have some simple surprises...but to open our arms to the people who have spied on us and betrayed us with such touching unanimity, not to throw out these innocent-looking Judases, that's what goes beyond all bounds.[26]

For eight long months this was the subject that dominated his attention and caused him to reconsider and embellish his recollections of the commune at a later date. During and after the siege and Commune his bitterest words were reserved for spies, real and imaginary. In this view he was not alone. His apprehensions reflected the fears of a generation.[27]

In his own way Drumont came to admire and hate the Paris Commune. He resolved this paradox in 1886 in this manner: "The Commune had two faces: one was irrational, rash, but courageous: the French face. The other was mercantile, greedy, thieving, contemptibly calculating: the Jewish face."[28]Drumont was to blame in particular an officer of Jewish origin, Simon Mayer, for his role in the uprising. But Mayer was no radical socialist; he was a staunch republican, a highly assimilated Jew and had tried to exert a moderating influence over the radical elements in the Commune. Apart from this figure Jews exerted almost no influence on the Commune.[29]

It may seem surprising at first to observe that in his later years Drumont did not attack the Commune as much as one might have expected. At the height of his fame he described himself as a "national socialist" and often praised what he called the "French face" of the revolt. One of his favorite radical participants was Benoît Malon, a fiery socialist who shared anti-Jewish sentiments in the tradition of Toussenel's and Proudhon's radicalism. Drumont maintained this admiration and later wrote: "If...I have not yet already been killed by the Jews, I will certainly have a mass said and I will recite more than one *ave* for the socialist Malon.[30]

In the wake of the war and the Commune there developed another strand of thought that powerfully influenced Drumont's thinking. It was widely considered in many circles that race had been a determining factor in the struggle between France and Germany. *The New York Times* of 16 August 1870 commented that "the Latin races have done their part-- and not always an inglorious one--in the world's history. Now more earnest and moral and free races must guide the helm of progress." [31]

Like many of his countrymen Drumont mourned the decline of France and the rise of Germany. Some were prepared to give credit to the factor of race. The logic of racial determinism was deceptively simple. If a hitherto strong race begins to regress, so goes the argument, it follows that something has entered the national lifestream. After the victory many Germans, flushed with national pride, viewed the French as a genetically degenerate race, and Wagner in particular saw them as so many "semiticized Latins." For Drumont the logic dictated that France would be returned to greatness once the land was purged of the debilitating agent. In a short period of time Drumont would come to identify these elements as Germans and Jews, principally the latter who he accused of being agents of the former. "They introduced themselves into all levels of French life thanks to the disorder which followed the Commune and passed themselves off as Alsace-Lorrainers." [32] After the war large numbers of Jews and Gentiles did flee the newly acquired German provinces and settled frequently in Paris. The spectre of spies within the gates was to remain one of Drumont's favorite battle cries.

What was important for Drumont during this period was the impact of defeat on a demoralized France. The new French government was to become militantly anticlerical and in response the clerical parties and factions reacted with vehement denunciations of liberalism and republicanism. The early years Drumont spent in the clerical press prepared him well to join ultimately the enemies of the republic. In the following decade the Right in France tried to regroup and it struggled mightily to overthrow the new republic. His conversion to Catholicism was the catalyst which allowed him to combine his journalistic experience with a devastating critique of contemporary society. His return to the faith must be reviewed and studied in the context of France's gradual recovery and the changing fortunes of the Jews in Europe in the 1880s. Examining these events in detail will be the task of the next chapter.

Notes

1 See Walter Benjamin, *Charles Baudelaire: A Lyric Poet in the Era of High Capitalism* (London: NLB, 1973).

2 On Drumont's genealogy see Edouard Drumont, *Sur le chemin de la vie* (Paris: Cres, 1914), pp. 107-108. Throughout his career Drumont was periodically accused of being an antisemitic Jew. He recalled a popular poster circulating in Paris and depicting him as a child at his "bar Mitzwa," and receiving the blessing of an old rabbi. Abraham Dreyfus, a celebrated newspaper figure, declared in the journal *Gil Blas*: "He (Drumont) looks like my old Hebrew teacher." For the most bizarre treatment of Drumont's background. see L'Abbé Charles Renaut, *L'Israélite Edouard Drumont et les sociétés secrètes actuellement*, (Paris: chez l'auteur, 1896), pp. 342-382.

3 For a description of Drumont's father, see Henri Rochefort, *The Adventures of My Life*, (London: Arnold, 1896), vol. I, p. 67.

4 In this journal on 29 September 1861 Drumont would have read an article "Le Chemin de Fer du Nord et l'Accident de Ronchin," in which d'Aunay accused the state and the press of covering up the line's malfeasance. This rail line had been started years earlier by Rothschild.

5) Edouard Drumont, *La Dernière bataille,* (Paris: Dentu, 1890), pp. 285-286.

6 Huysmans loathed the vulgarity of Lourdes and blamed much of it on the Jews. "Priests ought to think about how much the Jewish element now dominates among the dealers in pious objects. Converted or not, it really seems that even and above the passion for profit, these merchants experience the conscious need to betray again the Messiah, vending him under appearances inspired by the demon." Joris-Karl Huysmans, *Les Foules de Lourdes* (Paris: Plon, 1958), p. 72, (my translation). For a study of the anti-Jewish criticism concerning the shrine, see Alan Neame, *The Happening at Lourdes* (New York: Simon and Schuster, 1967), p. 155.

7 For comprehensive studies on Veuillot's career, see Lucien Christophe, *Louis Veuillot et les mauvais maîtres de son temps (Paris: Perrin, 1913).*

8) According to Philip Spencer, "Veuillot not only spoke for himself but for a generation of priests, and the echoes of his work went reverberating long after his death, down the distorting caverns of *La Libre Parole* and *L'Action Française*...Veuillot prepared the way for Drumont...Indeed, the Catholic press is still haunted by the figure of its most brilliant and injurious representatives." *Politics of Belief in 19th Century France,* (New York: Grove Press, 1954), p. 217.

[9] Quoted by Villemessant, *Le Diable à Quatre*, 7 Oct. 1868.

[10] See Edouard Drumont, *La France juive devant l'opinion*, (Paris: Marpon and Flammarion, 1886), pp. 187-188. For the most comprehensive treatment of Drumont's association with Charles Marchal de Bussy, see Stéphane Arnoulin, *M. Drumont et les jésuites,* (Paris: Librairie des Deux Mondes, 1902).

[11] See Edouard Drumont, *La France juive*, (Paris: Marpon et Flammarion, 1886), vol. II, p. 223.

[12] Francisque Sarcey, *Le Gaulois,* 14 July 1868 .

[13] Shortly before his death de Bussy viciously denounced Drumont as "that phony, obscene, degraded, vile snake of a writer...that squint-eyed, yellow, knock-kneed, hateful, drunken little clown..."in an article published in *La Tante Duchêne* of 6 Feb. 1870. For Drumont's reaction to this vilification, see *La France juive devant l'opinion*, p. 183.

[14] In his history of the press during the Commune, Firmin Maillard speculated on Drumont's role in the scandal. "Mister Charles Marchal, called de Bussy, had in 1868 as an intimate friend and associate by that name (Drumont) and who even figured in a trial for assault and battery and bearing illegal arms for Mr. Marchal de Bussy, if my memory serves me right, the same Edouard Drumont recommended Mr. Veuillot had gone from *Le Figaro* to Mr. Charles Marchal, then left him and found himself dragged through the mud by his former friend in a filthy rag of a paper called *La Mère Duchêne* (1870). Could he be the same one? *Histoire des journaux publiès à Paris pendant le siege* (Paris: Dentu, 1871), pp. 153-154. (my translation)

[15] *La Revue du Monde Catholique,* 25 Sept. 1865, p.4

[16] See Richard Wagner, *Judaism in Music, Stories and Essays,* selected, edited, and introduced by Charles Osborne, (New York:the Library Press, 1973), pp. 38-39. Leon Stein, *The Racial Thinking of Richard Wagner* (New York: Philosophy Library, 1950), and Léon Poliakov, *Histoire de l'antisémitisme* (Paris: Calmann-Lévy, 1968), vol. III, pp. 440-467.

[17] In order to convince French readers that Wagner's ego was immense Drumont compared his to that of Victor Hugo. One reviewer of Drumont's book, George Servières, felt that the comparison was "a severe judgment." *Richard Wagner jugé en France* (Paris: Librairie Illustrée, 1887), p. 141. See also Leon Guichard, *La Musique et les lettres en France au temps du wagnérisme* (Paris: Presses Universitaires de France, 1963).

[18] Edouard Drumont, *Richard Wagner, l'homme et la musique à propos de Rienzi* (Paris: Dentu, 1869).

[19] Even in death Magnan's name remained anathema in some Catholic circles. The occasion of the Marshal's burial in 1865 caused a scandal when Monsignor Darboy, the archbishop of Paris, blessed his coffin which bore masonic insignia of the grand master and was denounced by Veuillot and many conservative Catholics. See Drumont, *La France* vol. II, p.337.

[20] Concerning the impact of status deprivation on the development of fascist ideology, see Stanley Payne, "Fascism in Western Europe," *Fascism: A Reader's Guide,* ed. Walter Laqueur (Berkeley: Univ. of California Press, (1976), pp. 295-299.

[21] In his diary on the siege of Paris, American ambassador Elihu Washburn observed: "It may well be asked if there was ever before a city besieged which published twenty-three daily newspapers! Some of these papers are ably done, but the amount of trash, taken all together, surpasses anything in History. *"Recollections of a Minister to France* (New York: Scribner's, 1871), vol. I, pp. 399-400. See also Aimé Dupuy, *1870-1871, la guerre, la commune et la presse* (Paris: Colin, 1959).

[22] Concerning *Le Bien Public* and Drumont, see Giuseppe Del Bo, *La commune di Parigi (Milan*: Feltrinelli, 1957), pp.21,40.

[23] Drumont, *La France juive devant l'opinion,* p.63.

[24] See Michael Howard, *The Franco-Prussian War* (New York: Macmillan, 1962), P. 282.

[25] Félix Pyat, an important radical leader of the Commune, wrote in a similar vein in *Le Vengeur* of 28 April 1871: "Show yourselves, you bankers from *Le Siècle* and the ghetto so that we can have a look at your priestly or your Jewish yarmulke."

[26] See Pierre Dominique, "Edouard Drumont et la Commune," *Le Soleil,* no.7, Feb. 1966, p.8.

[27] On the widespread epidemic of "la spionite" Alistair Horne remarks: "In a pathological study of the Siege, one French doctor analyzed the symptoms of 'obsidional fever' as including such phenomena as spymania, mistrust and defiance of authority, the resplendent but hollow verbosity stemming from a need for self-assurance, and fear-created persecution complex, that pointed accusing fingers at the usual variety of 'enemies'--Freemasons, Jews, and Jesuits. With unprecedented fickleness even for France, the newspapers transformed heroes of one day

into traitors of the next." *The Fall of Paris* (New York: St. Martins, 1965), p.231.

[28] Drumont, *La France juive,* vol. I, p.404.

[29] On the role of the Jews during the Commune, see Zosa Szajkowski, "Di Yidn in der Pariser Komune," *Yidn in Frankraikh,* (New York: YIVO, 1942), vol. II, in Yiddish, pp. 93-154.

[30] Edouard Drumont, *La Fin d'un monde* (Paris: Savine, 1889), p.125. On anti-Jewish hostility in French socialist circles, see Byrnes, *Antisemtism in Modern France,* pp. 156-158. For a fascist appraisal of the Commune, see Maurice-Ivan Sicard, *La Commune de Paris contre le communisme* (Paris: Etudes et Documents, 1944).

[31] For similar American views see "The Great European Change," *Scribner's Monthly,* vol. II, No. I, May 1871, 94.

[32] Drumont, *La Dernière bataille,* p. 304.

2

Defender of Faith

> I always thought that Jesus Christ
> was a Snubby or I should not have
> worship'd him, if I had thought he
> had been one of those long spindled
> nosed rascals.
>
> --William Blake

If the experience of status deprivation was difficult for France, it was particularly more painful for its Catholic church. Certain Catholic reactions to the new regime's anticlericalism help explain why some of the faithful, like Drumont, turned to antisemitism as an explanation and solution to its decline. Catholicism abides a demonological explanation of evil, and because Jews were often found in the ranks of liberalism their actions could be understood as the work of the devil. This chapter will explore the rise of antisemitism in Europe, Drumont's friendship with the Daudet family, his writing at *La Liberté*, the collapse of the Catholic counteroffensive in France, and the influence of earlier antisemitic writers on the development of his social philosophy.

The decade following the war proved to be the most decisive in Drumont's life. From the rank of an obscure journalist in 1871 he was well on his way by 1881 to becoming one of Europe's leading antisemites. What determined this momentous development was his return to Catholicism at a time when condition were favorable to the spread of antisemitism as a modern political movement in Europe.

These years were also highly significant for the Jews of western and central Europe. For the first time in memory it appeared that widespread political emancipation for them was about to become a reality. In 1870 they were allowed to attend univerisity in Great Britain, a very large number were granted French citizenship in Algeria, and in Italy the papal ghettos were thrown open while the papacy retreated into the Vatican to sulk until the advent of Mussolini. In 1871 a triumphant Germany magnanimously granted them civil equality throughout the new empire. Thus this brief period of hope lasted from 1870 to 1873. After this date the fate of most European Jews moved slowly though inexorably and often imperceptibly downward.

In Austria-Hungary a few years earlier a similar emancipation program was also legislated but it was often the case that civil enforcement was resisted by popular resentment. In the Dual Monarchy the secretary of Napoleon III, Baron d'Ambès, noted: "to these thirty millions of ill-assorted inhabitants must further be added a million of Jews, scattered broadcast like stinking vermin everyone would exterminate if possible.'' [1]

In order to understand Drumont's return to the faith and his turn toward anti-Jewish hostility a brief review of antisemitism in Europe is necessary. Despite real progress, especially in the more advanced countries, popular resentments against Jews were not slow in developing there as well. It was at times abetted by governmental complicity in Germany where antisemitism as a modern movement was born. Ironically, antisemitism began to spread in Germany and later in France in the wake of their recently fought war. According to the terms of surrender France had to pay Germany five billion francs in reparations. These payments were often recklessly invested in industrial overexpansion. The collapse of the boom and the stock markets in Vienna and New York in 1873 touched off an international financial crisis and many Germans blamed their losses on Jewish speculators. This despite the fact that according to Hajo Holborn, ''the relative influence of the Jews on finance decreased after 1871. None of the big industrial fortunes that came into being were in Jewish hands, and the modern big banks which financed the German industrialization were not decisively directed by Jewish interests.'' [2]

As a result of the Stock Exchange crash large numbers of investors, members of the nobility, upper and lower middle classes, tried to fix blame for their misfortunes. The first anti-Jewish reactions to this financial disaster came in 1873 from a journalist, Wilhelm Marr, who brought out a popular pamphlet, *The Victory of Judaism over Teutonism.* Marr, who coined the term ''antisemitism,'' claimed that the Jewish problem was not a religious but a racial conflict. This marked a novel approach developing out of traditional Jew baiting which had been based on irreconcilable religious differences. Yet the argument was really the old one centering on the treachery of Jews living among Christians. What made this doctrine more appealing was that the new objections were couched in the fashionable intellectual terms of the period, i.e., the study of human races and their classification.

This initial anti-Jewish campaign seemed to diminish somewhat in intensity. However, it took the German economy six years to regain its equilibrium, and in the meantime social unrest against Jews was still felt. During this period Bismarck was set upon consolidating support for his new state by attacking the Catholic church. The basic aim of the *Kulturkampf* was to break the power of the Center Party, the political arm of German Catholicism. Bismarck's plans did not succeed completely. Turning his attack from the Center Party, he decided to break with the National Liberals who had been the dominant vehicle for middle class interests that advocated a parlimentary democracy for which Bismarck had no use. Jews were prominent in this faction.

In order to offset this major political party it seems that Bismarck was not above condoning antisemitic tactics. The Iron Chancellor had nothing personal against Jews; he merely found this ploy a useful political tool to play off one faction against another.[3] In 1879 the works of Marr and other antisemites were republished and an Antisemitic League was established and headed by the Lutheran court chaplain, Adolf Stöcker, the leader of the Christian Social Working-Men's Union. Other segments of society, especially in the academic community, supported this program. The strategy had limited success. The coalition of various conservative factions, including the antisemites, blunted the emergence of an effective liberal parlimentary system and created a national majority strongly patriotic and subservient to the state. It was not until the defeat of 1918 that German liberalism reasserted itself in the Weimar period. The presence of Jews in this movement was greatly resented by rightwing and ultranationalist forces.

The birth and growth of antisemitism did not go unnoticed in the rest of Europe. In Russia, after the first pogroms and expulsions of 1881, it commanded international attention. This date is important for Drumont claimed that he then returned to Catholicism and began writing his opus magnum. He also stated that as late as 1879 he was not aware of the Jewsih question. If by this he meant the official beginning of the antisemitic movement in Germany, the assertion would of course be true. But there is evidence that Drumont was already preparing the dominant direction of his career at an earlier date.

The testimony of one of his close associates, Léon Daudet, suggests that the obscure journalist from *La Liberté* was already making plans long before the time which most critics usually identify as the starting point of his life's avocation. Writes Daudet: "Drumont was working on *La France juive* which only saw the light of day ten years later."[4] According to this recollection this would roughly place its inception around 1876. What Drumont may have meant by identifying 1881 as the beginning of his book was that he actually began then to write it in its final draft. It is assume that he must have given the matter long and weighty thought before the actual composition of the book. Considering the years he spent in clerical press circles he could scarcely have avoided hearing denunciations of the Jews from Veuillot and his associates.

In all likelihood Drumont was already seriously discussing his plans with Alphonse Daudet five years after the Franco-Prussian war. The outcome of this conflict provoked random grumblings mainly over the conditions surrounding the treaty negotiations with Germany. The fact that Bismarck's Jewish banker, Bleichröder, had to deal with Rothschild (whose interests he handled in Berlin) on the French side caused mutterings about the two Jews who were allegedly dividing up the spoils of war. Rothschild's attitude toward Bismarck, however, was far from satisfactory, and he managed to reduce the amount of the debt to be paid to the victors. But even though Rothschild had his commission reduced by one half, his bank managed to make a generous profit for its services.

While the nation debated the condition of the restitutions and tribute to be paid, Drumont was a frequent guest of his close friend, Alphonse Daudet, His son, Léon, recorded the impression that the journalist made on him. On the whole he found him "friendly, considerate though a rather prudish individual." Every day Drumont would ride his horse to Champrosay. At night little Léon used to go out ahead to surprise Drumont on his return to Soisy. At the right moment the child tried to startle his father's friend by shouting, "Long Live the Jews." Drumont always took these escapades in good humor.

At Daudet's home Drumont mingled with the leading literary figures of the day. Zola, Goncourt, Coppée, and others offered a stimulating atmosphere for discussing literature and politics. Drumont, however, as Léon recalled, rarely discussed his project openly at this time. Not in front of the other guests but surely before Alphonse Daudet who strongly sympathized with Drumont's developing world view.

Without the intervention of Daudet *La France juive* would never have received its initial backing and publicity. The author of *Tartarin de Tarascon* fully agreed with Drumont's original project and he did all in his power to assure its success. Shortly after its publication Drumont recalled, musing on their respective triumphs, that their works seemed to pale before the vast design of Providence. Under a starry sky he would often remark: "How can you admit that all this was created and that we've been placed on this planet only to eat your melons or even for you to write *Nabob* and for me *La France juive?* [5]

But Daudet, according to Drumont, was no philosopher; he was a writer: "Others have better understood than Daudet the great laws of society, the collective evolution of peoples: no one, in our time, has penetrated the individual with a similar rapidity of intuition." [6] What Drumont admired of his works in particular was *Les Rois en exil.* This realistic novel reflected the decadence of contemporary society in the story of a deposed monarch at the mercy of the new class of exploiters. Though it is considered a minor work, Drumont thought it one of his favorites in which he found some of his stock themes expressed in muted tones. Daudet like Balzac was fascinated by the notion of shady speculators. One of his characters from this novel, J. Tom Lévis, made a practice of betraying the confidence of the gullible. His vast emporium was staffed by "frizzy-haired employees, all elegant but with foreign airs and accents....olive complexioned, pointed skulls, and narrow Asiatic shoulders." [7] The climax of this tale is the scene in which the ex-queen is forced to sell the crown jewels and discovers that they have already been sold by the king who replaced them with paste imitations. Drumont's first antisemitic article, appearing six years later, centers around the theft of France's crown jewels and their alleged sale by Jews.

Contemporaries of Daudet accused him of all sorts of reasons for writing the novel. Margaret Cunliffe, the biographer of the Empress Elizabeth of Austria, writes that the "Baroness Adolph Rothschild... had once been very kind to the Empress's favorite sister, the ex-queen of Naples, and that at the time this unfortunate sovereign, whom the French writer, Alphonse Daudet chose as the heroine of his celebrated book, *Les Rois en exil,* had just lost her crown and was leading a miserable existence in Paris." [8] In the imaginations of Daudet and Drumont this act of charity would be viewed as the perfect theme to demonstrate the decadence of hereditary monarchy and its fall at the hands of the Jews.

In his study of Daudet's career, Professor Murray Sachs felt confident enough to write that "there is nothing in his writings or public attitudes or choices of associations that can be properly called antisemitic..For as far as close study of his life and work can reveal there is nothing in his creative writing which was in any way influenced by any personal opinions he may have entertained on the Jewish question." [9] In his public utterances Daudet was extremely cautious on this matter, but in private, according to his son and Drumont, his views were violent. As Sachs observed Daudet was fascinated and repulsed by the spectacle of swindlers and cheats. Financial scandals and skulduggery intrigued him. Léon Daudet recalled that his father used to say to the author of *La France juive:* "Every time you lift up a stone, you'll find underneath one or several circumcised wood lice." [10]

This animosity spilled over into his novels in more subdued form. In his study of the Jewish images in literature, Moses Debré observed that Alphonse Daudet put into *Les Rois en exil* a "half-Jewess...one of the few female Jewish characters in modern French literature to be shown as an obnoxious personality." [11] According to the commonly accepted literary canons of the day Jews were usually depicted as repulsive and Jewesses as highly attractive. Daudet was one of the few to portray a Jewess, Sephora Leemans, the wife of J. Tom Lévis, as utterly reprehensible. This novel, the last chapter of which is called "the end of the race," can be read as a thinly disguised allegory on the decline of monarchism in France and the rise of the new society dominated by foreign financial interests.

Drumont was sensitive to Daudet's views on the Jewish question. Even without discussing publicly, Daudet managed to attract a sort of publicity that revolted him. He seemed to agonize at the suggestion that he might have been descended from Jews. In his memoirs Léon Daudet records that "a rather hateful imbecile named Poupard Daryl first recounted in the *Figaro,* more than a half century ago, that the Daudets were of Jewish origin and that their name came from Davidet." [12] In an article on the significance of names which appeared in 1880 Drumont too, speculated ont he accusation and came to his friend's aid: "Daudé-Diudet--shortened forms of Dieudonné (Langue d'oc). A tradition has been pointed out to me which gives Daudé, Daudet as a form of

David, pronounced Arab style, in a family from the Orient; but this exception does not weaken the law, because the names Daudet and Doudet, which assimilated to it, are rather numerous." [13]

Whatever these petty quarrels are worth, they certainly annoyed Daudet. He reported to Goncourt that when a journalist, Alfred Delpit, made similar accusation in 1883, Daudet promptly challenged him to a duel. Delpit had accused him of being a "Carthaginian," by which he probably meant a Semite of few scruples. For all his shortcomings Drumont deeply admired his powerful and influential friend and he made it a point to emphasize the positive side of his character. In *Le Livre* of 2 February 1884 he wrote that "Daudet is like those handsome lords who attack the Revolution. Theirs is nobility."

This charge of unreliability and lack of scruples continued to dog the career of Daudet. As a result of Delpit's allegations Drumont agreed to come to his assistance once again. The major controversy surrounded the authorship of Daudet's *Lettres de mon moulin,* and Drumont found himself embroiled in the mutual recriminations. While it seems impossible to determine exactly what actually happened, Paul Arène, a collaborator of Daudet, accused him of usurping all the credit for writing this collection of tales. In all probability Arène undoubtedly suggested and discussed certain themes, and he may even have helped in the revision of a work that Daudet claimed entirely to be his own.

Drumont took the side of Daudet and his article on the squabble prompted a reply from Arène in *Le Livre* of 10 March 1884. Arène imputed "the most perfidious of intentions" to Drumont's presentation of the conflict. In his rebuttal Drumont tried to set the record straight: "I add that Daudet has since written and verbally repeated to me that if I hadn't told the whole truth, I had told *only the truth.*" Such evasiveness earned Daudet an unenviable reputation in some quarters, leading him to be oversensitive about slurs against his integrity and ancestry. This was the same problem which Drumont would soon have to face himself. Although the public had little way of knowing about Daudet's scron for Jews, he ironically found himself condemned for the very traits he professed, in private, to find in those he most despised. [14]

These were quiet years for Drumont. Although he mingled in salons with the literary elite, he remained in the background at work in a difficult profession. His major publication after the Wagner book was a play, *Je Déjeune à Midi,* composed in collaboration with Aimé Dollfus, the city editor of *Le Bien Public.* They received 250 francs for this piece which was published in 1875 by Calmann-Lévy, thanks to the good offices of Alexandre Dumas *fils.* Later Drumont condemned Dumas for being half Jewish.

In 1878 Drumont published the book for which he was chiefly remembered before writing his masterpiece. The first series of *Mon Vieux Paris* was a collection of his journal articles dedicated to evoking the charm of medieval Paris. Those monuments, many of them long since demolished, held a special affection for Drumont. And if it is possible to identify what he loved most in his life it was undoubtedly the image of Paris and its past glories. The destruction and ruin of so much of the heroic past gradually embittered him against the agents of progress and modernity.

The nostalgic tone of these pieces foreshadowed by one year the sense of disgust he would again experience in reading *Les Rois en exil.* For both authors, Daudet and Drumont, modern Paris was overrun with high society riffraff that turned everything to profit with no regard for tradition. The image of the city had been usurped by "certain artificial segments" which only offered a "sickly neurosis" to those in search of the "high life."

Thanks to a rampant hedonism this period was called the Babylonian phase by Drumont in his work on the capital: "Foreigners, three fourths of them reproducing the only types they might know, the types of European *intrusion,* sketch weird and frightful portraits of us." This was a false image, pleaded Drumont. An agglomeration of people of this size is bound to have "many a horror stirring up in the subterranean darkness beneath the refined and artistic city." In their image they have cast Paris as "the sewer of the universe." [15] Interspersed among these nostalgic vignettes are found Drumont's social views on the modern metropolis. He quickly traces the ruin of the old nobility and also of the one created by Napoleon. In just one generation "the sons of these fearless men will be as degenerate as those descendants of Crusader barons were after five or six centuries." [16]

In 1879 Drumont published a novel which painted a vast historical backdrop for the adventures of just such a hero. *Le Dernier des Trémolin* is a sort of historical *roman policier.* This sentimental tale relates the exploits of a young man mixed up in the embezzlement schemes of a character who had acquired some *biens nationaux,* property confiscated from the church. He gambles away his mother's fortune and is almost executed (wrongly) for the murder of his libertine uncle. He repays his mother, distinguishes himself in the Crimean war, and on the same day that she dies he meets a glorious end, with the rank of general, during the siege of Paris in 1871. The novel was highly praised in Catholic literary circles.

Drumont's next book also reflected his major interest in the capital. *Les Fêtes nationales à Paris* (1879) had little pretensions of being a scholarly work. Consisting of more illustrations than text, this volume told the story of popular reactions to patriotic celebrations. The author could not resist commenting on the political aspects of these events which seem peripheral to the main theme. He chided, for example, Louis-Philippe for dealing the Jew Deutz, a central figure in a major scandal of his reign. The author showed a clear interest in the plots surrounding the various factions that staged patriotic festivals.

Many of the festivals in honor of the revolution were laughable in their naïveté, according to Drumont. Nevertheless he insisted that it was important to recognize who were the real instigators of social change. That nebulous term, the people, did not deserve the honors. For Drumont it was the result of a conspiracy hatched by the "monstrous Philippe-Egalité and abetted by foreigners who wished to change the course of French history to serve their own selfish designs. Drumont emphasized that this observation was applicable to the present state of affairs in the country: "To deny the role of England in the revolution is as absurd as denying the role of Prussia for the last fifteen years." [17] By implication the author attacked the current leaders of government in suggesting that they were truly serving the interests of the conqueror. These opinions hint at Drumont's long standing feud with republicanism in its actual embodiment. Ironically, however, Drumont's book was one of many contributions of the time which helped create a climate of public opinion favorable to establishing 14 July as the national festival day.

In 1880 Drumont edited, prefaced, and published some papers of Saint-Simon, the chronicler of Louis XIV's reign. During these quiet years for Drumont the country as a whole was occupied by debate over its form of government and its policy toward Germany. There was a good deal of soul searching and recrimination which was often aroused by fear of German espionage. From time to time the spy craze erupted on the national scene in politics and on one occasion in the theater. In 1873 Alexandre Dumas *fils* had produced a flawed though remarkable play, *La Femme de Claude,* which set forth a proto-Zionist answer to the Jewish question. The Jewish hero, Daniel, had an influence on the creation of George Eliot's Daniel Deronda. Dumas' triumphant pronouncement, "the wandering Jew is no longer on the march; he has arrived," caught Drumont's eye and he chose to interpret this line to indicate that the Jews would settle down in France as the new promised land. [18]

The main theme of the play which gripped Paris audiences dealt, however, with spying. The wife of Claude, Césarine, was a thinly veiled character whose name in German would be "Kaiserin" thus suggesting Prussia as the land from which the espionage plot had been launched. When this character tries to pass her husband's military secrets to the German embassy, he shoots her, an outcome which implies the eventual triumph of France and the deserved fate of a traitress. [19] A more convincing spy drama than *La Femme de Claude* was Sardou's *Dora* which was produced in 1877. Though the play had to be changed to avoid accusing

Germany directly of spying against France, the revanchist plot escaped no one.

Rumors and fears of spying were common fare in the early Third Republic. Apprehension provided the climate in which such plays were favorably received. Thus public reaction to a real instance of spying was already prepared in the form of a notorious case of espionage which was revealed in 1880. Early that year three Paris journals proclaimed that plans from the General Staff for army mobilization and frontier defense had been sold to Germany by a French officer, Colonel Jung. That his name was of Germanic origin made the story seem all the more plausible. According to Jung's chief accuser, Ivan de Woestyne, the real spy was Madame Jung who implicated her husband's superior and the former Minister of War, Ernest Comtot de Cissey. In fact the colonel and general were acquitted of the charges and in turn they brought their own charges against de Woestyne, a journalist with a bad reputation for scandal mongering. He had to pay Jung 5000 francs in damages and was sentenced to six months in prison.

The matter might have ended there but the gutter press refused to let a good story die a natural death. Three newspapers began a daily program of harrassment against de Cissey. The general brought action for libel against his accusers and got a verdict in his favor. The journal that led the packwas Rochefort's *L'Intransigeant,* and the muckraker, though fined 4000 francs and forced to pay de Cissey 8000 more, thought of raising a mob in his defense outside the court. Despite his loss in court, Rochefort regarded the affair as a symbolic victory for himself as the number one self-appointed vigilante of France's interests. [20]

This incident bears a striking resemblance to the Dreyfus affair: A French officer of Germanic background is falsely accused of spying, the real spy is exposed, a high ranking officer implicated, and the jingoist press inflames public opinion. All these factors were present but those wrongly accused had the chance to fight back vigorously and openly, opportunities which were to be denied Dreyfus. Like the rest of France Drumont followed the case closely. In *La Liberté* of 14 October 1880, echoing Rocherfort's charges, it was claimed that Jung was a friend of Gambetta, thus insinuating that the head of state (accused by many reactionaries of being a Jew) was keeping company with traitors.

Whatever Drumont's attitudes toward Jews after the war of 1870 may have been, he had no compunctions about returning to the Jewish owned newspaper, *La Liberté.* Here he remained until just before publication of *La France juive* fifteen years later. At this stage of his journalistic career his praise of prominent Jews was just as flattering as his later denuntiations were vicious. When Moïse Millaud died, for example, Drumont wrote his obituary in the 15 October 1871 issue of *Le Bien Public* and praised the deceased as one of the great benefactors of his time, which indeed he was. Millaud, along with Girardin, was a giant of journalism. Like Girardin, who sold him *La Presse* in 1856, Millaud was one of the first to realize the benefits of a mass circulation press which could be sold to more subscribers in order to assume greater accessibility to the public.

Like many other prominent French Jewish families Millaud had been born in Bordeaux. [21] Another famous Jewish family of that city, the Pereires, were also involved in the press and many other innovative enterprises of the period. Promoters of the Saint Simonian ideal of wedding capitalism and socialism, the Pereires established the most daring banking system during the Second Empire, and they were also the owners of *La Liberté* while Drumont was a member of the staff. It was the flagrant discrepancies between Drumont's opinions on them in 1878 and 1886 that astonished the public when *La France juive* brought him instant, widespread recognition. He claimed that during his early years on the newspaper he did not know who the owners were. But in January 1875 he was able to write a pompous eulogy on Emile Pereire:

> This millionaire in no way resembled the financiers of the past...For the first time one saw a man move enormous capital with nothing more than the force of an idea..All these generous spirits, these progressive intelligences, they dreamed of regenerating humanity by a more broadly based solidarity, by a loyal renumeration of work.. The hour has come to judge once and for all the work in which Emile Pereire took so preponderate a part, the group of which he was, with his luminous and just practical sense, the venerable and uncontested leader.

Again in 1878 Drumont expressed similar praise about Emile's brother, Isaac, another "apostle of progress." Using the same words, he glorified the two brothers for "cooperating together on the marvellous organization of the economy of the nineteenth century. Both will share the admiration which their peaceful revolution will inspire to posterity."

It seems probable that while writing these flattering pieces Drumont was already working on *La France juive* in the sense that he was already collecting material and doing research. When this appeared, six years after the death of Emile Pereire, his opinion of the two bankers had completely changed. This new evaluation of his long time employer was cast in the framework of the famous rivalry between the Pereires and the Rothschilds and the financial dynasties which they created. His comments on the vendetta are important insofar as they prefigure the greater outcry over Rothschild's confrontation with the Catholic banking enterprise, the *Union Générale*. The passion aroused by this duel in the realms of *la haute finance* were perhaps the most powerful immediate catalyst in the inception of French antisemitism. Drumont's attitudes were crystallizing while this drama was unfolding. [22]

The fundamental thesis of Drumont's social philosophy was that the Jews have conquered France and that Rothschild was their king. In most of his writings every conceivable evil was attributed to this family. Even the destruction of fellow Jews would contribute to the insatiable appetie of the Rothschilds. This Drumont attributed to the more rapacious nature of the German Jew in contrast to his milder Mediterranean cousin. Although he acknowledged a bit of the praise he formerly heaped on the Pereires for their civility and French airs, certain physical traits always were pointed out by Drumont to indicate the root of the problem: "The hands alone, grasping and light-fingered, betrayed the race." To obscure this defect Drumont claimed that the Pereires "had to keep their hands gloved." [23]

The Pereire family seemed relatively acceptable to Drumont. Unlike their Germanic competitors, these descendants of Portuguese Jews were highly assimilated. But there was limits to Drumont's indulgence and tolerance. In comparing these two branches of Jewish people, the Sephardic and Ashkenazic, he declared that "one is the gay and dancing fly, the other is the slimy, sticky louse, living inertly at the expense of the human body." [24] Images of this sort abound in Drumont's writings and thought: they serve to indicate that at the heart of the antisemitic arguments there stands not a criticism of society's ills or a critique of religion and culture, but a radical attempt to portray the alien as a sub-human form beyond the pale of human recognition and compassion.

For the years he spent on the staff of *La Liberté* Drumont complained bitterly about his low salary: "I earned 300 francs per month for *three articles a week,* and not the worst I've written." [25] He claimed that he would have stayed on another few years but he feared the journal would be taken over by the enemies of the Pereires: "These Bordeaux Jews were destined to be eaten by German Jews, the way our domestic rats, which have totally disappeared, have been eaten by Norwegian rats." [26] The northern specie of rodents he referred to here were of course the Rothschilds. The staff room of *La Liberté* must have been an excellent spot to overhear gossip about the famous vendetta between the two families. Drumont sketched some vague details of the affair and came to the conclusion--reached by many other Frenchmen--that "Pereire, who had crushed Mirès, was crushed by Rothschild." [27]

Drumont held the opinion that Pereire had been driven from the field by the house of Rothschild. A closer look at the famous struggle suggests that such a view is less clear that the facts would indicate. Emile Pereire had worked for the Rothschilds but abandoned their services to strike out on his own. He decided to apply Saint-Simonian principles to the financial world to "democratize" banking by opening up his establishment to general public investment. The *Crédit Mobilier* was born and immediately it challenged the Rothschild hegemony. For two years Pereire enjoyed the Emperor's favor, but in the end a combination of factors destroyed his financial empire.

There is no doubt that Rothschild and Pereire's other rivals did their best to defend themselves against the upstart financier. Rothschild was convinced that what Pereire called banking innovations were nothing more than rash speculation on capital raised by fickle public subscription. Public confidence in the *Crédit Mobilier* was shaken when its stock dropped, and when one of its directors, Jules Mirès, was arrested for fraud. The last straw was the collapse of Maximilian's Mexican adventure which had been backed by Pereire. By 1867 the *Crédit Mobilier* had fallen apart.

It is difficult to say whether Pereire was destroyed by Rothschild's opposition or whether his bank died a natural death as a result of his unwise investments. There is no definite proof that would put the blame directly at the feet of his rivals. What was more important was what public opinion thought, how it interpreted the recovery of Rothschild control over the state's banking system. In its broad outlines this sort of banking rivalry foreshadowed a similar confrontation, the rise and fall of the *Union Générale.* [28] The repercussions of this struggle, from which the Rothschilds again emerged triumphant, provided the chief impetus that guaranteed the success of Drumont.

After the war of 1870 it was doubtful that many recalled the exact details of the rivalry between the two Jewish bankers. Once again, however, Rothschild faced a new challenge. Instead of coming from a coreligionist, this assault stemmed from an ambitious attempt by financiers with heavy support from Catholic circles. The Holy See and other Catholic states had been content to do business with Rothschild, but the prospect of a Christian banking operation with all its political implications seemed even more attractive.

The director of the rival Catholic enterprise was Paul-Eugène Bontoux. Among his accomplishments was the management of the Austrian State Railway which had been organized in 1857 by Pereire. Whatever resentment Bontoux developed toward the Rothschilds in these years was turned against them in full when he launched his own concern which he baptised the *Union Générale.* It had the complete support of clerical elements and was supposed to protect its backers from "the dishonesty and rapacity of Jewish banks." [29]

From the onset Bontoux and his followers heralded the *Union Générale* as the vehicle to save Christian Europe from "the yoke of Jewish finance." But for all its support and the director's proclaimed rectitude Bontoux himself was susceptible to irregular practices. The cause of his undoing resembled what had befallen Pereire. Again it was a question of rash speculation, over-extension of credit, and conflict with Rothschild. Bontoux's bank profited from a brief period of accelerated prosperity from 1878 to 1881, but it was one of the victims of the long depression that began in 1882.

While proof has never been established that Rothschild ruined this Catholic banking enterprise, scholars agree that there is ample evidence to show that internal factors played a major role in its collapse. [30] At the time of the crash there were only the vaguest mutterings against Bontoux's sworn enemies. The only major figure to blame Rothschild was the socialist leader, Jules Guesde. [31] The theme of Rothschild's central responsibility came later and was exploited, among others, by Drumont.[32] What dominated public attention in 1882 were the circumstances in which Bontoux's bank collapsed, particularly since several thousand investors lost heavily when it became apparent that Bontoux could not cover their repayment demands. Many were curious about the role of government in bringing charges against the bankrupt director. Bontoux was arrested and while denying most charges of irregular practices, he did admit guilt on certain points. He was condemned to five years in prison, but he decided to choose exile instead of serving the sentence.

Bontoux's supporters believed that the republican government was overzealous in prosecuting their champion. The crash of the *Union Générale* was far more than the collapse of another financial venture. The entire operation was part of a larger political and religious struggle, and the controversy surrounding it went on for years and grew more bitter. While Drumont profited from this resentment, it should be remembered that he had already started his secret project before Bontoux's firm collapsed. He devoted much space to the affair in *La France juive,* the inspiration of which had its roots deep in the political climate of the 1870's.

If the crash of the *Union Générale* had merely been considered a financial disaster, it would have been remembered as just another minor chapter in the boom and bust cycle of capitalism. But because its directors also had political ambitions as well, the crash was inextricably linked with the perennial conflict between church and state. After the war the nation was preoccupied with reorganizing itself and above all with paying off the debt to Gemany. The political machinery of France was in the hands of a conservative caretaker government the majority of whose members expected that ultimately the monarchist cause would stand the most likely chance to lead the new regime.

The Bonapartists had been discredited by the debacle of war, and the logical choice fell on the house of Bourbon. The Bourbons had still not learned or forgotten anything, and both branches, the Legitimists led by the Comte de Chambord and the Orleanists by the Comte de Paris, failed to reach a common accord. The latter, however, for the sake of the cause, was willing to cast support to the former even though the Comte de Chambord never really forgave this branch for its ancestor's behavior during the revolutions of 1789 and 1830. A reading of Drumont's writings shows that he closely followed these developments.

Most parties assumed that when the Comte de Chambord was to be offered the chance to favor restoration that the matter would be settled. But in 1873 Henri de Bourbon, duc de Bordeaux, comte de Chambord, refused to retain the tricolor as the national standard because it was the symbol of the revolution. Only the white flag of the *ancien régime* would be acceptable to this living relic out of the past. He was adamant in his refusal despite pleas from several quarters, and his decision, though regretted, was sadly accepted by most monarchists.

Although they were exasperated, almost all supporters applauded the Comte de Chambord's archaic sense of honor. Veuillot was most pleased by this decision even though it spelled the death knell for the cause of monarchy in France. Members of the lower orders who might have supported a monarchy had grown wary of rule be absolute divine right. Once the figure of the benevolent pretender disappeared, the list of ultra-conservative candidates, often drawn from the local nobility, seemed rather unattractive to the electorate.

Like Veuillot, Drumont had high praise for the Comte de Chambord, describing his as "a soul made in the image of God, one of those beautiful eucharistic souls which evaporates in the aromas of kindness like the lily bent over its branch and dies while emitting perfume."[33] According to Drumont, Chambord, unlike the Jacobins, had no taste for shedding blood to seize power. In his portrait of the noble pretender he underscored the influence of the Comtesse in disuading her husband to abandon his quest for the throne.

The monarchist cause, though severly curtailed, refused to capitulate. It rallied as best it could behind its traditional support, especially the church, and waged a spirited effort to make its influence felt. This was the main factor which led to the creation of the *Union Générale,* and when it failed, it was felt that the enemies of Christian monarchy were responsible. The Comtesse de Chambord was especially upset by the defeat of the Catholic royalist bank. Born in the ducal house of Modena, she and her husband were, in the words of Thiers, "a family from the Middle Ages, they have political ideas of the most reactionary kind and their religion is outrée."[34] When the bank crashed, she immediately saw the hand of the devil at work. Among its victims, writes scholar James Parkes, "were the French pretender, the Count de Chambord and his Austrian wife, the Archduchess Maria Theresia. The archduchess, who was particularly furious with the Jews for her losses, sent a colleague of Bontoux to study the new antisemitic movement in Germany. Among others he made contact with Stöcker and brought back a mass of literature and ideas."[35] This was the type of muttering heard in certain French royalist circles, thus it is not surprising that Veuillot and his followers like Drumont came into contact even indirectly at an early date with antisemitism in its modern political form.

Drumont was aware of the development and sentiments in anti-republican quarters. Because he worked for a newspaper owned by the Pereire family, he felt he could not freely express his ideas on the subject. Those articles of his touching on the church question were of necessity moderate in tone, simply defending clergy against the growing hostility of the government. Once the initial monarchist bid for power was dissipated, the political establishment continued to develop among the lines of a republican regime. By 1875 the Third Republic was officially created in the National Assembly by a majority.

Thanks to the tireless efforts of Gambetta the republicans gradually increased their popularity. They made a solid show of surpassing their more conservative colleagues who were not idle despite the setbacks which they had experienced. Because of Chambord's reluctance to fight for power, ultra-conservatives increasingly turned for support to the Catholic church. Both church and monarchy were united in opposing the growth of secularism as personified by the republicans. From the very beginning and throughout the history of the new republic the school system was seen as the battle field where the struggle for public opinion was fought.

Judging by his essays and articles Drumont was a supporter of clerical policies. For the church this was an agonizing period, one which was totally new in its long history. For the first time it found itself confronted by a secular philosophy that claimed to set the tone and standard for national life. The lines were sharply drawn, and the worst speculations on both sides were not without some foundation. For the Left the issue was clear when Gambetta uttered the cry: "Clericalism, there's the enemy!" For the Right this new order was the work of the devil. For the Catholic church status deprivation from traditional privileges to exclusion caused it to perceive itself as a fortress besieged by the enemies of God. Drumont came to see himself as its self-annointed champion.

Apocalyptic signs were evident for the faithful to behold. The pope was a prisoner in the Vatican, and France, his traditional protector, was unwilling to come to his defense. In France, the government seemed to embody all the evils denounced by Pius IX in the Syllabus of Errors. In 1879 the pope decried the restraints placed on Italian bishops and he appealed for support throught the Catholic World. Previously goaded by the church authorities in France, conservatives had retaliated when on 16 May 1877, for example, President MacMahon dismissed Jules Simon, the Minister of the Interior, in what was considered the high water mark of the reactionary counterattack. One cleric, Cardinal Bonnechose of Rouen, went so far as to urge MacMahon to stage a coup d'etat to establish a Christian state. THus comprised for meddling in affairs of state, the church had assured that the contest for control of the country would be fought along the lines of social legislation and foreign policy. Drumont's newspaper articles from this period give testimony to his growing hatred of the early Third Republic.

Just as similar clashes had made the reputation of Veuillot in the 1840s, the same issues would serve to guarantee Drumont's in the 1880s. Unlike Veuillot, however, Drumont took a longer time in reaching the public, but in both cases they were viewed by many as the champions of clerism. Even on this score there was one important distinction between them. Although much of Drumont's anti-Jewish resentment undoubtedly sprang from Veuillot's circles, the quality of this hatred derived from another source as well. It stemmed from the nature of his return to Catholicism. As Robert Byrnes wrote: "It is significant that between 1879 and 1885, the period of Opportunist rule, Drumont both rejoined the Catholic church and became an antisemite." [36]. The two experiences went hand in hand and yet they call for some explanation and qualification.

It is not so much a question that Drumont returned to Catholicism: what is more important is the quality of that conversion and the character of the church that received him back to its bosom. Drumont almost took the step to re-enter the church a decade earlier when, under the influence of Henri de Lasserre, he began writing for the clerical press. Its leaders made a tremendous impression on him, but it was really the national defeat suffered in war and what conservatives saw as the disintegration of traditional Christian society that finally made up his mind.

The sincerity of Drumont's conversion was rarely questioned, though were were doubts about its quality. While the clericalists were delighted by his return to the fold, members of the literary circles he occasionally frequented were puzzled. When Victor Hugo heard of his plans to convert, he responded: "Look, old friend...you know that I appreciate you, that I like you, that I find you a noble mind, a noble heart...but Catholicism, really...No, no Catholicism, give it up." [37] Drumont never gave it up; he faithfully performed his religious duties and always saw himself (as did others) as one of the frontline defenders of the faith against the works of Satan.

Maurice Talmeyr, who recorded Drumont's encounter with Victor Hugo, noted that Drumont questioned the exact religious convictions of his own beliefs and admitted that he was really a "historic Catholic," one who believed the Catholic church was right because it was a rampart of western civilization, especially in its French manifestation. This viewpoint seems similar to that of Charles Maurras, the future leader of Action Française. But there is an important difference. Maurras clearly did not believe in the divine claims of the Catholic church: for him it was good insofar as it promoted his idea of French nationalism. Although Drumont was not as orthodox as Veuillot, he was not as cynical as Maurras. He truly thought that he was acting according to the dictates of his religious convictions and conscience. And if many of his religious views can scarcely be called Christian, this speaks volumes about those in the church who saw him as one of their strongest supporters.

Drumont may have had the same mass appeal as Veuillot and derived many of his ideas from the famous Catholic journalist, but the nature of his Catholicism had more in common with that of the lesser known Henri Gougenot des Mousseaux, a Catholic writer who pioneered the idea of anti-Judaism prior to the war of 1870. There were differences between them: Gougenot des Mousseaux was a nobleman and a scholar whereas Drumont was a petty bourgeois and a journalist. But the quality of their Jew hatred was quite similar, and the career of this man from whom Drumont borrowed so much is worth a brief review.

The general tone of most of Gougenot des Mousseaux's works were highly illiberal. One of his early books defended the cause of slavery in the French colonies. For him "emancipation destroys the role of master," and slavery was really for the African race, "the first step to civilization." [38] Two years later in 1846 writing on the working class, he discovered that France's troubles stemmed from the designs of foreigners at home and abroad. [39] But it was the series of books on religion that assured his reputation. His master work, *Dieu et les dieux* (1854) is a long erudite treatise on comparative religion in which parallels between Christianity and paganism were discussed at length. One source of information used by this author was the works of the renegade Jew Drach who had been named the "librarian of propaganda" by the pope in Rome. What is curious about this treatment of religions is that what used to be considered prefigurations of Christianity in the Old Testament were identified as pagan symbols. There was in this volume a good deal of talk about sacred symbolism and magic stones, but the most startling analysis was drawn between Abraham and Chronos, the god that devours his children. Thus Judaism was seen as the father religion that persecutes its offspring.

Subsequent volumes deal exhaustively with such questions as vampirism, spiritism (principally in the United States), magnetism, magic, and occultism. In *La Magie au 19ᵉ siecle* (1860) the Reverend Father Ventura de Raulica in his preface referred to the Damascus affair of 1840 in which Jews were accused and persecuted on charges of ritual murder. This priest who also specialized in anti-Jewish polemics proclaimed that such ghastly events were linked down through history by "an uninterrupted chain." Gougenot des Mousseaux also believed in the charges of ritual murder but the object of most of his books up to this date was to demonstrate the falseness and to denounce what he termed the contemporary pseudoscientific explanations of demons and magic. It became his appointed task to reaffirm the orthodox teaching of Catholicism on the reality of devils and evil spirits. In the year after his death, Léon Pagès, in the *Annales de Philosophie Chrétienne,* wrote: "all his work, it can be said, could be summed up in the demostration of the supernatural diabolical life." [40]

Four years before the Vatican Council and the publication of his major antisemitic work Gougenot des Mousseaux wrote a remarkable book in which all these themes were explored in great detail. In *Les Hauts phénomènes de la magie* (1865) the author upheld the existence of vampires which have been "attested by reliable witnesses," and in a prophetic note he linked the theological and political concerns that would later determine papal policy: "The more my life goes on, the more experience reveals to me the cause of things, the more my eye contemplates the efforts and plots of the visible and invisible enemies of the church, that is to say, the real enemies of civilization, burning to revolutionize the world by uprooting all truths..the more my conviction grows strong that papal infallibility must be a dogma no less philosophical than religious." [41] Small wonder that this early champion of papal supremacy was eagerly greeted and praised by the Vatican.

This same remarkable book by Gougenot des Mousseaux reflected an important change of attitude found in certain Catholic circles regarding race and by analogy the Jews. It is a long and fascinating passage containing a weird mixture of theology and eroticism that isolates the hysterical element underlying much of modern antisemitism. First the author asks the question: "Will a demon be able, by crossing himself with our species, to give birth to a race of mongrels?" To this he emphatically replies in the negative, but the qualifications he then offers are worth examining: "No, above all no, the matter is from all sides impossible if we're dealing with a succubus...a demon who, in these monstrous unions, play the part of a woman..But, oh surprise! oh unexpected phenomenon! The demon, which doesn't possess the body's life, the demon which cannot make the germ of human life come out of the nothingness of its generative power, the demon will be able to snatch this germ and plant it! Yes, either by infusing its damned inspiration or caressing with its warm breath those voluptous dreams which provoke those eruptive fermentations of the flesh, or even bu using it with a man its infernal role of succubus, the demon knows how to appropriate this germ...The mother in whom the process of conception operates, then receives the germ of an absent man, but she has the *demon* for a mate and *spouse.*" [42] The significance of this fantastic mating with demons is to be found in the fruit of this unholy union: "Wretched children can then be encountered who owe their birth to the *Spirits* of evil, and not at all like a bastard race, deeply infected as it may be by these travellers from hell..." Gougenot des Mousseaux may have derived his demonology from the Middle Ages, but what is important here is how he applied this knowledge to his and future generations. According to his conclusions "the frequent reproduction of the human race aided by the techniques and help of the incubus spirits is in all probality one of the ongoing and higher means by which the future will carefully guide us." [43]

What Gougenot des Mousseaux was concerned with was nothing

less than the destruction of Christian civilization by diabolical forces. Max Milner in his definitive work on the image of the devil in French literature felt that although these and similar works had a "morose agressiveness against the spirit of the century," they were marked by a "naive and amusing pathos." [44] These books could be viewed as merely a reaction to the widespread interest in demonology among writers of that period. But Gougenot des Mousseaux's works were different and explosive in that he linked his findings to politics by specifically identifying these malignant creatures as Jews.

And for all this quaint subject matter his brand of antisemitism was quite modern, culminating in 1869 with *Le Juif, le judaïsme et la judaïsation des peuples chrétiens,* which was highly praised all the way from Pius IX to Rosenberg and Hitler. The modern demon, according to this Catholic scholar and aristocrat, will not necessarily resemble those of the Middle Ages although they are all eternally related. The contemporary devil will resemble other men, making them all the more difficult to identify. In short what Gougenot des Mousseaux described is the image of the assimilating Jew who is supposed to retain his millenial hatred of Christ while bearing the shape of modern man. This would be a major them developed by Drumont is thousands of pages and editorials.

Drumont often affected the pose of a socialist and in this regard his work could be seen as a continuation of the polemics initiated by the anti-Jewish progressive spirit, Alphonse de Toussenel. But the main outlines of Drumont's thought were prefigured in the writings of Gougenot des Mousseaux. In both authors there was the concern for racism, then interest and belief in the supernatural and occult, and finally the conclusion that the Jews are the cause for the decline of Catholicism and civilization. Unlike Gougenot des Mousseaux's erudite tomes Drumont's fascination with magic was vulgar, a trait which made his ideas all the more popular with a reading public given to forms of superstition.

Drumont had close contacts with various psychic prophets and seers in Paris. He always carried a mandrake root to ward off evil spirits and he fancied himself an accomplished palmist. It was not uncommon for him to seize the hand of a new acquaintance or that of a reporter so that he could tell them their fortune. After the Boulanger affair, for example, he declared that the abortive coup d'état was inevitable because the general's hand did not reveal those qualities recognizable in a leader. When he launched his paper, *La Libre Parole,* Drumont employed Gaston Méry who was also the editor of the leading spiritualist journal, *L'Echo du Merveilleux.* [45]

These acquaintances were to lie in the future. But there was one contemporary association that Drumont was accused of having that dogged him throughout the rest of his career. When *La France juive* came out in

1886, he was accused of being a stooge of the Jesuits because of their desire for revenge against the anticlerical legislation of the new republic. In particular critics like Joseph Reinach and Stéphane Arnoulin directly linked Drumont and the name of the famous Jesuit priest, Father Stanislas du Lac. [46]

Drumont vehemently denied ever receiving money or special encouragement from this wealthy Jesuit. [47] He had been bitter about the dissolution of certain church run schools, and as early as 1880 the plight of the Jesuits, personified by this priest, came to his attention. Referring to the expulsion of clerics, he commented with acerbity: "Will you force Father du Lac to take up residence in Belleville?"[48] Expulsion and exile were only short term measures to be taken against such martyrs and Drumont further commented: "There's only one way to prevent those people from living as they wish, people who commit reprehensible acts, and that's to kill them." Du Lac must have appreciated Drumont's support for the latter admitted travelling all the way to Canterbury, England, to have a priest correct the proofs of *La France juive* for any theological errors.

This, claimed Drumont, was the extent of their association. His enemies, however, without any real proof, asserted that he was part of a massive clerical cabal directed against those modern ideas which were condemned by Pius IX. Though for lack of conclusive evidence the matter cannot be resolved to the satisfaction of all parties, there is one bit of information that suggests that Drumont received a bit more than proof reading from his Jesuit contacts.

Among the numerous references found in *La France juive* Drumont mentioned the series of antisemitic articles published from 1880 to 1882 in the Italian Jesuit journal, *Civiltà Cattolica*. [49] These lengthy pieces, mainly written by Father Giuseppe Oreglia, were exceptionally vicious in that they signaled in this instance a step from the church's traditional anti-Judaism to the modern form of antisemitism. As the pope's own shock troops the Jesuits were the only holy order which refused to accept members who had been Jews and later converted to Catholicism. This special animosity toward Jews increased their perception of the church beleaguered on all fronts by mortal enemies. In Italy the Society of Jesus was faced with the same type of republican style government, an anticlerical regime, as it did in France. Father Oreglia avoided denying all value to Judaism and claimed that the ancient Hebrews were good as followers of the Mosaic law and as precursors of the advent of Christ. Modern Jews, however, according to this cleric, were supposed to be inspired by rabbis and Talmud, were evil and enemies of God. This had been traditional church teaching regarding the Jews, but Oreglia added a new element. All crimes were imputed to them especially ritual murder and the blood libel, accusations which had formerly been denounced by various popes but which were spreading once again in Europe. These were the sorts of tales which particularly appealed to Drumont.

On the matter of ritual murder as described by the *Civiltà Cattolica* one comes across a classic example of psychological projection. By accusing the Jews of kidnapping children for diabolical rites, these church spokesmen turned attention away from the long standing practice in the Papal states of kidnapping and forced baptism of Jewish children. The Papal states were among the worst ruled areas of Europe. Its central policy was a rule of bigotry and obscurantism that had been on the wane in other parts of the continent. Throughout the nineteenth century the Papacy's reputation had been tarnished abroad by cases of kidnapping children from Jewish parents. Even after the reunification of Italy the Papacy continued to nurture a throwback attitude to the days of its temporal supremace. The articles appearing in the *Civiltà Cattolica* were just a part of the church's reaction to the forces of liberalism, anticlericalism, and Freemasonry whose doctrine the Jews were accused of propagating. [50]

The *Civiltà Cattolica* was a specialized journal, but it had some following in Italy, France and Austria. Since Drumont did not read Italian someone who did must have indicated those antisemitic articles to him. It can therefore be assumed that the help he received from his Jesuit contactswas perhaps less than his enemies claimed and a bit more than he cared to admit.

If Léon Daudet's already mentioned memoirs were trustworthy it seems that Drumont was discussing among his closest friends his first book on the Jews as early as the middle 1870s. As the conflict between church and state increased, he became more defensive about the traditional religious beliefs and heritage of France. By the end of the decade Drumont had returned to the church of his childhood and by 1881 he considered himself an antisemite. At this date work on his massive study was probably beyond the rough stages. It was during the next five years that he had the time and inspiration to complete in secret what would become the largest bestseller in nineteenth century France.What Drumont later was able to do through *La Libre Parole* was to convince many Frenchmen that France's ills were the fault of the Jews. Drumont exploited the general malaise of France's relative loss of great power status by combining a sense of deprivation to displacement of anger against the Jews. This combustible combination served to set the stage for immediate and distant hostility towards France's Jewish community.

## Notes

[1] Baron d'Ambès, *Intimate Memoirs of Napoleon III* (Boston: Little, Brown, 1912), vol. II, pp. 238-239.

[2] Hajo Holborn, *A History of Modern Germany* (New York: Knopf, 1973), vol. III, p. 279.

[3] James Parkes, *The Emergence of the Jewish Problem* (London: Oxford University Press, 1948), p. 200. See also Fritz Stern, *Gold and Iron.* (New York: Knopf, 1977).

[4] Leon Daudet, *Les Oeuvres dans les hommes* (Paris: Nouvelle Librairie Nationale, 1922), p. 146.

[5] Drumont, *La dernière bataille,* p. 313.

[6] Ibid., p. 314.

[7] Alphonse Daudet, *Les Rois en exil* (Paris: Flammarion, 1879), p. 152.

[8] Margaret Cunliffe, *The Martyrdom of an Empress,* (New York: Harper & Brothers, 1901), p. 15.

[9] Murray Sachs, *The Career of Alphonse Daudet* (Cambridge: Harvard University Press, 1965), p. 209.

[10] Léon Daudet, *Panorama de la troisième République* (Paris: Gallimard, 1936), p. 92.

[11] Moses Debré, *The Image of the Jew in French Literature* (New York: Ktav, 1970), p.26.

[12] Léon Daudet, *Quand vivait mon père* (Paris: Grasset, 1940), p. 10.

[13] Edouard Drumont, *La Liberté,* 11 February 1880, p.3. In his exhaustive study on Daudet's early years Jacques-Henry Bornecque comes to a similar conclusion about the problem of ancestry although he does not rule out the possibility that Daudet might have been descended in the very distant past from less than purely French stock. Jacques-Henry Bornecque, *Les Années d'apprentissage: Alphonse Daudet* (Paris:Nizet, 1951), pp. 17-18.

[14] Daudet confided to Goncourt that the charge that he was a "Carthaginian" was extremely annoying. See Sachs, *The Career of Alphonse Daudet,* pp.207-208.

15 Edouard Drumont, *Mon Vieux Paris* (Paris: Flammarion, 1893), vol. I, xiv, xv, xvii.

16 Ibid., p. 28.

17 Edouard Drumont, *Les Fêtes nationales à Paris* (Paris: Baschet, 1879).

18 Drumont, *La France juive,* vol. I, p. 43. See also Paul Duclos, "Catholiques et juifs autour de l'affaire Dreyfus," *Revue d'Histoire de l'Eglise de France,* LXIV, No. 172, Jan.-Feb. 1978, 39-53.

19 See Benjamin Szold Levin, "Prophet of the Lord: Dumas Fils' Vision of Israel," *Judaism,* Summer 1974, 23, no. 3, 351-368.

20 Albert Vandam, *Men and Manners of the Third Republic* (New York: James, Pott, 1904), pp. 219-244.

21 Livois, *Histoire de la presse française,* vol. I, p. 273. On the Jews of this region, see Frances Malino,*The Sephardic Jews of Bordeaux* (University: The University of Alabama Press, 1978).

22 Drumont, *LaFrance juive,* vol. I, p. 354.

23 Ibid., p. 37.

24 Ibid., p. 39.

25 Drumont, *La France juive devant l'opinion,* p. 178.

26 Ibid., p. 179.

27 Drumont, *La France juive,* vol. I, p. 374.

28 Bouvier, *Les Rothschild,* p. 187.

29 Parkes, *The Emergence of the Jewish Problem,* p. 204.

30 Jean Bouvier, *Le Krach de l'Union Générale* (Paris: Presses Universitaires de France, 1960), pp. 171-185.

31 Jeannine Verdès-Leroux, *Scandale financier et l'antisémitisme catholique* (Paris: Le Centurion, 1969), pp. 36, 57, 153, 154.

32 The best known fictionalized account of the scandal is Zola's novel, *L'Argent* (1891).

33 Drumont, *Figures de bronze,* p. 293. On the politics of this era, see

Robert R. Locke, *French Legitimists and the Politics of Moral Order in the Early Third Republic* (Princeton: Princeton University Press, 1974).

[34] Frank Brabant, *The Beginning of the Third Republic in France* (London: MacMillan, 1940), p. 244. See also Daniel Halévy, *The End of the Notables* (Middletown, Conn: Wesleyan University Press, 1974), p. 33.

[35] Parkes, *The Emergence of the Jewish Problem*, p. 204.

[36] Robert Byrnes, *Antisemitism in Modern France*, p. 146.

[37] Quoted by Georges Bernanos in *La Grande Peur des bienpensants,* p. 128.

[38] Henri Gougenot de Mousseaux, *Emancipation aux Antilles* (Paris: Darvoir & Fontain, 1844), p. 92.

[39] In Gougenot's opinion the working class was stirred by ''a few high bankers and opulent, impudent capitalists and some bold speculators.'' *Des Proletaires* (Paris: Mellier, 1846), p. 560.

[40] Léon Pagès, ''Le Chevalier Gougenot des Mousseaux et ses travaux sur la magie contemporaine,'' *Annales de Philosophie Chrétienne,* October 1877, no. 82, 306. Followers of Gougenot claimed that he had been killed by a poisoned communion wafer which had been planted by Jews in the chapel where he heard daily mass.

[41] Henri Gougenot des Mousseaux, *Les hauts phénomènes de la magie* (Paris: Plon, 1865), pp. 462-463.

[42] Ibid., pp. 395-396.

[43] zibid., pp. 399, 419.

[44] Max Milner, *Le Diable dans la littérature française* (Paris: Corti, 1960), vol. II, p. 355.

[45] See Byrnes, *Antisemitism in Modern France,* p. 165.

[46] Stéphane Arnoulin, *Edouard Drumont et les jésuites,* p. 109.

[47] Drumont, *Sur le chemin de ma vie,* p. 138.

[48] Drumont, *La Liberté,* 8 May 1880, 3.

[49] Drumont, *La France juive,* vol. II, pp. 401, 419. See also Pierre Pierrard, *Juifs et catholiques français* (Paris: Fayard, 1970), p. 28.

50 See Andrew Canepa, *"La Civiltà Cattolica* and Clerical Antisemitism in Italy, 1880-1900.''* (submitted article). For a recent study on Daudet's personality, see Roger Williams, *The Horror of Life* (Chicago: The Univ. of Chicago Press, 1980), pp. 275-312.

3

La France Juive

*Slander lives upon succession*
*For ever housed where it gets*
*possession.*

--*Shakespeare*

By the 1880s Drumont was gradually emerged in the public eye as a self-proclaimed champion of Catholicism. His growing antisemitism developed along parallel lines with his spiritual devotion. After reconciling himself with the church, in February 1882 he fought a duel with Charles Laurent, a fellow journalist who had denounced the Benedictine order and cheered their expulsion from France at the government's order. Drumont saw these monks as an integral part of France, and although dueling was forbidden by the church, he gladly took up the sword in its defense. He also took up the pen in the same cause. In his voluminous writings Drumont often justified composing his *opus magnum* as a response to the liberals and radicals, and behind them the Jews, whom he charged with waging a campaign to drive literally the Catholic church out of France. For some members of the church status deprivation was not just a matter of lost privileges but rather the experience of forced expulsion. To this challenge Drumont proposed antisemitism in part as a radical means to expel the enemies of Christendom.

It is necessary therefore to analyze in detail the circumstances surrounding the creation, arguments, and reception of his most important book, *La France juive*. It immediately became the bestseller of the age and was responsible for changing the attitudes of many Frenchmen toward the Jews in their country.

As his religious views became better known the self-annointed Christian paladin thought it prudent that same year to marry according to church law the woman with whom he had been living for some time. Her name was Louise Gaète and Drumont almost never referred to her in any of his writings undoubtedly out of embarrassment over their liaison which was scandalous in he eyes of the church. She had been the former mistress of Charles Marchal de Bussy and had been in poor health for some time, and in February 1884 she died. After her passing Drumont claimed that "now no human consideration holds me back any longer: I am finally going to be able to speak!" [1]

By the time of his wife's death his secret book was well under way. After working at *La Liberté* he would carry on research at the *Bibliothèque Nationale*. At night he busied himself with glue pots and newspaper clippings to put together the work for which he would always be remembered. When it eventually appeared he was roundly accused of being an agent for the clerical party, a charge he vehemently denied. He claimed instead that "Christ saw that my soul was straight and that I obeyed no personal thoughts since I had not been raised by priests, had never been protected by them, and in a word owed nothing to what is called 'the clerical party', and He rewarded me." [2] Whatever he owed the priestly faction may never be completely known, but by his own admission he remained in contact with them, having had his manuscript checked for theological errors by the Jesuit Father du Lac.

Whether Drumont's talents were solicited by some clergymen to denounce the liberal republican party may thus never be fully revealed. With all the fervor of a fresh convert he had little trouble in identifying his motives: "I obeyed a call...perfectly...I heard in a moment like an inner voice that repeated to me from morning till evening: 'Go...go...go!' and I ended up by going." [3] Drumont saw himself as an instrument of providence. He was also aided by therapeutic considerations: "I was only guided by the hatred of oppression which is my basic nature. Oppression makes me physically ill. Forced, for many years, in order to execute my family duties, to repress what I thought, I ended up with stomach aches, and a lack of appetite which caused my throat to contract at mealtime. This suffering completely disappeared the day I could freely express my vision, to offer my words, which I did in *La France juive*." [4] In his study of antisemitism in the nineteenth century Poliakov recorded that Wagner underwent a similar experience when he read the Jew-baiting works of the priest Father Rohling. The contribution of the latter, for which Drumont wrote the preface to the French edition, was so efficacious that it helped relieve Wagner of eczema. [5]

With his health restored and his faith buttressed, Drumont began to put his plans into action. He was not by any means the first Frenchman to write against the Jews. Such works had been around since the beginning of the century, but they had only limited appeal. Until 1886 anti-Jewish literature of the doctrinaire sort was confined to certain Catholic circles on the Right and to some socialists on the Left. [6] What was unique about Drumont's contribution was that he succeeded in merging and magnifying the Catholic and socialist criticisms into a vision that would soon be characterized as "national socialism."

Most of these early anti-Jewish books seemed to have passed largely unnoticed by the general public. They were aimed at special audiences. So it was with Drumont's first published assaults upon the Jews which were printed in his literary column in the journal *Le Livre*. In March 1884 in a review of Heine's memoirs Drumont wrote: "This Semite, artistic and refined, consumed by the great sadness of all things, is the particularly successful example of a type which you always meet on the streets of Paris, that you have either for a companion, comrade, or master." But Drumont was not concerned with Heine alone. In this column he used the German poet as a foil to characterize the basic quandary facing contemporary Catholicism: "If it hasn't totally destroyed the Christian religion, this stubborn, intriguing, political, subtle people have almost completely demolished it." Drumont ended this attack by declaring himself willing "to sacrifice the interests of the artist and scholar to the needs of the suffering masses" in order to restore the Christian order of things.[7]

Other reviews of Drumont appearing in *Le Livre* were less explicit, almost cryptic in tone. In the 4 April 1884 issue where he examined the correspondence of Frédéric LePlay, he recalled that newspaper directors were forced to confess that to tell the truth would run the risk of losing subscribers. Two months later, in reviewing Huysmans' novel which he called *Au* (sic) *Rebours* he recognized in the hero "a representative of that former race..." Years later the great novelist would reciprocate Drumont's praise and lend support to his world view.

Drumont's next assault came in 1885 in *La Revue de la Révolution*, a recently founded journal of counter-revolutionary tendencies. It was a long piece which later was to be printed as a brochure dealing with an episode which took place just before the outbreak of the great revolution. Here Drumont claimed that the crown jewels had been stolen and used by Jews and Freemasons to bribe the English to help organize anticlericalism in France. Then Drumont tried to trace the history of other historic precious stones up through modern times. In every case he found that they had been sullied by passing through the hands of shady types like financiers and republican politicians. He even claimed that "one could see appear on these brilliant fiery diamonds the blood of so many wretched suicides, so many luckless sorts reduced to despair following some killing on the stock market." Though the attack on Jews almost seemed obscured by the rest of the article, it becomes apparent that this was Drumont's way of announcing to the world his views on the Jewish question.

In order to protect himself he resigned from *La Liberté*, when on 28 December 1885, he informed his readers of his departure, "all choked up writing this article which will be the last that I will write in *La Liberté*." He was about to leave his old journal to accept a high position at the Catholic paper, *Le Monde,* which was directed by Oscar Havard and A. de Claye. No sooner had he made the transition that he began to denounce the republic and Freemasonry with renewed vigor.

Drumont had been careful not to reveal his plans to anyone outside of a small circle of close friends. Only Alphonse Daudet, Octave Uzanne, and Raoul Duval were aware of his secret project. Drumont liked to tell the story about the old Jew from whom he gathered bits of information about Jewish subjects. He merely told him that he was writing a history of the Jews and could use any kind of help. Once the book appeared the writer claimed he never heard from him again.

The times were ripe for a book like Drumont's. In 1886 the faculties of

Catholic theology in the universities were abolished by the state. Such attacks on religion inspired Drumont to persevere in his task. The clandestine author had carefully put his plan into operation. With his wife no longer a hinderance and protected by a position on a Catholic newspaper, he completed the two enormous volumes. The Goncourt journal for 5 January 1886 records this entry: "At the Spartiate dinner today Drumont officially announced the forthcoming publication of his book attacking the Jews--that book written for the personal satisfaction of hatred by a Catholic and reactionary in the midst of the complete and insolent triumph of republican Jewry. If he is unbearable and even a little despicable sometimes because of the narrowness of his ideas on everything, at least Drumont has the valiance of spirit of a man of another age and almost an appetite for matyrdom."[8]

Drumont may have been ready for the world but the world was less than enthusiastic at first for him. He had tried to peddle his bulky manuscript to various publishing houses only to meet rejection at almost every turn. One major complaint was that Drumont refused to present a balanced treatment of the subject, that his language was too bitter and outrageous. With a flair for the public's taste, Drumont replied that to water down his message would lessen its impact. He wanted to give the masses a bomb not a treatise. He was especially bitter about the lack of interest expressed by his old schoolmate, Fouret, who had become one of the directors at Hachette. After the book finally caught the public eye, many critics concluded that the miserly Drumont must have been financially backed by reactionary circles.[9]

Despite these setbacks, Drumont received the help he needed, that extra support that got his book into print and reviews in the leading journals of Paris. He was forced to turn to his old, close friend Alphonse Daudet, one of the most successful writers of the time who wielded much influence in publishing circles. Daudet believed in Drumont and his mission. Though his good offices he convinced the new publishing house of Marpon and Flammarion to print his friend's book. This firm, like many others, was suffering from the general economic recession that plagued France. It had hoped to expand sales by issuing reprints of Daudet's already successful earlier novels, thus it seems likely that Daudet's drawing power and prestige convinced them to accept *La France juive* under certain conditions.

Marpon was hesitant about running the risk of publishing such a work. He thought it might be a good seller but that Drumont would have to bear the costs of the first edition of 2000 copies and any libel suits that might be brought by outraged readers. Drumont paid the sum of 8000 francs and hid twenty-five copies in a friend's house out of fear that the police might seize the entire printing.

At his parish church Drumont could be found praying for success, resigning himself to divine will. Finally on 14 April 1886, the two enormous volumes of *La France juive* went on sale. During the week only twenty-five copies were purchased. Drumont frequented the bookshops and lamented over the piles of unsold copies of his life's work. The book-dealers, too, were disappointed and were on the verge of withdrawing the stock from display. But Drumont's faith never wavered: he redoubled his efforts and prayers, believing that "God, who guided all these matters, protected this book, however imperfect it might be, because without doubt he knew that it was inspired by the love of justice."[10]

His prayers were answered. Help came again in the shape of Alphonse Daudet who persuaded his friend, Francis Magnard, to give Drumont a boost by writing something about his book. Magnard published a brief piece every day in the consevative *Figaro*. He, too, had been troubled by republican anticlericalism and was glad to lend his hand to the cause of attacking its influence.

In his column of 18 April 1886 Magnard wrote a review that was designed to arouse public opinion. He found *La France juive* a work "where the fury and at times inflammed eloquence of his sincere convictions are joined with a childish credulity which indiscriminately accepts the most trivial gossip." Magnard's tongue-in-cheek article was a challenge to the leftist politician, Charles Freycinet, to read Drumont to see for himself "what kind of fanaticism produces persecution." As for Drumont "he seems to be given to a peculiar obsession which makes him see the Jew everywhere where others monomaniacs see the police, the Jesuits or Freemasons." Magnard's shafts were well directed and calculated to arouse controversy. No one seemed to be spared. He then intimated that because of Drumont's clerical associations, past and present, the polemicist was probably writing at the behest of the Abbé d'Hulst, rector of the *Institut Catholique* and vicar of the archdiocese of Paris. Magnard claimed it was unlikely that Drumont, editor of *Le Monde,* the archbishop's quasi-official journal, would have gone to so much trouble without consulting high church leaders.

Whatever the truth of these suggestions they reached their mark. Catholic papers published the archbishop's denial of financing the book. While the clerical press praised Drumont, "this respectful son of the church," other important journals began to decry the work. Drumont was glad to profit from this public bickering and sales began to increase.

At *Le Figaro* on 23 April Albert Wolff denounced Drumont as a former associate of Charles Marchal and linked his present notoriety to German inspiration: "In Berlin it is the preacher Stoecker who leads the movement and in Paris it is the Catholic Drumont...Above the Rhine separating them these two dervishes dream of shaking hands in a fond embrace..." Other Jews, too, took exception to Drumont's attacks. The most memorable reply came in the challenge of Arthur Meyer to fight Drumont in a duel.

It was not Drumont's antisemitism which offended Meyer. On this point he largely agreed with his adversary. Meyer, though born a Jew, became a Catholic and antisemite and later an anti-Dreyfusard, in an attempt to placate the conservative clientele he catered to as the editor of the Bonapartist journal, *Le Gaulois.* Meyer was the consumate dandy, a snob, who, according to Goncourt, slept wearing pearl gray gloves. He had carefully aped the ways of the upper classes and he was thoroughly annoyed when Drumont's book accused him of being the son of an old clothes peddler. This and this alone prompted him to challenge Drumont to a duel. The test of strength turned out to be one of the more notorious journalists' duels of the nineteenth century.

As soon as Meyer demanded satisfaction, he had second thoughts. Drumont had a reputation as an extremely aggressive swordsman. Goncourt's journal dated 22 April 1886 graphically captures Drumont's confident mood on the eve of combat: "I eat dinner this evening with Drumont, who will fight a duel on Saturday with Meyer of *Le Gaulois,* Daudet and M. Albert Duruy acting as his seconds. Drumont arrives nervous, tense, yet droll and gay. 'Today', he exclaims, 'fifty-five people. The bell never stopped ringing. Crowds began to stop in the street in front of the house where they saw all those people entering it--coming to say to me: 'Oh, how we thank you for having said what we feel!' Some Carmelites sent word they would pray for me on Saturday...and my lay sister, who has just come into my household and was told that I was sort of a lay priest..she doesn't know what to make of it. Yes, there's not a copy of the book left, the 2000 are all gone. Marpon is urging me to make another printing. They are going to put eight presses to work. It's aggravating just the same. I have talked eight hours today, and my voice is gone." [11]

The duel ended as the most humiliating experience of Meyer's life and turned into a boost for Drumont. Again Goncourt captures the mood of Paris reacting to the scandal on the following day: "Young Lavedan, who gets around, was present when Meyer got off the train on his return from the duel. The whole boulevard in front of *Le Gaulois* was full of Jews: and broughams, such as one sees in front of the Saint Augustin church on the day of a big wedding, were pouring out a Yid a minute onto the boulevard. There were all the Dollfusses and the Dreyfuses in creation..." It was Daudet who filled in Goncourt on the details of the duel. As Goncourt recalls: "There was a first encounter in which, when Meyer parried with his left hand, Daudet called him a scoundrel and told him he ought to have his hand tied behind his back. A second attack followed, and this time Meyer grasped the sword with his hand and wounded Drumont. And Daudet describes the scene at the entrance to the barn where he had been carried, of Drumont, his trousers already removed, slapping his bloodstained shirt tail and shouting angrily at Meyer and his seconds: 'Back to the ghetto with you, you dirty Jews! You are bunch of murderers! You are the ones who chose this house belonging to Hirsch which was bound to bring me bad luck! Daudet adds, 'Yes, indeed, that man, behaving incorrectly, that guttersnipe giving vent to a vulgar outburst, was superb, whereas Meyer, that correct Semite, looked like a haberdasher's clerk.''

All Paris was talking about the sword fight. Later that week Goncourt records in his memoirs on 6 May: "The real truth about the duel, as told by Daudet in confidence, is this: Meyer, who was expected to give way, to turn tail and run, conducted himself very staunchly at first and carried out the thrust which he had told his intimates about, a thrust in prime, I believe, which was to get Drumont in the belly. But when the thrust was made, and very well made, not parried at all by Drumont, and Meyer had at length withdrawn his sword--bent apparently not by a pants button but by a truss--he completely lost his head and behaved like a cad." [12]

Meyer and Drumont had to answer to the courts for such public combat. The judge thought the contest was more of a "knife fight" than a duel and fined Meyer 200 francs. The editor of *Le Gaulois* was mortified though not enough to prevent him from rebuilding his reputation. In part his praise of Drumont's philosophy helped to rehabilitate him in the eyes of his conservative readers. Of Drumont he later wrote: "I learned to know him. I could admire in him one of the great writers of our time-- a percursor who remained an apostle."[13]Drumont never tired of reminding his public of Meyer's famous "left hand," which was described as a symbol of Semitic treachery, comparing him and all Jews, to that kind of parasite one meets on the beach, that one teases and covers with sand: "As soon as it shakes off the sand, it starts off again following the line it was following before." [14]

The publicity aroused by the planted pieces and the duel produced the desired results. The book sales began to move upward rapidly. In the following months it ran through several printings and eventually became the most popular work of its time. After *The Protocols of the Elders of Zion* and *Mein Kampf* Drumont's book is perhaps the most influential piece of classical antisemitic literature in Europe. For all its faults it should be carefully examined in order to understand and appreciate its author's special talent to mold and direct public opinion.

Analysis would show that *La France juive* is chiefly a political pamphlet. Despite Drumont's pretensions of being considered a philosopher, historian, observer of society, and economist, his masterpiece bears the stamp of a journalist's work with all the techniques and appeal of that calling. Essentially the book deserves the description it was given by Sartre who wrote of its author: "He bathes his hands in ordure. Read again *La France juive* of Drumont; that book of a high French morality is a collection of ignoble or obscene stories. Nothing reflects better the complex nature of the antisemite.'' [15] What is complex about this work is the fact that its author was aiming at two distinct reading publics: the average Frenchman and the militant antisemite. Drumont is not really interested in providing a psychological portrait of the modern Jew. His aim to ransack history to paint the most negative portrait of the Jew.

Even before Drumont launched into what he called the historical foundations of the Jewish question, he found it difficult to refrain from expanding that area where his talent became unsurpassed: scandal and gossip are at the heart of his elephantine pamphlet. All the same it is important to recall that Drumont claimed that his work was a serious study which he intended to serve as a beacon focusing on the conditions which caused the decline of France and Christendom.

*La France juive* is divided into six parts. The introduction succinctly states Drumont's thesis and intention: "Taine wrote *The Jacobin Conquest.* I want to write *The Jewish Conquest.*" From this perspective the author claimed to be revealing the hidden motives behind the revolution of 1789. In his hostility to the Third Republic he believed that by casting it as mainly beneficial to the Jews he would somehow weaken its authority. Through his simple logic the defeat of monarchism, the chief vehicle of Catholic political interests, from 1789 to 1877, was the work of Jews and their lackeys.

Drumont was the first antisemite in France to explain this conflict in racial terms. Although he often mocked and misrepresented the Jewish religion, he insisted that his arguments were based on racial and not religious factors. It is doubly ironic, therefore, that Drumont rarely indulged in explicit racist arguments and did not refer to the racist thought of his countryman, Gobineau. The latter in fact had little that is negative to write about Jews, and it was in Germany that his racist theories were twisted to serve antisemitic causes. By adopting other pseudo-scientific notions, Drumont presented a Semitic-Aryan struggle of cosmic proportions, "of distinct races irremediably hostile to one another, whose antagonism has filled the world in the past and will still trouble it in the future." [16]

It should be noted that in comparing races similar notions had been commonly accepted in respectable European intellectual circles although their import was not necessarily malicious. In 1869, for example, Matthew Arnold wrote in his essay "Hebraism and Hellenism" that "science has now made visible to everybody the great and pregnant elements of difference which lie in race, and in how signal a manner they make the genius and history of our Indo-European people vary from those of a Semitic people." [17] Arnold, of course, intended nothing malicious, and neither did Ernest Renan for the most part when he later characterized the Semites as decidedly inferior to the Aryans in the creation of civilization. Still, for Renan, whom Drumont quoted for his own purposes, Semitic qualities were in the main negative. It was a major misfortune in western intellectual development that these particular terms were taken from the history of languages and applied to the history of races.

In the hands of German academics and demagogues such notions about radically different races turned explosive when applied to politics. This was the tradition from which Drumont heavily borrowed and grafted onto an existing anti-Jewish sentiment already lingering in certain segments of the French population. For Drumont "the Aryan or Indo-European race alone possesses the virtue of justice, the feeling for liberty and conception of beauty." As for the Semite, he is "mercantile, greedy, intriguing, subtle, tricky," whereas the Aryan is "enthusiastic, heroic, chivalrous, disinterested, forthright, confiding to a fault."

Hundreds of millions of Aryans are so naive, according to Drumont, that they cannot see that they have been duped by a handful of Jews. If so few Semites are so dangerous, then their increasing numbers can only suggest a larger peril. As the great modern exodus began, resulting from Tsarist pogroms, eastern Europe, that *"Vagina Judeorum"*, as Drumont put it, threatened to overwhelm France. It should be observed that native French Jews were also apprehensive about the arrival of their uncouth cousins from the East whose presence might "stir up antisemitism". They did not wish to admit that Drumont and his admirers made little distinction between such regional differences. For the latter a Jew always remained a Jew with no exceptions. Thus the Jews of France helped organize the passage of eastern Jews through their land and on to the New World where they caused no embarrassment to their Gallic benefactors.

Although Drumont was a proclaimed racist it is ironic to note that he did not dwell long on the pseudo-scientific rationalizations for modern racism. He did endorse the modern zoological form of racism, but the bulk of his writings reflects his preference for ransacking history and theology books and recounting the gossip of contemporary events and scandals.

The first part of Drumont's book is devoted to the stereotyped image of the Jews down through history in the West. No crimes were unknown to them and Drumont eagerly depicted them as given to child sacrifices, espionage, fomenting wars, causing capitalism and socialism, and alcoholism. So carried away by this monomania, Drumont was forced to cite false statistics to exaggerate his claims. It has been estimated that the number of Jews then residing in France figured roughly 80,000. However for Drumont, who saw them everywhere, the figure 500,000 was more effective and appealing to the curiousity of the general public.

Not only are Jewish spiritual values dangerous in this narrative, but physically as a race Drumont found them revolting. He offered a long disquisition on the *foetor judaicus* and attributed this stink to their love of goat and goose meat. He was quick to add that baptismal water could never wash away this defect because Jews were essentially a race and not a religion. Drumont did not have much to say about Judaism per se because he was too ignorant to know its basic tenets and history. What little he had to say was culled from contemporary antisemitic tracts. Even where he began to touch on an engaging subject such as the fabled Jewish drive to social movements and advancement, he could only see it in terms of mental illness: "Neurosis is the implacable sickness of the Jews." And it was this illness which Drumont believed was causing the ruin of France.

Drumont had little talent for handling historical subjects and theory. His most powerful passages were devoted to concrete depictions of Jews as the most loathsome, repulsive creatures ever to walk the face of the earth. Here is his most celebrated portrait of his enemy: "The principal signs by which the Jew can be recognized are these: that famous hooked nose, blinking eyes, tight teeth, protruding ears, square fingernails instead of round, ankles sticking out, the soft and melting hand of the hypocrite and the traitor. They often have one arm shorter than the other." [18] The first reaction to this description might be laughter, as if such a being ever strolled the streets of Paris. The second reaction, after reflection, is one of uneasiness, of the feeling that makes the flesh creep. What Drumont was doing, essentially, was drawing the portrait of the bogyman in his classic medieval incarnation.

The image of Jewish women fared little better in Drumont's hands and it seemed to be an exaggeration of a trend already noticeable in Daudet's technique of characterization of Jews. For Drumont they were all nothing less than whores: "The prostitute, moreover, serves Israel in her way; she fulfills a sort of mission by ruining and pushing into dishonor the sons of our aristocracy; she is a marvellous instrument for Jewish politics." [19] Racial and social contamination, he averred, always result in the destruction of the Aryan upper classes. Towards the end of his long description of Hebrew horrors Drumont furnished a list purporting to identify all those prominent Gentiles who married Jewesses and who came to violent ends. All in all, however, negative erotic references to Jews in this work are relatively rare. They only are used as one of many categories of invective. Speculation on the alleged prudery of Drumont and the origins of antisemitism are in this instance misplaced. Non-erotic social gossip served up as history is the main feature of this book.

After the general introduction the second part of *La France juive* was devoted to the Jew in French history. Drumont, finding the thought somewhat inconceivable, condemned Renan's assertion that there were converts to Judaism among the Gauls. He did acknowledge important Jewish communities in the Middle Ages only as a pretext to blame them for causing the Albigensian heresy. Although Dumont like many historians could not accurately identify the source of Albigensian beliefs, he was certain that "Judaism was at the bottom of these troubles." One gnostic trait about Albigensianism, however, was that it was more hostile to Judaism than Catholicism. Drumont did not mention this fact because it would contradict his theory of Jewish responsibility for this heresy.

Like Louis Veuillot, Drumont hailed every instance of anti-Jewish persecution as a great moment in French history. With lavish detail and approval he related how Saint Louis had the Talmud burned at the behest of Pope Gregory IX in 1240. As the king of France Louis earned a reputation for piety as a model of Christian charity. But according to the Jewish historian Graetz "the otherwise noble and well-disposed monarch, Louis IX, was so ruled by his prejudices that he could not bear to look at a Jew...the command of Gregory to confiscate the Talmud was entirely disregarded in Spain and England, at least there is no record of any hostile measures in these countries. Only in France, where the priest-ridden and weak-minded Louis IX, having attained his majority, had nominally assumed the reins of government, was the Talmud really confiscated. The Jews were compelled under penalty of death to surrender their copies." [20] For Drumont, on the other hand, "the holy king displayed an extraordinary mildness." [21] Forced conversion, separation of children from parents, bribes, destruction of religious practices and livelihood were prompted by Saint Louis' fanatical scruples. These were the kingly qualities which Drumont admired and longed for. [22]

Drumont recounted their fate at the hands of other French monarchs. Whereas Saint Louis was moved by religious zeal, his successor, Philip the Fair, was mainly prompted by political and economic considerations in his persecution of the Jews. Louis had toyed with the idea of having them expelled but that plan would have thwarted his conversion efforts. King Philip in 1306 actually decreed their banishment before which their money and possessions were confiscated by the state. In his book Drumont hailed this turn of events, viewing it as a foretaste of his own social philosophy.

According to Drumont one year after stripping and deporting the Jews the king still in need of money turned his wrath on the wealthy order of the Knights Templar. Concerning this policy Norman Cohn writes: "to Philip the religious megalomaniac the existence of the Temple presented an infuriating obstacle, which to Philip the politician the destruction of the Temple offered financial relief." [23] In a series of baseless trials and forced confessions the powerful order was exterminated and its funds despoiled. Because this order of Christian knights derived its name from the Temple Mount where its headquarters stood in Jerusalem, Drumont claimed the "knights Templars were often in contact with the Jews on money matters." [24] He also rehashed all the unfounded, ghastly anti-Christian arguments against them which tended to link them to the Jews. Drumont's main purpose in so doing was to connect them with the Free-masons of his own time whom he treated as another arm of a world-wide, eternal international conspiracy against the Christian order of things.

Throughout this book Drumont continued to ransack history in search of details to buttress his central thesis. A case in point was the question of Montaigne's ancestry. Because scholars had recently discovered that Montaigne's mother might have been of Jewish descent, Drumont concluded that the great essayist's advocacy of moderation was a typical manifestation of Jewish cowardice. Following this kind of logic Rembrandt fared no better and was severely condemned for having lived in the Joodenbreestraat of Amsterdam and used its inhabitants as models. According to Drumont: "his work has the Jewish color, it is yellow, that hot, bruning yellow which seems like the reflection of gold..." [25]

Drumont's habit of identifying the Jewish origins of all those who dis-pleased him went to absurd lengths. In cases where there were no Jews to be found, he invented them, and when they could not be invented, he insinuated their presence. As one example of the old regime's decline he cited the South Sea bubble of the Scot John Law. "You can't possibly identify the Jewish origins of Law although that name of Law (Lewis, Levy) really has a Judaic character." [26] Drumont knew that there were no Jews as such in Paris during those tumultuous times. But in order to blame them for causing the French revolution, he exaggerated the roles of the few who might have been there and then he denigrated the sup-posedly Jewish aspects of Freemasonry characterizing it as another branch of those secret societies dedicated to the overthrow of France.

The theme of the cryptic Jew occupies a large place in his writings. Unable to find those who openly displeased him, Drumont asserted that those who have assimilated into the general society have only pretended to do so. Thus their acceptance of the dominant culture was merely a pretext in their plan to dominate society. At the slightest opportunity they were supposed to be ready to shed the mask of bourgeois conformity and "insult priests, smash sanctuary doors and throw down the crosses." [27] In short for Drumont assimilation was a hoax. [28]

In Drumont's eyes this sort of assimilated Jew was the true enemy of Christian civilization. "The dangerous Jew is the vague Jew," he was fond of repeating. "Socialist in word, agent provocateur, foreigner's spy, he simultaneously deceives the workers who trust him, the police who pay him, and the government which employs him...he is the noxious animal par excellence and at the same time the elusive beast; he has thus bur-rowed into so many things that you don't know how to grab him." [29] This was Drumont's favorite theme which he fully developed in his treatment of contemporary society. By deliberately qualifying the Jew as a slippery character and difficult to notice, he thereby preyed on the reader's paranoia and sense of helplessness in understanding the workings of the modern world.

From the conspiratorial view of history the revolution of 1789 could be made to appear to have been instigated by those who professed so-called Judaic principles and who were easily taken over by crypto-Jews themselves. When, for example, Louis XVI was beheaded Drumont identified his executioner as a Jew named Simon. To account for the ferocious character of Jean-Paul Marat, Drumont acknowledged that his father was a Sardinian Catholic whose name had been Mara and had converted to Protestantism. Drumont then insisted on claiming that Mara was originally a descendant of Spanish Marranos, crypto-Jews who for centuries managed to retain a chance to seek revenge on Christian society. This scenario was thus supposed to explain the period of the Terror during the revolution. These denunciations of Jewish conspiracies had their parallel in anti-Masonic literature which was rampant during this period and enjoyed a wide audience in mainly Catholic circles.

Drumont's imagination was so fertile that it led him to make contradictions on the question of conspiracy. Since Jews were reputed to be bold parvenus, what else, he speculated, could explain the meteoric career of Napoleon Bonaparte, the greatest parvenu of all time? Taking some speculations of Michelet at face value, Drumont postulated that Corsica like Sardinia had once hosted various large Semitic populations in the past and that Napoleon and his tightly knit family were representatives of the type of social unit that could under favorable circumstances take over the government in time of turmoil.

This theory encountered difficulty when Drumont was unable to deny that Napoleon was ultimately opposed to the great Sanhedrin which he had convened. Then, according to this scenario, Napoleon the grasping Semite, was miraculously transformed into Napoleon the leader of the French and victim of the Jews. Only when this descendant of Marranos was opposed to the Rothschilds working for the allies did he become the great national hero. Thus Drumont had it both ways: Napoleon was first damned for his reputed Semitic origins and then praised when he stood in opposition to Jewish interests. As in most of this book's narrations Drumont's guiding principle was hatred of Jews everywhere. History had to be contorted to conform to his vision of things.

The outcome of this tumultuous period--the revolution, republic, empire, the result of these upheavals, declared Drumont, was the total triumph of the Jews. "The peace was signed on the ruins of France...They (the Jews) monopolized all the world's money. Nations and kings were no more than puppets whose strings were pulled by Jews."[30] In the fourth part of his book Drumont entered into the modern world and vividly related its rapid development from this point of view. Mainly echoing and repeating the socialist arguments of Toussenel, Drumont in effect was chronicling the decline of the old order during the restoration and the rise of the middle class.

What makes Drumont's work superficially resemble the socialists' denunciation of the same society was the fact that they largely were tracing the same social developments. But where those socialists unaffected by antisemitism themselves chose to stress the class struggle Drumont saw the same conflict as a racial struggle. Like many Catholics of the period he was unaware of the scientific study of social development. It never occurred to him and many others that the development of their society would have proceeded in just about the same direction even without the presence of Jews. The Jews themselves, and not in all cases, were doing no more than following and participating in the rapid rise and growth of the bourgeoisie. But Drumont like the church that inspired him chose in too many instances a demonological explanation for the forces that threatened their traditional status.

Drumont painted in the most sordid and lurid colors the revival of the old Jewish section of Paris. The entire Saint-Paul quarter had been taken over and "today the parish of Saint-Eustache is almost completely contaminated..." These final portions of the second part of his book are devoted to the Second Republic and Second Empire and the Commune, those periods in which Drumont and his family were growing up and with which they were most familiar. Following his line of exposition he treated all these governments and upheavals as just so many milestones on the Jews' road to total domination of France. Wars were started and stopped on their occult command. All other factors were superficial in the face of this racist explanation of history.

When writing about the early years of the Third Republic Drumont was especially vehement and trenchant. He regarded the aftermath of the 1870 war and the Paris Commune as the Semites' moment of "complete triumph." From then on the government was, in his eyes, at the beck and call of the Jews. A critical analysis of certain topics treated by Drumont reveals how he tailored historical fact to suit his theory.

One of the more common charges repeated by Drumont, one that would have devastating repercussions during the Second World War, concerned certain policies of the revolution toward church property. When the immense land holdings of the church were sold off almost a century earlier, the middle class, just as it had in the England of Henry VIII, made a substantial profit. Drumont traced the impetus for the sale of these *biens nationaux* to the Jews and their frontmen who supposedly acted out of greed and hatred of Christianity. Unfortunately for this thesis careful re-

search of these events shows that at the time Jews were actually chided
by their new compatriots for not benefiting from confiscated church pro-
perties. [31]

Drumont's accusation, nevertheless, made good propaganda and he
proposed a scheme to re-establish justice as he saw it under the Third
Republic. His plan consisted of nothing less than an administration of
*biens juifs confisqués,* the proceeds from which would go to promote various programs for giving the money back to the people and the church.
Confiscation of Jews' property and their eventual deportation were at
the heart of Drumont's political antisemitic program, and this program
was to become the exact policy to be adopted by the clerically-backed
Vichy state fifty-four years later.

When he discussed the social question Drumont indulged in populist
rhetoric. He fancied himself a friend of the people, their tribune and
spokesman and he never tired of repeating, "for the worker, the social
revolution is an absolute necessity." On this score it might seem that
Drumont was echoing a certain type of Christian socialism that was
then developing as a reaction to the rise of materialistic secular socialism.
Regarding the quality and nature of Drumont's Catholicism many complex factors come into play that shed light on the church's attitude towards the social question. [32]

Was Drumont a Catholic and a Catholic writer? He surely thought he
was, and so did most of his friends and enemies. Once his reputation was
established he was viewed as another vigorous spokesman for Christian
France. However it has been at times argued that because of his racism
and hatred Drumont should not be considered to be a real Catholic.
There is some truth in this assessment. But the central question regarding his religious attitudes has more to do with the concrete reactions
of Catholics to his politics rather than measuring them against an ideal
standard of what constitutes Christian behavior.

A Catholic historian, Pierre Pierrard, has observed that many, perhaps
most of France's Catholics could hail various aspects of Drumont's work.
But endorsement of his basic attitudes was less than complete in certain
clerical quarters. For Drumont the battle he was waging was supposed to
be a radical struggle and strictly speaking the church had no purview in
this area. While antisemitism is an outgrowth of pagan and Christian
hostility towards Jews, its modern pseudo-scientific garb makes a mock-
ery of the church's spiritual claims. A baptized Jew for Drumont was
still a Jew, whereas in the eyes of the church, except for the Jesuits of
this period, the convert must be treated like one of the faithful. It was on
this point that Drumont differed from many fellow Catholics. He could
justify this break because he was not really a clerical writer,
one who always submitted himself to prior consultation with church authorities. Indeed Drumont often claimed France's episcopate was indul-

gent towards Jews. And this special brand of antiauthoritarian anticleri-calism served to make him popular with some segments of the lower clergy.

There is no denying that at times some leaders of the Catholic social movement in France made some limited use of antisemitic themes as part of their program. Albert be Mun, for example, a leading social ac-tivist, in 1886 solicited Drumont's help on occasion as a representative of the Paris press who was sympathetic to church interests. [33] However the layman in the street might view Drumont's personal peccadilloes such as anti-episcopal criticism and occasional superstitious beliefs, various Catholic worker organizations were divided about supporting his polic-ies. In short the church and its lay spokesmen were often ambivalent about the Jewish question. What was an occasional tactic for some of them was a total strategy for Drumont, however. They were mainly try-ing to infuse Christian principles into the working class; Drumont was trying to drive Jews out of France. At times their paths and interests crossed, but as Drumont's career progressed he became more and more bitter about the lack of total official support he felt he deserved from the church he had sworn to defend.

The message of Drumont to large numbers of Catholics struck a sym-pathetic chord. It could scarcely have been otherwise because generations of the faithful had been trained by the church to prefer a demonological explanation of history. Drumont like his ideological predecessors con-stantly exploited this tactic. To read Drumont at his most socialist mo-ments one has the impression that society would radically improve some-how once the Jews were deprived of their livelihood. In this way the dan-gerous ebb of social upheaval would drastically change when they were driven from the land, their capital confiscated, baptized, and turned over to church hands.

Psychologically, what Drumont proposed was an updated version of that logic earlier developed by Gougenot de Mousseaux. The latter be-lieved in his day that experiments with the occult and the supernatural were the work of diabolical agents. Somehow Gougenot hoped all would be well if persons given to such experiments realized that they were dealing with the devil. In his later works the devil was revealed to be the Jew. In this way Drumont's brand of socialism was based on the same ap-proach. By sanctifying capital, by putting it into Christian hands, and ex-pelling diabolical agents, the social question would supposedly be solved.

By the time Drumont had composed the third and fourth sections of his book he could write with the assurance of a first-hand observer of society. The basic themes of these parts expose in lurid, lengthy detail how Jews had secretly undermined national morale and Christian morals, provoked wars and taken over the government. On one fantastic detail Drumont prefigured Céline when he accused Jews of wishing to depopulate Paris by violent measures in order to make more room for their own kind. He accused them of trying to chase off Christians and "to exterminate men whose ancestors for centuries have been on the land of France." [34] When it was a question of Jews the word extermination was not slow in forming on Drumont's lips.

All these fantastic plans were allegedly plotted and carefully coordinated by a small though cohesive group of pro-German factions residing in France. To the ardent nationalist that Drumont thought himself to be no other explanation could account for the defeat of France. The drive to discover all the causes of France's decline led Drumont to denounce, for example, the influence of Jacques Offenbach, "the Jew who, after obeying his race by mocking, for the world's laughter, the pure creations of the Aryan genius of Greece, consciously worked for Prussia, by teaching soldiers to insult their generals." [35] Such was the power of the Opera bouffe.

There were different accusations of a more serious nature that show how Drumont distorted history. One to which he devoted much attention was the statute proposed in 1870 by Adolphe Crémieux for the naturalization of Algerian Jews. Crémieux, one of French Jewry's outstanding figures, succeeded in having this law enacted on 24 October 1870. For Drumont this was supposed to represent the height of Jewish interference in the affairs of state. He and other antisemites denounced this attempt to pass favorable legislation while the country was in the agony of the war. What Drumont did not say was that such a measure, granting French citizenship to these Jews, had been considered long before the war. As recently as 19 July 1870 it had been proposed by Emile Ollivier. Drumont's main argument against the law was that it discriminated against the Moslems. What he also neglected to mention was that the history of its long birth showed in 1859 naturalization was proposed for all the natives of the colony which had been made into an integral part of France. Similar measures favoring Jews were put forward in 1860 and again in 1865.

In Algeria the Jews were happy to flock to the banner of France and the Moslems preferred to remain faithful to their own national identity. More importantly, the European settler population did not wish to face a much larger Moslem community on equal terms. It was resigned for the time being and not without some bitterness to find itself on an equal footing with the much smaller Jewish community. This would change as soon as the European tried to arouse Moslem feelings against the Jews whom the latter traditionally held in contempt. For the most part the Moslems semed to be ambivalent about the new status of the Jews. On the one hand it appeared intolerable to have Jews hold a higher position than Moslems, yet on the other the latter dimly realized that Europeans, not Jews, were the ones who were frustrating their nationalist aspirations. There was friction between the two different native groups that Drumont endlessly exploited. His long passages in praise of Arabs was clear proof that in practice antisemitism has little to do with so-called Semites and is nothing more than another form of millennial Jew hatred.

One of the signers of the Crémieux decree was Léon Gambetta. He was also one of Drumont's favorite bugbears. As an erstwhile supporter of Chambord he could never forgive Gambetta's energetic campaign that effectively stopped whatever serious ambitions the monarchist parties had entertained. Since monarchism was the traditional vehicle of Catholic political aspirations, Gambetta was viewed as an enemy of Christiandom, a state of affairs which both rival parties fully and gladly accepted. In Drumont's imagination it was a short step to cast the energetic republican as the leader of an atheistic, Jewish, Protestant, Masonic conspiracy to destroy Catholicism. To emphasize this point Drumont always accused Gambetta of being a Jew although research shows that this charge is baseless. [36]

Much of Drumont's book is colored by contemporary anti-Jewish politics and polemics in Europe. Inevitably his attention was drawn to a sister Latin land, Romania, where the Jewish question had aroused international concern. Here Drumont's portraits reflect his Manichean view of the world: "The Italian type has taken on among the Romanians a sort of oriental grace both masculine and poetic. They love to sing at night under the clear stars." As for the Jews they constitute "a sort of perpetual discharge which is impossible to stop...dropping vermin wherever they pass, offering a constant danger for public health."

Underlying most of Drumont's descriptions of Jews is the thinly veiled assumption that they are not human and at best they are really monsters who occasionally assume human form only to trick Gentiles. By constantly portraying Jews in this light it seemed logical that some type of hygenic measures be taken to protect public health against their presence. Thus it is not surprising that a genocidal impulse often surfaced throughout his works. Referring again to the Romanians, he commented that "they would be in short perfectly happy, just like the French, if the Jews did not exist." [37]

What aroused Drumont's wrath regarding Romania was the attempts of the French foreign minister, William Henry Waddington, to obtain favorable or at least equitable treatment for Jews there at the time of the Berlin Congress of 1878. For Drumont, Waddington was the agent of Jewish interests. What Drumont neglected to say was that such intervention was part of a general drive on the part of France to assert its international influence. Because it suited domestic interests Waddington's foreign policy extended French influence and direct protection over the Christian minorities of the Ottoman Empire, especially those in Lebanon who were the victims of Moslem Arab atrocities. This form of humanitarian intervention was much more serious and far-reaching and persecuted minorities, Christian and Jewish, were its beneficiaries.

Drumont had other reasons for hating Waddington. It was during the presidency of Jules Grévy that he brought into the cabinet one of the outstanding statesmen of the Third Republic, Jules Ferry. What is curios about Drumont's long attacks against Ferry is that they were voiced with pseudo-radical eloquence against his foreign policy, especially in Indo-China. It was Ferry who revived and expanded the French empire under the republic.

Drumont was not really concerned with foreign policy. What he truly detested about Ferry was his more successful and enduring domestic campaign to establish compulsory education. The Catholic church loathed Ferry's aggressively republican educational policies because he was also in favor of educating women. Charles Péguy's famous remark that Jews have been reading since biblical times, the Protestants since the Reformation, but Catholics only since Jules Ferry has passed into legend. The church felt bypassed and vehemently opposed secular education among the broad masses, especially women. Ferry's policies made many new converts to the republican cause and made many enemies among the clerical factions. Because of his policies France entered a new phase in its historical development.

Drumont was not really a historian but mainly a gossip monger. However intriguing those chapters may have been which dealt with historical subjects, his main appeal was undoubtedly appreciated in the two long sections that he was saving for last. These parts, "Jewish Paris and French Society" and "Jewish Persecution," purport to unmask the occult operations of society at the time they were published. To many general readers uninterested in racist theorizing these must have been the most titillating chapters. Paradoxically this also seems to be the part of the book that has become the most dated for twentieth century readers. Most of it bears the stamp of journalistic sensationalism, forgotten scandals, trivia and gossip.

These concluding sections consist largely of hearsay portentously served up as criticism of society. One example is sufficient to show at which level Drumont's talents were functioning. He felt it important, for instance, to mention the fact that in March 1884 in Berlin the daughter of the Jewish banker Bleichröder had trouble finding a dancing partner during a ball. Therefore "the Prince Heir of Germany took pity on the young Israelite and ordered an officer to go offer himself to make her dance." [39] As Drumont went on to explain the average German officer was so antisemitic that only a royal command could make him lower himself to dance with a Jewess. Drumont liked this sort of detail and so, presumably, did his readers. This aspect of *La France juive* undoubtedly explains its tremendous popularity among general audiences of the period.

This critical analysis of Drumont's work demonstrates the various themes which the author has interwoven into his central thesis of Jewish perfidy. It cannot account for the phenomenal success which the book acquired. Despite the footnotes and scholarly apparatus, Drumont largely comes across as a master of that kind of journalism known as the *chronique scandaleuse*. The average reader could be counted on to delight in these revelations about the entrance of Jews into high society. From this perspective Drumont posed as a socialist castigating the upper middle classes and aristocratic circles, elaborating a theme that found favor among a wide audience. What makes Drumont's campaign special is that he attributed the gradual assimilation of some Jews into these circles as proof of a Semitic plot to control France.

This theme is emphasized with terms couched in nostalgic reminiscences for an earlier age when Jews were confined to ghettos and France was the master and not the mistress of Europe. By Drumont's logic the fact that France was no longer the major arbiter of Europe was supposed to be due to the increase of Jewish influence under the new republican government. What Drumont was describing was the gradual embourgeoisement of society, a social phenomenon which was also taking place in lands that had no Jews to speak of.

In France some Jews of means assimilated and inter-married into Gentile families. For Drumont this more tolerant social interaction was treason to God, race, and country. Echoes of this societal phenomenon were immortalized in the pages of Proust's masterpiece. [40] Drumont was opposed, needless to say, to these trends, indeed to most of modernism. He keenly felt the erosion of traditonal values was almost overwhelming and that the removal of Jews would somehow restore France and the church to their former glory and power. Modernism and industrial society were threats to his ideal way of life, and the assaults were being mounted from all sides: "Americanism has invaded Paris as much as Semitism...the professors at the *Ecole des Beaux Arts*, scornful of the most elementary duty, preferably receive American students; the Salon jury gives Yankees medals that it refuses to old artists for whom it would be a joy, a testimonial also for today's stupid public." [41] Such scorn and jealousy prompted Drumont to denounce the government that sent to America the Statue of Liberty, the symbol of the system he felt was ruining France.

In the last and longest section of the book Drumont denounced Freemasonry. Then he attacked the Protestants, accusing them of having introduced Jewish practices into Christianity. He saw these two religions as working hand in glove for the ruin of Catholicism. But to call Protestants supporters of the Jews was stretching the limits of historical credibility. It should be remembered that the word Jewish was a general term of abuse which the Protestants themselves were capable of hurling at the Catholics. An analysis of this final section shows that it was devoted to listing all the traditional complaints of Christianity against Judaism. Drumont liked to dwell on those fraudulent versions of the Talmud hawked by antisemites who claimed that it was not a sin for Jews to cheat, lie, deceive and murder Christians. That was the extent of his knowledge of Judaism. Taking a cue from Gougenot des Mousseaux, Drumont regaled the readers with a list of supposed ritual murders throughout history up to the present time. [42]

The religion of Israel, about which Drumont knew little, was distorted in gruesome detail: "What they adore in the ghetto isn't the god of Moses, it is the frightful Phoenician Moloch whose human victims were children and virgins." [43] This statement formed the heart of Drumont's ideological campaign, and it is taken directly from the anti-Jewish literature often propagated in certain circles of the Catholic church, particularly the Jesuits. It holds that the ancient Mosaic code or its fulfillment has been assumed by the new Israel, the church, and the Jews, after divine favor had been withdrawn from them, reverted to a form of occult devil worship embodied in what Drumont and others claimed were its holy texts, particularly the Talmud. That such calumnies were repeatedly denied and refuted made little impression on Drumont and those who were sympathetic to his program.

Ironically, Drumont sometimes cast himself in the role of the Old Testament prophet who castigated the wayward people against vice and corruption. As far as he was concerned the struggle between Gentile and Jew remained unchanged, encompassing a timeless realm, a cosmic battle continuing into the heart of the nation's capital: "Such was Christ in Jerusalem, so he is in Paris." The new money changers to be punished were the money lenders of the stock exchange and banks. In the period of prolonged depression when this book first appeared, it did not fail to provide a handy explanation of economic woes to the curious reader. As an ardent nationalist Drumont also offered up many of his arguments in patriotic language: "Love of fatherland and love of God are but one." This volatile mix of politics and religion gave special urgency to his call for a savior to rid France of her troubles.

By way of conclusion Drumont confessed that he had only given a detailed account of the hitherto occult forces responsible for France's decline: "As for myself, I repeat, I have only claimed to undertake a work of good will..Have I prepared our rebirth? I do not know, I have done my duty...In proclaiming the Truth, I have obeyed the imperious call of my conscience, *Liberavi animam meam...*" [44] With these words Drumont closed the best selling French book of the nineteenth century. Like Hitler in the twentieth century he too proclaimed that he was "doing the work of the Lord."

Drumont was not the first writer in France to try his hand at Jew baiting. He was the first to be successful and he even surprised himself by the *succès de scandale* that his book enjoyed. Why was Drumont, a relatively unsecure journalist, able to achieve recognition when others had failed? It goes without saying that circumstances and the book coincided to give the public something of what it wanted. But it should be kept in mind that the book was a long time in the making and was not occasioned by any one sensational event. Even the duel with Meyer cannot explain its steady and growing popularity.

The last portion of *La France juive* was probably what appealed to most readers. In it Drumont offered numerous anecdotes and vignettes of contemporary society and corruption, all accompanied by a lengthy index of names. One critic, after seeing this feature, quipped that the book was a "guidebook of defamation." Despite its bulk and frequent obtuseness, it did contain many passages of powerful rhetorical quality.

To what audiences did the book appeal? It would be safe to assume that there were at least two groups of readers who enjoyed *La France juive* and read it avidly at least until the end of the Dreyfus affair after the turn of the century. The book was designed to appeal politically to the Left as well as the Right. For a relatively limited number of vehement antisemites it was a reaffirmation of their beliefs. But more importantly it must have struck a responsive chord among a very large number of people who while not exactly being violently opposed to Jews probably did not care for them either.

The latter category seems to be the only one which can account for the steady number of reprintings of *La France juive*. The book ultimately surpassed two hundred printings before the First World War. It was among this vast diffuse body of readers that Drumont achieved his greatest triumph. As an organized political movement antisemitism in France unlike that of Germany remained for the most part somewhat peripheral. The far-reaching impact caused by *La France juive* must be located as much in its insinuations as in its accusations. It helped to condition generations of Frenchmen to look upon Jews as a group unworthy of their sympathy, as a foreign body living off the naive hospitality of France.

Drumont was a master publicist. He practiced many of the very vices that he labeled as specifically Jewish. With regard to Jewish talents in the field of publicity he observed: "The obsession of a name, constantly repeated, is such that the most skeptical and informed people cannot prevent themselves from hesitating" before this influence. [45] By this Drumont meant that constant repetition of a name or word can exert an influence over the perceiver which is difficult to ignore. This was precisely what Drumont himself did throughout his books and later in his newspaper. It is important to note that even in this first major work readers would already be exposed to the names of the principal figures in what would become the Dreyfus affair one decade later. Not in the actual protagonists themselves but their names were already mentioned by Drumont long before the affair began. Just as he would later protect the son, he protected the name of the father, General Walsin-Esterhazy, who, according to Drumont, was the object of Jewish wrath in Algeria at the time of the Commune. [46]

More significantly, it was the name of Dreyfus which reappeared quite often in all Drumont's writings before the celebrated affair began in 1894. In *La France juive* it stands out prominently after the names Rothschild, Lévy, and Mayer. Dreyfus is a name that is not uncommon among French Jews. Even a few Gentiles share this same appellation. It stems from a place name, the French form, Trèves, of the German city of Trier from which these families must have originated during the Middle Ages. By dint of constant repetition these Jewish names, including that of Dreyfus, were dragged through the mud of scandal and vilification. As will be later demonstrated Drumont's growing leadership became conditioned to associate the names with crimes and treason.

The skyrocketing sales of *La France juive* were fueled by widespread critical reaction. Within a short period of time three hundred articles were devoted to its impact. In *L'Evènement* of 22 April Arsène Alexandre reflected: "It cannot be repeated enough that the best way to force the Jews to deal with us is to act like them, to work stubbornly. Surely not by the same means! We don't have the same temperament, the same education." Alexandre then mused: "Does he think that his solution has any chance of being put into practice at the present time?"

The distinguished critic Ferdinand Brunetière wrote a balanced, subtle review in *La Revue des Deux Mondes* which he began by setting forth his qualifications: "As for myself in general it is not that I like the Jews. I even believe, while thinking about it, that I don't like them at all. I don't like music or mountains either." For the most part he could not accept what Drumont, "blinded by his hate for Jews," put forward as his basic premise. Brunetière reasoned that Christians did not need Jews to corrupt them, that they really could be worse than Christians, stating that "people loved money before there were any Jews, and if Jews had to disappear one day, money would not cease being loved." When it came to examining Drumont's last inflammatory passage Brunetière summed up the book's major flaw: "If it were true that there still subsists deep in their (the Jews) hearts an old leaven of hate against the word Christian, who put it there if not ourselves? Who cultivated it? Who will take care to make it ferment if it isn't M. Drumont himself with pamphlets like his own?"

Many other reviewers were also forthright in praising and condemning

*La France juive.* Arsène Guérin, writing in the *Revue du Monde Catho-lique,* echoed the dominant tone of clerical publications which were quite receptive to the new book. It might have seemed unlikely that a religious publication would uncritically accept Drumont's claim that he was not attacking Jews as a religion but as a race. But Guérin justified anti-semitism as a legitimate form of "anti-banditism" proclaiming that Jews were "insatiable vampires." For his efforts Guérin praised Drumont for having "carried a veritable hot poker into this gangrene." His praise became at times rhapsodic: "It cannot be mistaken or denied in Mon-sieur Drumont the devoted wish to serve, the praise of having served the cause of Christ."

And if Guérin is be believed, Albert de Mun, the leader of Catholic labor circles, wished to congratulate Drumont for his endeavors. Dru-mont's old collaborator, Jean Drault, furnished details "to show the reac-tion that Drumont's work could have on the average Catholic conser-vative bourgeoisie among which were initially recruited his most faith-ful readers and later his most ardent subscribers to *La Libre Parole.* "[47] In Veuillot's journal, *L'Univers,* the book was hailed as a masterpiece and *Le Monde* thanked the author for having "kicked over the Jewish Masonic anthill." Oscar Havard, in the same journal, tried to outdo his colleagues in praising Drumont, that "outstanding Catholic spokesman for having so magnificently flagellated the executioners of the father-land....Drumont, and this will be his glory---will have been that long-awaited trumpet that we've been wanting and yearning for." Of Dru-mont's work the chief editor of *Le Monde,* A. de Claye, wrote that "it is a book of great value and vast implications, a sincere book overflowing with a ardent and courageous faith....the work has confirmed our sym-pathy for M. Drumont."

In the words of the Catholic historian Pierre Pierrard: "the reception given by the Catholic press to *La France juive* and Drumont's other pamphlets was a general rule very sympathetic, even gushing and en-thusiastic." [48] Drumont himself was encouraged by this support because he was altogether uncertain at first about how his work would be judged. Its immense success was so startling that he immediately wrote a spin-off volume, *La France juive devant l'opinion,* in which he reviewed its origin and critical reception.

In this subsequent work Drumont collected a good deal of the praise that was personally directed toward him. Officers, he reported, told him: "In the next Commune, count on us...Now we know who to beat on and who are the real instigators of civil wars." [49] He was particularly pleased by the humble country priests who "love force and gladly pardon excess even in certain generous indignations."

Drumont knew that his appeal was not limited just to clerical circles. As for republicans and patricians, he was satisfied with their common agreement on the Jewish question: "A light nuance separated these two Aryans. Regarding the fate of Israel's princes, the republicans seemed to wish that they be shot and the patrician seemed to me to prefer that they be hanged..." The only item that Drumont regretted about his book was that he had mistakenly accused certain Gentlies of being Jews for which error he offered apologies. Otherwise he believed that he had rendered a great service to Aryans of all political persuasions.

In his follow-up volume, *La France juive devant l'opinion*, Drumont filled in details on specific topics that he had raised in his *opus magnum*. He insisted that his quarrel with the Jews had nothing to do with religion: he only intended to assail what he misnamed their legendary (sic)"Houptza" or *chutzpah*. In practice, however, he often condemned their religious beliefs but he claimed that his main arguments were meant to be directed against Jews as a race and how they could be overcome. "In the end, the forthcoming Semitic crisis, like all the analogous crises in the past, is explained by a simple error in the appreciation which Semites make of Aryans; they look upon us as idiots while we are only prodigiously naive."

Much space was devoted to answering personal attacks and recounting his version of the sensational duel with Arthur Meyer. In this volume he went on to attack various Jews in the legislature for their role in government, Alfred Naquet, who had been described by his enemies as "the ugliest man in France," was an easy target for derision. He had been responsible for the enactment of a divorce bill and came in for special opprobium. And so did Camille Dreyfus for promising legislation on income taxes: "This project being supported by Dreyfus, that is to say by all Jewry, has a chance of being voted, and I would be happy, because it would contribute to exasperating against the Jews the middle class which would be the most directly affected."

Success proved heady for Drumont. He became ambitious and planned grandiose campaigns to implement his recommendation for a new political order. One of them proposed creation of the *Alliance anti-Israélite Universelle* as an antisemitic force to counteract what Drumont claimed were the politics of the charitable organization, the *Alliance Israélite Universelle*. Its constitution, intoned Drumont at the end of this volume, "announces that we've had enough of you. The Arab chef in the evening at the edge of his tent in the balmy silence of oriental nights, conjures up the same thoughts as the artist and the writer who gossip on the boulevard in bustling Paris." [50]

Drumont concluded this tirade with a direct challenge to the Jews, a call for a massacre on a grand scale. Working himself up to a paroxysm of prophetic rage, he called for a "great organizer" to set in motion the anti-Jewish crusade. "Who is to say that he is not already at work?" Viewing his campaign in cosmic terms, Drumont harkened back to

Rome's struggle with Carthage, predicting a similar fate for modern Semites, specifically the Jews, who defied the Aryan will. "Many of us will die without seeing victory, but they'll have their bloody testament." *La France juive devant l'opinion* ends with Drumont's imploring the church to grant absolution to soldiers who go forth to kill the infidel Jews. It should be remembered that technically speaking the church was not supposed to have a hand in formulating and propagating the racist variant of its anti-Jewish tendencies. In the eyes of the faithful the distinction, however, was easily blurred. Drumont is a good example of a racist who is eager to use traditional Christian anti-Judaism and to adapt it to the latest intellectual and political fashions.

If Catholicism is not racist in theory, why did so many Jew baiters like Drumont feel they could pose as its champion? The answer is complex and can be explained by contemporary ideological and political factors. The church in France had in fact spoken out against Tsarist persecution of Jews in Russia. But at home such charity was not so easily mustered. Because liberalism was considered the church's greatest domestic threat and French Jews by and large were flocking to support this movement, it became a short step to consider attacks against Jews as an attack against liberalism. More than any other factor this desire to welcome all allies accounts for Catholic tolerance even encouragement of Jew baiters in the struggle against all that liberalism symbolized.

With few exceptions Catholics supported in varying degrees of enthusiasm Drumont's new campaign. There was at first, however, one Catholic writer, Léonce Reynaud, who stood up to challenge Drumont. There would be a few others but their random responses were swamped by the large number of co-religionists who supported Drumont. Reynaud, in his book, *La France n'est pas juive* (1886) tried to answer point by point many of Drumont's assertions. The following year he published *Les Juifs français devant l'opinion* which employed the same tack by showing how ritual murder accusations that delighted Drumont had been frequently condemned by the highest church authorities down through history.[51] But such a sober refutation could never expect to counteract Drumont's flamboyant, sensationalist style. Drumont had become a great pamphleteer, he knew what the public wanted to hear and how it listened to his racy essays which provided his generation of Frenchmen with a source of entertainment and food for thought.

Considering the amount of controversy generated by this book, the Jewish response was singularly negligible. Arthur Meyer was credited with an unusual attempt to denigrate Drumont's book after the duel. One version of an anecdote then making the rounds of Parisian society told of how Meyer tried to commission the eccentric symbolist writer, Villiers de L'Isle-Adam, to write a refutation of Drumont's work. When he supposedly made his offer to Villiers, the Catholic writer retorted: "My price, sir? It hasn't changed since the time of Our Lord Jesus

Christ....It's thirty pieces of silver.'' [52]

The targets of Drumont's vilifications did not answer for various reasons. A student of their social behavior, Michael Marrus, observed ''a distrust and persistent tendency on the part of Jews to minimize the importance of antisemitic outbursts in France and to respond passively to its assaults.'' When *La France juive* appeared ''no systematic refutation ever came from the Jewish community. One Jewish freethinker sought some form of collective response, but was unable to obtain support.'' [53]

The Jewish response was not to respond. In the words of the scholar Theodore Reinach, they would answer with ''the silence of disdain.'' This would remain the typical reaction of France's Jews, the policy of the ostrich with its head in the sand. It has been observed that whereas Jewish groups in Germany did respond somewhat to the growing challenge of anti-semitism, those in France were inert. Energy there could be mobilized to help Jews in distress abroad, but not very much for self-defense at home. Highly assimilated French Jews had more confidence in the institutions of their bourgeois democracy than did their coreligionists in Germany.

Perhaps the major reason that they failed to respond collectively was because Jews in France no longer formed a cohesive community. As the last century drew to a close French Jewry was largely an anemic body, incapable of such collective endeavors. Even when the Grand Rabbi Zadoc Kahn spoke out against antisemitism his voice sounded more like that of an individual than that of the spiritual leader of the country's Jews. Despite their legendary cohesiveness French Jews thought themselves so much a part of the nation's fabric that they put their trust in its laws and traditions which had served them so well since their emancipation in 1791. Besides, was not France, so they reasoned, the most civilized land in Europe? What was occuring in Russia and Germany was to them unthinkable at home.

One of the few replies to Drumont was voiced by a Jewish freethinker, Alexandre Weill, dubbed by Robert Dreyfus ''the prophet of the Faubourg-Saint-Honoré.'' His life spanned the century and he rarely shrank from a good fight waged in the cause of justice. Weill's first pamphlet on the subject, *La France catholique et athée, réponse à la France juive* (1886) was followed two years later by *Epîtres cinglantes à M. Drumont.* These ''scathing epistles'' hit the mark and threw Drumont into a frenzy and they remain perhaps the strongest denunciation of his entire career.

In this pamphlet Weill wastes no time in identifying the source of Drumont's hatred. After accusing him of not being a true Christian and blaming him for vilifying Jews, Weill gets to the heart of the subject: ''You attack them as Jews because Catholicism, such as it has become deformed by pagan or it you like Aryan idolatry, in whose name you speak, would like that there be left on earth only one Jew--Jesus....According to this idolatrous Catholicism it is necessary that the Jew they have not yet been able to exterminate be at least a vile creature, a slave or dressed in way with a special badge to distinguish him from the Drumonts and Daudets who could be mistaken for Jews. You wish Jews, the honest and dishonest, to be outcast from humanity for your fanatical priests." [54]

Weill specifically scored Drumont's claim to be a defender of the faith. By singling out Jews as the unique source of the crisis of belief in Christendom, Drumont, Weill reasoned, had missed the point: "But as a so-called Catholic, you're the last person capable of successfully combatting rampant atheism. Atheism is not a random phenomenon, it's the ravaging worm fresh out of the whitened sepulcre where the cadavre of Catholicism lies. Catholicism is a dead religion that hasn't yet been buried." [55]

As a freethinker Weill was no less harsh regarding the religion of his ancestors. In his concluding passage he uttered a tentative Zionist alternative to the Jew who was incapable of adhering to traditional beliefs: "If there were in Palestine a Jewish republic proclaiming not the stupid religion of rabbis whose religious idiocies border on senile decay and from which has developed that insane, dogmatic Christianity bordering on madness, but the universal religion purified by Moses, such as I have exhumed it from its triple layer of biblical, rabbinical and evangelical dust, I would gladly leave you and go die in Jerusalem." [56] Since there was then no such land Weill exhorted his fellow Jews to struggle for equality and political rights at home.

Weill himself was no less sparing of crooked Jews. But he found Drumont's scheme of expropriation insane and ultimately unworkable: "And then when your Jews will have been burned and exiled, where will you get the money so that you and your horse Bob can ride through the woods, because this scandalous money, thanks to the Jews you insult, that you'd invent if they didn't exist, you won't be keeping it? It's as illgotten as the money of the Erlangers and Dreyfuses and others. You will finish up miserably and it will be a Jew who will take pity on you and your children." [57] This last part of Weill's prophecy was uncannily accurate. Many years later the journalist Lucien Corpechot recalled in his memoirs that he received "one day a visit from the widow of Drumont. She told me that since the death of her husband Arthur Meyer had been sending her for years a little income." [58] This considerate gesture on the part of the aristocratic Jew and gentleman could be seen as an act of charity. It could also be taken as a peculiar form of self-flagellation that was not uncommon among the belles lettristes of that era.

To understand the general spiritual climate of France in 1886 is to understand how Drumont's book came to be so well received. Assailed by economic depression, jingoist and radical politicians, and the extreme elements among the clergy, the mood of French public opinion was conditioned to be receptive to *La France juive*. This book was not triggered by any one particular incident. Drumont wrote it to express rage over an accumulation of grievances which arose under the liberal order of things.

More than any other factor the great reception that Drumont enjoyed was perhaps aided by the bizarre shape of dominant and religious moods and controversies. [59] That this was an age dominated by two major hoaxes goes a long way in explaining how *La France juive* could be accepted by a gullible public. Drumont's book was published in the same year that two reviews, *Le Décadent Littéraire et Artistique* and *La Décadence* were founded. The mood of the artists who were called decadents was one of world weariness, indeed of the end of the world. Such extreme pessimism was in fashion. Although Drumont railed against what he termed a decadent society, he himself was deeply moved by what he saw in certain features, notably pessimism, of the decadent movement. One need only recall his flattering review of Huysmans' novel *A Rebours* to note how much Drumont was sympathetic to the esthetics and mood of decadentism. [60]

The element of fraud played an important role in establishing this spiritual climate. The previous year, for example, saw the publication of a slim volume of decadent verse, *Les Déliquescences* by one Adoré Floupette. Despite the silly pseudonym adopted by Gabriel Vicaire and Henri Beaucaire, their volume of fraudulent verse became an instant success in parts of the world of letters. While many journalists laughed and dismissed this parody of avant-garde poetry, various critics sang it praise. The controversy reached such proportions that the poet Jean Moréas suggested changing the name of the new poetic trend from decadents to symbolists. Thus one of the more significant modern literary developments took shape in the wake of a hoax. [61]

Another deception on the public of a much broader significance was also forming during these years. It involved the antics of Gabriel Jogand-Pagès, alias Léo Taxil, perhaps the greatest charlatan of the century. His strange career is worth mentioning in passing not only because his path occasionally crossed Drumont's but mainly because of the type of propaganda in which they were both involved. As historian Robert Byrnes observed: "The remarkable feats executed by Taxil from 1885 to 1897 are extremely significant also because they demonstrate again the connection between the entire antisemitic campaign and the general current of anti-rationalism manifested at that time also in symbolism, impressionism, spiritualism, and varous utopias which could be gained only through violence." [62]

Briefly, what Taxil did was to dupe an entire generation of Frenchmen from rival ideological camps. His appetite for scurrilous journalism was whetted by observing the career of Rochefort, especially during the scandalous matter of the *Inflexible* affair in the summer of 1868. Shortly after the war of 1870 Taxil became the editor of various anti-clerical journals which specialized in a form of political pornography against the Right. In 1879 Taxil and his wife started a Bibliothèque Anti-cléricale which published vitriolic anti-Catholic pamphlets whose titles speak for themselves, works such as *The Female Pope, The Pope's Mistress, The Loves of Pius IX*, etc. After a costly trial for defamation in 1885, Taxil decided suddenly to switch sides and converted to Catholicism. For the church his conversion was like that of Saint Paul. He promptly set to work playing the other side of the street by writing a flood of lurid literature againts the Masons. Catholics were so pleased by his powerful pen, now in their service, that Taxil was warmly received by the pope, bishops, and priests and hailed as a new defender of the faith. In 1887 Pope Leo XIII personally told him: "Thy life is still very useful in combats for the faith."

Like most other Catholics Drumont initially accepted Taxil's conversion as authentic. In 1886 he noted: "Superior in character to Renan, Léo Taxil has extirpated himself from degradation. He was ashamed to be the Jews' handyman and he braved their wrath by separating himself from them." [63] Drumont's praise, however, was shortened when Taxil in 1890 challenged his candidacy in a Paris municipal election in which the latter received more votes from clerical followers.

In the meantime the themes of Taxil's many books had become more outlandish in direct proportion to his audience's growing gullibility. Finally in 1897 he was forced to admit publicly that all he had done was a hoax. It is revealing to note that many Catholics could not accept Taxil's apostasy. They had invested too much in him and preferred to believe that he had been seized by the devil (or Jews) and forced to renounce the religion he had so brilliantly defended. Though Taxil faded from public view, he managed to achieve an apotheosis of sorts. James Joyce was so impressed by his spectacular career and adventures and his ambivalent relationship to Catholicism that he used Taxil as one of the principal models for Leopold Bloom and Stephen Daedalus in *Ulysses*. [64]

Drumont was delighted by his rival's second confession but as Byrnes' remarked: "It is extremely significant that Léo Taxil was so successful during the period from 1885 through 1897 and that had such great influence upon French Catholic priests and laymen, for it was during this same period and over this same group that Drumont exerted his greatest influence." [65]

The antics of Adoré Floupette and Léo Taxil were hoaxes whereas Drumont's campaigns were seriously conceived and sincerely believed. The thread that binds them all, however, is the penchant for gullibility on the public's part. A people that could believe such charlatans would not find it difficult to accept the basic arguments of Drumont. Some of these stupendous machinations were ultimately exposed and discarded. But Drumont's went on to greater heights, reinforced by his new books and ultimately a newspaper.

In summary, *La France juive* launched Drumont as a major propagan- ist of antisemitism. It established his reputation throughout Europe as an exponent of racist politics. Drumont was not the theorist that some fancied him, but rather a journalist, and as such he had scant ability or patience to develop a unified, philosophical, original justification for racism. It would be accurate to state that Drumont used racism as one of many weapons to attack Jews and through them the liberal republic he hated and believed was destroying Christian France. Of his career George Mosse observes: "Drumont was above all a publicist; but unlike Gobi- neau and Chamberlain, he attempted to found political and social move- ments that would advance his cause."[66] Before he could put these plans into action, Drumont wrote more books and, more importantly, he event- ually endeavored to establish a newspaper. Around this journal he would gather supporters to spread the gospel of antisemitism on a daily basis. This journal, *La Libre Parole,* represented the second phase of Drumont's ultimate aim to rid France of Jews.

## Notes

1 Drumont, *La Dernière Bataille,* p. 252.

2 Ibid., p. 321.

3 Quoted by Bernanos in *La Grande Peur des bien-pensants,* p. 145.

4 Ibid., p. 179.

5 Poliakov, *L'Histoire de l'antisémitisme,* vol. III, p. 466. See also Leon Poliakov, *The Aryan Myth* (New York: Basic Books, 1974, p. 276).

6 See Pierrard, *Juifs et catholiques français,* pp. 3†-79.

7 Edouard Drumont, *Le Livre,* April 1884, 142.

8 Edmond de Goncourt, *Paris and the Arts: from the Goncourt Journal,* edited by George Becker and Edith Philips (Ithaca: Cornell University Press, 1971), pp. 229-230. See also Lazare Prajs, *La Fallacité de l'oeuvre romanesque des frères Goncourt* (Paris: Nizet, 1974).

9 Arnoulin, *Monsieur Drumont et les jésuites,* pp. 114-115.

84

10  Drumont, *La France juive devant l'opinion,* pp. 17-18.

11  Goncourt, *Paris and the Arts,* pp. 234-235.

12  Ibid., pp. 235-236.

13  Arthur Meyer, *Ce que mes yeus ont vu* (Paris: Plon, 1911), p.254.

14. Drumont, *La France juive devant l'opinion,* p.215.

15  Jean-Paul Sartre, *Anti-Semite and Jew* (New York: Schocken, 1948), p.45.

16  Drumont, *La France juive,* vol. I, p.5. For thorough studies of Gobineau's racist thought, see Michael Biddiss, *Father of Racist Ideology* (New York: Weybright and Talley, 1970) and Janine Buenzod, *La Formation de la pensée de Gobineau* (Paris: Nizet, 1967).

17  Matthew Arnold, Hebraism and Hellenism,'' *Culture and Anarchy* (Cambridge: Cambridge University Press, 1957), p.141.

18  Drumont, *La France juive, vol. I, p.35.*

19  Ibid., p.91.

20  Heinrich Graetz, *History of the Jews,* (Philadelphia: The Jewish Publication Society of America, 1894), vol. III, pp.570, 575, 576.

21  Drumont, *La France juive,* vol. I, p.164.

22  Twentieth Century antisemites are still attracted to the image of this monarch. On the 800th anniversary of Saint Louis' death for example, the extreme right-wing journal, *Ordre Français,* in June 1970, published this commemorative note:

"Since Christianity has renounced its faith, it has given free rein to the Revolution. The land of Saint Louis, the land of crusaders, still produces sons capable of courageous battle without the hope that defense of a sacred cause imposes...Thanks to these hardy souls, hope remains, but legal France more and more stifles the real country and sterilizes it; faced with a rampant Revolution, would the authentic sons of France, of Saint Louis be numerous enough, those whose courage and clairvoyance hasn't been deadened by the poisons of the Revolution?'' pp.2-3.

23  Norman Cohn, *Europe's Inner Demons* (New York: Basic Books, 1975), p.82.

24 Drumont, *La France juive,* vol. I, p. 173.

25 Ibid., p.207.

26 Ibid., p. 264.

27 Ibid., p.232.

28 For a modern version of the question of Jewish assimilation, see John Murray Cuddihy, *The Ordeal of Civility* (New York: Basic Books, 1974).

29 Drumont, *La France juive,* vol. I, p.322.

30 Ibid., p. 334.

31 See Soza Szajkowski, "Jewish Participation in the Sale of National Property during the French revolution," *Jews and the French Revolution,* p. 475.

32 See Byrnes, *Antisemitism in Modern France,* p.146. on the church's response to working class movements, see Lilian Wallace, *Leo XIII and the Rise of Socialism* (Durham: Duke University Press, 1966).

33 Henri Rollet, *L'Action sociale des catholiques en France* (Paris: Editions Contemporaines, 1947), p. 263 n. See also his *Albert de Mun et le parti catholique.* (Paris: 1949), and Benjamin F. Martin, *Count Albert de Mun* (Chapel Hill: University of North Carolina Press, 1978), pp.130, 133-134, 239.

34 Drumont, *La France juive,* vol. II, p. 285.

35 For a similar complaint against Offenbach, see Peter Kropotkin, *Memoires of a Revolutionist* (Cambridge: Houghton, Mifflin, 1899), p.252.

36 See J.P.T. Bury, *Gambetta and the National Defence* (London: Longmans, Green and Co., 1936), p.288. On Arab attitudes towards Jews, see Charles-Robert Ageron, *Les Algériens musulmans et la France*(Paris: Presses Universitaires de France, 1968), vol. I, p.600.

37 Drumont, *La France juive. vol. I, p.456.*

38 See Alexandre Israël, *L'Ecole de la république* (Paris: Hachette, 1931), and Thomas Power, *Jules Ferry and the Renaissance of French Imperialism* (New York: King's Crown Press, 1944).

86

[39] Drumont, *La France juive,* vol. II, p. 106.

[40] See Seth Wolitz, *The Proustian Community* (New York: New York University Press, 1971), and Sherban Sidéry, "Israel's Way," *Marcel Proust, 1871-1922: A Centennial Volume* (New York: Simon and Schuster, 1971), pp.79-102.

[41] Drumont, *La France juive,* vol. II, pp.258-260.

[42] On the use of the word Jew as a term of opprobrium, see Louis Israel Newman, *Jewish Influence on Christian Reform Movements* (New York: Columbia University Press, 1925).

[43] Drumont, *La France juive,* vol. II, p.416.

[44] Ibid., pp.576-577.

[45] Ibid., vol. I, p.547.

[46] Ibid., vol. II, p.17.

[47] Jean Drault, Drumont, *La France juive et la Libre Parole* (Paris: Societe Francaise, 1935), pp. 11-12. On the question of de Mun's influence an anonymous article in *Le Journal des Débats* commented:

"The ideas which he defends are not personal ideas. The clerical party, like all others, has its extreme Left...with its revolutionary demagoguery...The socialism of M. de Mun is proper, respectful and the opression it threatens us with is quite legal...Look beyond the border: we see the pietist Protestant, the Reverend Stoecker, dealing in the same manner with Mr. Bebel and Mr. Liebknecht, and we see him preaching the great antisemitic crusade. M. de Mun and M. Stoecker are still theoreticians; but there exists at their sides, in Berlin as in Paris, minds which are absolutely ready to put their doctrines into practice. M. Drumont is one of those minds. And he reflects so well the instincts of his party, he so faithfully represents certain of its tendencies that not a single of the religious journals of Paris had the courage to disavow him."

[48] Pierrard, *Juifs et catholiques francais,* p. 61.

[49] Drumont, *La France juive devant l'opinion,* p.5.

[50] Ibid., p.288.

[51] See also Léonce Reynaud, *Les Français israélites* (Paris: Lahune, 1901).

[52] See A. W. Raitt, *Villiers de L'Isle-Adam et le mouvement symboliste* (Paris: Corti, 1965), p.23.

[53] Michael Marrus, *The Politics of Assimilation* (Oxford University Press, 1971), p.141.

[54] Alexandre Weill, *Epîtres cinglantes à M. Drumont* (Paris: Dentu, 1888), p. 2.

[55] Ibid., pp.12-13.

[56] Ibid., pp.23-24.

[57] Ibid., p.14.

[58] Lucien Corpechot, *Souvenirs d'un journaliste* (Paris: Plon 1936), vol.I, pp.99-100.

[59] See A.E.Carter, *The Idea of Decadence in French Literature* (Toronto: Univeristy of Toronto Press, 1958), and Noel Richard, *Le Mouvement décadent* (Paris: Nizet, 1968).

[60] See Francois Livi, *J.K. Huysmans, A Rebours et l'esprit décadent* (Paris: La Renaissance du Livre, 1972).

[61] See Augustin Thierry, *Les Grandes Mystifications littéraires* (Paris; Plon, 1913), vol. II, p.176, and Hubert Juin, *Ecrivains de l'avant-siècle* (Paris: Seghers, 1972), pp.23-30, and Henri Peyre, *Qu'est-ce que le symbolisme?* (Paris: Presses Universitaires de France, 1974), p.161.

[62] Byrnes, *Antisemitism in Modern France,* p. 304. See also Eugen Weber, *Satan Franc-Macon* (Paris: Juilliard, 1964).

[63] Drumont, *La France juive,* vol. II, p.469.

[64] See Marvin Magalaner, *Time of Apprenticeship* (New York: Abelard-Schuman, 1959), pp.49-71.

[65] Byrnes, *Antisemitism in Modern France,* p. 318.

[66] George Mosse, *Toward the Final Solution: A History of European Racism* (London: Dent & Sons, 1978). p.156.

4

La Libre Parole

> *Every newspaper, from the first*
> *line to the last, is nothing but a*
> *tissue of horror...And it is with*
> *this loathsome appetizer that*
> *civilized man daily washes down*
> *his morning repast.*

> *--Baudelaire*

In 1886 Drumont was enjoying the heights of popularity and success. For the next six years he mainly lived off spiritual and financial capital derived from his best seller. He wrote other books but did not regain the degree of attention he had known until he founded his newspaper, *La Libre Parole* in 1892.

This chapter will examine Drumont's career between these two dates. Critical emphasis will be devoted to his other books, the formulation of proto-fascist and national socialist ideologies in France and Germany, his new associates such as the Marquis de Morès and Jules Guérin, his failed political candidacy and rivalry with the Catholic apologist and propagandist Léo Taxil, in order to understand the circumstances under which his influential newspaper came to be founded.

*La Libre Parole,* under Drumont's brilliant editorship, was to become a major instrument in exposing the great Panama scandals which were unfolding during the year of its founding. Drumont's leadership and talent in this new field demonstrates his exceptional abilities as a journalist of the first order. Because so many of the personalities that were to figure in the Panama scandals were later associated with the Dreyfus affair Panama is often viewed as its precursor. Before Drumont created his newspaper he spent many years in preparation and in propagation of his message. He passed the next half decade in trying to forge alliances and seeking out sympathy at various levels of society.

Prior to the founding of *La Libre Parole* Drumont was obliged to content himself with consolidating his forces and living off the considerable reputation which fame had brought him. A series of books inspired by his initial success kept Drumont's name in the public eye. Writers beseeched him to add a kind word to their works. In 1887 he prefaced, for example, a semi-pornographic booklet entitled *Joseph et Mardochée: symboles du monopole et du proxénétisme juifs* by Paul Devaux. This author began his diatribe by cautioning readers not to confuse Arabs "with the descendants of a damned race," which this volume described as a menace to public health and security. [1]

In his preface for Devaux, Drumont suggested reading the recent work of Jacques de Biez, *la Question juive,* the approach of which more closely approximated his own. In this book de Biez's dedication to Drumont indicates how the latter could appeal to a wide audience:

> *You have sounded the call to arms to lead us*
> *to the fire.*
> *Here I am!*
> *You mount a white horse. I mount a red horse.*
> *You are Catholic. I am Republican.*
> *No matter, we are both Frenchman.*
> *Let's lower our vizors and go forward!*
> *The country is helping us! and may France keep*
> *us in her holy care!*

One feature of this long work was de Biez's insistence that Jews intended to massacre all Frenchmen. For self-protection this was what he recommended to his followers even if they "had to act like wild beasts." From beginning to end in this tract he was obsessed with the Eiffel tower project, claiming that it was part of a Jewish plot to build a tower of Babel to dominate France. His advice on the Jew: "We'll have to throw him down from his tower of Babel to crush him below."

As for those politicians he hated the most Jacques de Biez devoted ten pages to denouncing Camille Dreyfus and his support of a legislative bill advocating separation of church and state. This proposal especially angered de Biez "because at last among the signers of this bill I see the name of M. Camille Dreyfus." In de Biez's book this republican politician was treated as a very dangerous character: "Whether it's the right hand of M. Rothschild or the left hand of M. Camille Dreyfus, it's always the same result. You'll be handing yourself over to the Jew, because these two apparently enemy hands are the two arms of the same individual: the Jew." [2]

This same politician was also pilloried in 1887 by Father Georges de Pascal in his book, *La Juiverie.* It was prefaced by Drumont who hailed the priest as an "exorcist and social doctor." Pascal was one of the many priests who were inspired by Drumont's success to write antisemitic tracts. He devoted a good deal of space to the role of Jews in the press. Pascal was particularly upset by the press campaign against the proposed state funeral for the deceased Cardinal Guibert. The author singled out "the *Lanterne* of the Jew Mayer...the *Nation* of the Jew Dreyfus..who is his mouthpiece in the Chamber." Then de Pascal continued at great length about a tax law proposal which had been put forward by this Dreyfus. [3] All these antisemites found Dreyfus the politician and journalist annoying in the extreme. What mainly bothered Father de Pascal was "the army...don't we know the power which Mayer and his *Lanterne* engages in the offices of the War Ministry? In truth, the Jew has invaded everything, conquered everything..." A statement such as this dealing with the Jew who invades the heart of the military establishment helped establish the climate of opinion which precipitated the Dreyfus affair.

People like Devaux and de Biez came to represent the sort of confederates with who Drumont was associated. In a similar vein of writing Drumont continued to publish more books of this line of argument. In 1889 he published *La Fin d'un monde* which many consider to be his best book. In it Drumont took up several of his favorite themes and presented them in a coherent fashion. Through each successive book he continued to see Jews celebrating black masses and consorting with Satan to ruin Christian lands. Alongside the Epinal images of old France he contrasted the decadence of modern times: "Hatred and envy which are everywhere today were then rare in that noble country of France." [4] What caused this loss of innocence was for Drumont the Jews whom he compared with a disease in the body politic. Relying on the opinion of the great Charcot, Drumont mused: "That's the way races are: destined to finish in all manner of epilepsy, arthritis, and seizures. The Jew jumps up and down like those wretches who are touched by the dance of Saint Vitus."

Modern France, reasoned Drumont, was ill, almost incapable of resisting contact with Jews who he labeled as foreign bodies. Only healthy societies have been able to survive and such thoughts led Drumont to praise the Inquisition. The impulse to genocide was never far from his lips:"Undoubtedly the Inquisitors did not pronounce the death sentence themselves, but one shouldn't push this argument too far like those fakers from the liberal school; when the leaders of the Holy Office turned a Judaizer over to the secular arm, they had few doubts about what would happen to him...." [5]

As in his other works Drumont inveighed mightily against current events in society. At one point he condemned the Eiffel tower the aim of which "is to be insolent and stupid like modern life." [6] What made this volume a favorite among his readers was its idological tone. Drumont presented his brand of socialism in this volume by reviewing the history of the working class in this period. Long sections of this tract denounced the activities of Jewish capitalists: "All you've got around here are Dreyfuses, Lévys, and Lehmans." Several chapters are devoted to Christian labor circles and their successess and failures. Particular attention was directed at Albert de Mun, the Catholic social reformer, whom Drumont found "a bit worn out." What he mainly noticed missing in such quarters was a certain reticence to exploit the anti-semitic program which was so popular in other parts of Europe.

This failure to mobilize opinion for political action is perhaps best illustrated by Drumont's long relationship with the son of the famed photographer, Paul Nadar. In an unpublished letter to him dated 14 April 1888 Drumont commented: "I offer you great thanks and take note that you have decorated a copy of *La France juive* which will some day be a bibliographical rarity...It is evident, my dear Nadar, that we will always love one another, but that we will rarely understand one another." To the question of whether he was responsible for fomenting a religious conflict Drumont replied: "But this war I am provoking, who's following it with the most ignoble means? If this not your opinion I have for your disposal an illustrated prospectus which will be distributed in the street." Judging by the other fragments of this correspondence it seems that Nadar, father and son, got along with Drumont on a personal level, even to the point of admiring something of what he was trying to do with regard to the fate of the nation. But Nadar appeared unwilling, like some other famous figures of accepting *in toto* Drumont's social philosophy. [7]

Antisemitism was not unknown to some of his coreligionists and compatriots, but in France it never gained the mass organized following which it acquired elsewhere. Drumont felt that his country lagged behind central and eastern Europe where antisemitism was often looked upon as a popular form of Christian socialism. Thus one of his contemporaries, Francesco Nitti, wrote in his *Catholic Socialism* that 'in Austria, as in Germany, Antisemitism is neither more nor less than a form of Socialism." [8]

In fact in many parts of Europe antisemitism was just about the only form of crude socialism that appealed to the peasantry and middle class. This was the type of social movement which Drumont wished to develop in France. Such ideas were not alien to Catholic and some secular socialists there, but as an independent mass movement it failed to capture the homeland of revolution and socialism.

This failure was not due to any lack of activism on Drumont's part. In late 1889 the National Antisemitic League of France was founded and its chief officers were Drumont as president supported by Jacques de Biez, Millot, and the Marquis de Morès. From any point of view its members form a strange group. De Biez, whose antisemitic writings were as early as Drumont's, was a sidewalk cafe intellectual who believed in a spurious form of Celtic nationalism and racism. He thought that Christ was a Celt and he had a habit of asking priests: "Are you sure that Jesus Christ was Jewish? Drumont tolerates the idea, but it bothers me." [9] On another note de Biez proclaimed: "We are national socialists, because we attack international finance so that we may have France for the French." [10] This talk of Celtism reflects a curious strand of French popular political racist folklore which holds that France was largely a Gallo-Roman land dominated by those of Germanic descent. Drumont updated this bizarre belief by claiming that the modern domineering race was Jewish and mainly descended from German Jews.

The National Antisemitic League held its first meeting on 18 January
1890 at Neuilly, and it supported the candidacy of Francis Laur, a former
member of the socialist faction headed by Guesde and now a partisan of
Drumont's ideology. Laur's election to the Chamber of Deputies had been
invalidated and because he was an ex-Boulangist he felt himself like the
movement to have been betrayed. He and Drumont grew close to one another. Drumont was convinced that General Boulanger had been misled
into defeat by Jewish associates like Naquet and Meyer.[11] This support
from left-wing Boulangists gave antisemitism a certain progressive appeal. Drumont himself was influenced by it to the extent that he always
predicted France would ultimately be saved by an antisemitic military dic-
tator, the proverbial man on horseback. This prophecy was to be sufficiently fulfilled by Pétain exactly fifty years in the future.

Another one of Drumont's new confederates was an ex-Communard
named Millot who claimed that his business was ruined by Jewish com-
petition. Chavinistic and irascible, Millot reaped his revenge by manu-
facturing antisemitic jewelry for the League members who wanted such
items as tie pins, buttons, and even a watch-charm depicting Drumont
dressed like Saint Michael, slaying a long nosed dragon. Till his death
Millot remained one of Drumont's closest associates.[12]

A more important personality and cofounder of the Antisemitic League
was the mercurial Marquis de Morès who became one of the leading
figures and quite controversial member of Drumont's band. An examination of his spectacular career illustrates the sort of follower whom Drumont recruited to his cause in the years before the founding of his newspaper. Exploits in the United States and France made Morès a dashing,
fearsome opponent. Born into an old noble family, he trained for a military career and in 1877 he went to Saint-Cyr where Philippe Pétain was
one of his classmates. After resigning his commission in 1881, he married
Medora Hoffman, the daughter of a New York banker and sought out a
new life in the United States. He tried his hand at various business enterprises in the wild Dakota Territory, and when they all failed he later
blamed these setbacks on Jews. The only momento that Morès left behind in Dakota was a small town named after his wife and a number of
dead men whom he shot in gun fights.[13]

Upon leaving the United States, the dashing aristocrat sported a som-
brero he acquired in the Wild West and cut a figure as a bellicose dandy
and jack-of-all-trades. After more adventures and failures in India and
Indo-China, Morès returned to France where after reading Drumont's
books, he became convinced that his setbacks were truly caused by a Jewish cabal directed against him personally. It was during the Boulanger
campaign that Morès openly sided with the antisemitic faction. He

brought a touch of class to a movement that claimed to be for the working masses and all upright Frenchmen. At their rallies proletarians, journalists, shop-keepers and some aristocrats from the Jockey Club rubbed shoulders in an atmosphere that created the illusion in miniature of national solidarity against a common foreign enemy within the gates.

Following the collapse of the Boulanger movement Drumont published *La Dernière bataille* early in 1890. In this new volume dedicated to Morès he insulted and condemned the popular general, accusing him of having feet of clay and being a dupe of the Jews. As an avid palm reader, Drumont also stated that he knew the general and his followers were destined to fail because he had read the right signs in their hands. Exasperated by the conservatives' inability to overthrow the republic, Drumont and his friends decided to put their campaign into action. But he first took pains to outline the main features of his program. Above all, he insisted that he had nothing against the Jews on religious grounds, and he was careful to demonstrate that the animosity he claimed they aroused was not uniquely prompted by Christian beliefs: "The meaning of deicide was such a slight determining cause of the public safety measures taken against the Jews in the past that we see Moslems pursue with the same hatred or rather protect themselves with the same energy against a people they've never accused of crucifying Mohammed." [14] In this preface dedicated to Morès Drumont also played the prophet: "The Jews, these eternal agitators, will have once again tried to set upon other people that abnormal and factious domination...The Jews will have succeeded perhaps in destroying France, but they will die on the ruins."

*La Dernière bataille* was offered as a "new social and psychological study." Despite its ambitious claims the book is mainly a collection of nostalgic reminiscences of the immediate and distant past. Still Drumont lost none of his vitriol especially where he attacked Rothschild describing him as a rodent seeking his prey. What really upset Drumont on this occasion was the Paris Centennial Exposition of 1889 in honor of the revolution. He was particularly annoyed by the foreign presence which had flocked to Paris. Strolling through the various exhibits with Jacques de Biez, Drumont recalled only seeing Jews everywhere.

When he was not strking the pose of the prophet Drumont saw himself as a "social doctor" who diagnosed society's ills and prescribed appropriate remedies. Many of his arguments were couched in a pseudo-clinical language meant to impart an air of objectivity and authority. In this book Jews as described in terms of the Arab designation reserved for them as "the children of death." Drumont saw them as "swarming barbarians, microbes, fathers of putrefaction, who invade decomposing societies." [15] France, once healthy and Christian, has been attacked, he claimed by these "parasitic worms" and "swarming vampires."

The last part of *La Dernière bataille* dealt with the most recent revelations of what was becoming known as the Panama affair. At this point in the investigation the public only had an incomplete picture of this monumental financial and political scandal. More sensational details would be later published by Drumont in a form of muckraking journalism that helped revive his flagging career. For the time being he had other plans. He thought that his successful books could be turned to political advantage by his running for local office.

The Marquis de Morès had similar thoughts. He had made an impression with his blunt language at the Antisemitic League meeting at Neuilly. He told the audience that Frenchmen were too tolerant of Jews: "In America, by God, they would have been lynched in no time at all." [16] Two months later during the election campaign Morès made an appeal to Boulanger's followers, but the publication of Drumont's book dedicated to him was critical of the general and thus helped dash any hope of support from this political alignment.

In order to demonstrate his seriousness Morès decided to press the attack during the campaign. He set up headquarters near the Stock Exchange and the *Banque de France* and gathered about him a group of bully boys that he dressed up in sombreros and purple cowboy shirts. With this gang he led attacks against stockbrockers and bankers in the financial district. This sort of thuggery at first appealed to Drumont's same sense of violent activism. Like Drumont, Morès preferred to fancy himself a paladin defending Christian Aryan France against the Semites.

The wild tactics of Morès began to raise concern in some quarters. While he and Drumont were running for seats on the Municipal Council of Paris he made a speech on 15 April in which he declared that "at the time of the Commune 35,000 were killed. Well, this time only 200 or 300 usurers need to be killed." [17] Because of these calls to bloodshed those who should have supported Drumont and Morès declined to vote for such candidates capable of demagoguery. When the voting was over Morès lost by only 950 ballots and so did Drumont with less in a district in which he should have had more support.

The election defeats only spurred Morès on to more reckless statements. At one anarchist meeting he shared the podium with Louise Michel, the celebrated anarchist, and he repeated his inflammatory speeches and calls to class warfare. Just before the May Day celebration of that year Morès had called for 40,000 unemployed Parisians to join other malcontents and demand immediate action from the government. The authorities reacted by arresting immediately Morès on 28 April 1890. Drumont became concerned by this turn of events and warned his disciples to dissociate themselves from any demonstrations on May Day. Just to make sure that he would not be implicated Drumont left Paris by train.

Drumont did not blame his defeat on the critics of Morès. What particularly annoyed him was the lack of support he received from official Catholic circles, the very people he thought he was defending. Most galling of all was the fact that many of them had supported the candidacy of that master charlatan, Léo Taxil, who had become known as a favorite son of the church. That fact that both men posed as true protectors of the church suggests that many believers could be misled and convinced by such types. Their rivalry illustrated how split church factions were regarding the quality and character of their champions.

For Drumont, who had originally hailed Taxil's conversion, he had become "the spoiled darling of the conservative Catholics." At the time Drumont and no one else had any inkling of the massive swindle that Taxil was playing on such clerical circles. Drumont's main objections were directed at a rival who was appealing to the same block of votes. What Drumont was saying about the Jews Taxil was saying about the Freemasons. Perhaps because of the bad publicity which Morès attracted to the antisemitic cause Drumont lost votes which should have emanated from conservative factions in this district.

Drumont calculated that his electoral campaign should be directed at the same groups he sought to attract through his books. The Catholic petty bourgeoisie was thought to be his natural base of support. However because of poor organization and perhaps his difficult personality Drumont was unable to exchange his writings for votes in this small local election. The defeated candidate was bitter over this experience and did not try his hand again for elective office for almost one decade.

For fifteen years Drumont had been living in an apartment at 157 bis Rue de l'Universite in the seventh arrondissement. According to an article in *Le Figaro* dated 20 October 1890 his flat was decorated with old furniture and rugs. He loved this quarter near the *Invalides* and its church, Saint-Pierre du Gros Caillou, where he usually attended daily mass. It was this constituency which he counted on to carry him to the Paris Municipal Council. But his campaign slogan, "Down with the German Jew, the monopolistic, conniving, parasitic spy!" was not enough to make his neighbors vote in his favor.

In 1891, the year following defeat at the polls, Drumont published a bitter memoir, *Le Testament d'un antisémite*. Although he did not receive nearly the amount of Catholic votes he expected and needed to win, he did thank those of his co-religionists who offered their support. Indeed he had paid his dues for eight years to the *Cercle Catholique* and de Mun had spoken on his behalf. Nevertheless half the members of this group voted against him. He estimated the conservative vote at around 1500 in his district and of the 613 ballots which he received he was somehow certain that only 300 came from Catholic circles.

Bitter criticism was directed at the influential Catholics in his district, notably the Baron de Reille. Drumont thundered: "Take note that by conspiring against me, this Reille committed veritable treason." [18] The fact that de Reille was also influential in Bonapartist circles show how little Drumont was able to count on this bailiwick of traditionalist support. This rejectionwas particularly galling because these were the very people which he claimed to be saving.

The hardest words in this book were reserved for Leo Taxil and his high level clerical support. Drumont fulminated and accused his rival of hypocrisy for once denouncing Jewish influence and later for stating that "the names of Rothschild, Pereire, Cahen d'Anvers, Hirsch, Ephrussi, and Camondo are universally estimed." The slighted champion of the church spared few details reminding readers of Taxil's recent virulent anticlerical campaigns. It was only after meeting Taxil at the polls, however, that Drumont began to doubt the sincerity of his conversion to Catholicism. [19]

The height of exasperation was reached when Drumont discovered that Taxil had received the support of the apostolic nuncio, Monsignor Rotelli. At his sardonic best Drumont linked the papal diplomat's name with quotations from Taxil's more scurrilous anticlerical writings. For him the Roman prelate was typical of the ruffians, as he termed them, who ran the church government. All these recriminations were part of a growing trend on Drumont's part to castigate high ecclesiastical officials who were less than enthusiastic about his social views.

Taxil's reply to Drumont's candidacy was no less revealing and spirited. During the year of the election campaign he published a long work of denunciation, *M. Drumont, étude psychologique* (1890). In this virulent pamphlet Taxil wasted no effort in attacking his opponent's brand of Christian socialism, accusing him of being "a two-faced character" who appealed to Catholics and anarchists for votes. Taxil pointed out examples of Drumont's violent language and program. What kind of Christian, Taxil wished to know, could utter words like these: "Saint Bartholomew was a half-measure. We'll start it all over against the Jews, and this time we'll exterminate them all!"

To emphasize his point that he was a better Catholic than Drumont, Taxil reproduced the kind of letter he received from the pontifical secretary, Charles Nocella, and then he casually mentioned some letters "from seventeen cardinals, archbishops and bishops completely approving of my works on Freemasonry." By also affirming his Aryan descendance he then denied Drumont's insinuations that his pseudonym concealed a Jewish name. Taxil left Catholics with a choice of only two explanations for Drumont's campaign: he was either insame or insincere. Taxil himself one of the more notorious charlatans of the century inclined to emphasize the former category.

For Taxil, Drumont was simply a madman. His monomania would be harmless if it were merely a personal aberration. But Drumont unversalized it and demanded that everyone else follow in his steps and see Jews everywhere. In a satirical mood Taxil imagined a typical day in Drumont's life, an ordinary episode that pinpointed his feverish state of mind:

"An omnibus passes--Driver, stop!...Stop, please!..I'm in a hurry to get home..So stop! The driver whips his horses all the more. That driver, obviously, is a Jew. Then, M. Drumont lets the bus pass and runs after it. He makes a desperate sign to the conductor. It's useless, the conductor doesn't pull the stop signal...Oh horrors! the bus is full. You see, these wicked Jews have conspired to fill up the vehicle that should have taken M. Drumont. It's an unseakable persecution. They're watching him, waiting for him, they play the worst tricks on him. With orange peels they keep him from walking about. And then they fill up public transportation so that he can't get himself transported." [20]

In the first chapter of this diatribe Taxil depicted Drumont as a madman and with tongue in cheek he suggested that the police should have put him away because of his public calls to violence. This drastic measure should be taken "because it's wild incitements like M. Drumont's, which lead to catastrophe." Taxil took his rival to task on two more serious counts by drawing attention to Drumont's anarchistic sympathies and to various papal pronouncements in favor of protecting persecuted Jews down through the centuries. Above all Taxil berated Drumont for his lurid, obsessive tales about ritual murder, by speculating that he "must have at hand in his bag a new religion of which the main practice will be to get drunk on the blood of Jews."

According to the author a sign of Drumont's delirium was manifest in seeing Jews everywhere, even in command of Catholic publishing houses. On this point Taxil castigated Drumont for criticizing his own publisher, Victor Lecoffre, for not being receptive to his violent brand of anti-Judaism. Taxil reported a letter from the head of this venerable Catholic firm which showed that it had no fear of Jews when it published the works of a Jewish convert to Catholicism, the Abbe Lémann, who wrote in the more traditional vein of Catholic anti-Judaism. Drumont had also complained that this publishing house was not receptive enough at first to one of his young admirers, Jean Drault. In fact, as Taxil pointed out, Lecoffre eventually published some of this acolyte's popular novels about army life. Still Drumont persisted in his charge of Jewish influence over this publishing firm.

What probably annoyed Drumont most of all about Taxil's broadside was his apparent defense of Rothschild. Taxil, who never claimed to be a socialist like Drumont, simply failed to understand Drumont's myopic brand of socialism. In short, Taxil wished to know why Drumont only attacked Rothschild and not rich Christians as well. This was a question which most antisemites rarely answered satisfactorily. And if Drumont was indeed a Catholic socialist, why, asked Taxil, did he frequently denigrate the Catholic workers movement in France? For these charges Drumont had an answer, one that did not endear him to the faithful. On the one hand he claimed that so-called Christian bankers were truly imitating a Jewish form of exploitation, and he also argued that clericals interested in the social question were dupes of the Jews and enemies of the working classes.

Armed with his reputation as an expert on Freemasonry, Taxil went on to show how Jews had nothing to do with initiating the anti-Catholic bias of the continental lodges. Jews, he observed, may presently belong to such societies, but in the not too distant past they were excluded for various reasons not the least of which was their religious convictions. Christians and Jews, Taxil argued, have so much in common religiously that an attack upon one is really an attack on the other. Taxil then effectively exploited Drumont's tentative praise of anarchists, socialists, and former communards and their calls to political violence. In particular, Taxil indicated Drumont's approval "that in Oran in November 1882, some Jew baiters like himself had put up on walls posters bearing these words in big red letters: 'All means are good and must be used to annihilate the Jews' " [21]

There was just enough truth in Taxil's charges about the quality of Drumont's Catholicism which made him a bit suspect in the eyes of some devout Catholics. Taxil's accusations seemed to be confirmed with the appearance of *Le Testament d'un antisémite* in 1891 in which the author bitterly attacked the church's hierarchy in one hundred and fifty pages of vilification. After discoursing on the subject of "episcopal tyranny" inflicted on poor parish priests, Drumont spiced up these pages with charges of fiscal irresponsibility and lack of will on the bishops' part to combat effectively the secular, republican regime which ruled France.

"Why," asked Drumont, "were the bishops unwilling to lead the fight?" His reply held that they preferred to frequent a society which had been taken over by the likes of "the Rothschilds, the Cahens, the Lipmanns, Morpurgos, Oppenheims, Bernheims, Helbroners, Kahns, Dreyfuses..." [22] Since the church could no longer count on its traditional backers for support, Drumont reasoned that it should look toward the lower clergy which still retained contact with the ordinary people. These anonymous country parsons and curates would soon make up a good portion of Drumont's reading public, once he expanded his operations.

Drumont's denunciation of the church hierarchy was so severe that there were rumors about that his last book would be banned by Rome. But Drumont preached no heresy. Thus his books, however controversial, could not be censured from the angle of dogmatic error. Upset over lack of official church support for his candidacy the previous year, he continued to lash out at those who should have been his natural allies and supporters. They were so confounded by the tone of *Le Testament d'un antisémite* that Paul de Cassagnac felt obliged to write in *L'Autorité* on 20 March 1891: "My dear Drumont, you're wrong to shoot into the masses without aiming. You're firing on everyone and often on those whom you shouldn't, on your own troops. As a Catholic, you pose a more severe reformer than the clergy. As a conservative, you're harder on conservatives than on your natural enemies, the Republicans. It's a role with no pity and also no modesty. Because to play it with absolute authority, it would take an ideal perfection which you have not yet attained." [23]

By and large this self-defeating approach dogged Drumont throughout his career. It can be equally applied to his views on the social question. Here his program has been described as a form of "national socialism" or more euphemistically by one of his biographers, Emmanuel Beau de Lomenie, as "national anti-capitalism." But anti-capitalism should not be mistaken for socialism. Like its antonym, anticommunism, it is sterile and negative as a concept and it does not lead to reflection and growth but to recrimination and regression. For all the modern features of his social philosophy, Drumont's vision was resolutely anchored in the past. His social views may have seemed more advanced than those of many monarchist Catholics, for example, but both positions followed reactionary tendencies which harkened back to the golden age of the medieval Christian commonwealth. On one point, however, Drumont's ideology was resolutely modern and original. He preached a radical solution to social ills through the extermination of those whom he dubbed the exploiting class, the Jews.

It is obvious to recognize that France's political and social climate was in part responsible for the success which greeted Drumont. However these circumstances were not strong enough to enable him to expand the base of support for his cause. One major factor which inhibited Drumont's potential political effectiveness was his personality. By most accounts he was of a difficult nature, more capable of dividing than uniting his followers. This would be an individualist trait that plagued many right-wing factions in French politics. Drumont was too independent an individual, too timid in public, a poor speaker, in short he lacked those very qualities which make a great leader of movements.

Long after his death Drumont's disciples were fond of viewing him as a precursor of Hitler. It would be instructive, therefore, to compare in passing his career with that of Hitler's. According to Drumont's followers both men were essentially trying to do the same thing, to weld together a new force in their respective nation's politics, one which would take over the mantle of nationalism where more traditional conservatives had failed after disastrous wars and defeats. Revanchism, economic depression, political uneasiness, all these were the conditions for carrying our these modern anti-Jewish outbreaks, and circumstances were similar in Germany and France. France, before the First World War and Germany after the conflict, however, differed on the degree and not the nature of circumstances favorable to promoting national socialism. In both lands status deprivation played a major role in the development of extreme rightist ideologies.

To the best of his ability Drumont exploited the sense of uneasiness which underlay much of contemporary French society. The defeat of Germany in 1918 was, however, much more severe than France's had been in 1870. Even taking into account Germany's different political traditions, it is important to observe that Hitler actually succeeded in appealing to many of the same elements whose support Drumont also sought in his time. Thanks to more favorable circumstances and his personal magnetism, Hitler was able to unite factions whereas Drumont sowed dissension. Counterrevolutionary conditions were more aggravated in Germany after the First World War, but in both cases the means and end were identical: a national socialist regime which was pledged to remove forcefully Jews from all spheres of activity.

The age of Drumont was the period of Hitler's infancy. It is significant to note that in both lands antisemitism was simultaneously developing thanks to the efforts of similar groups and circles. A student of this period, Jehuda Reinharz, observed that in Germany "the supporters of anti-Semitism had been more or less obscure journalists and politicians whose ideology had been considered eccentric and demagogic." [24] Although this statement refers to Germany it is equally applicable to France, in particular to Drumont, and in his case this was the category in which he largely remained because of his inability to translate directly his ideology into votes. His influence over fellow Frenchmen especially affected political consciousness at the point where his views coincided with the interests of others in the highest quarters of society. It was this merging of common interests which later sparked the Dreyfus affair.

Despite the success of his books Drumont's plans to drive out French Jews had not borne fruit. He had reason for concern. Lack of immediate results drove some of his supporters to a more violent course of action. After his own defeat at the polls, Morès, for example, attacked the mainline socialist groups for not giving him the kind of backing he felt he deserved. To compensate for such loss he decided to press the attack more forcefully. In March 1891, the Marquis founded a group called "Morès and His Friends," whose members adopted a sort of American cowboy outfit and were recruited from among the butchers of La Villette, the slaughterhouse district of Paris. Most of these dedicated butchers were bosses and one of them, Gaston Dumay, for example, like to hang up outside of his shop a huge painting showing him dressed as a killer crushing a Jew with the words beneath: "Death to the Jews!"

Morès the dashing duelist soon gained some credence when he was able on one occasion to denounce the sale of rotten meat to the military authorities by a firm run by Jews. With his band of thugs Morès moved toward direct, physical confrontations. Of this movement Robert Byrnes writes:" A precursor in many respects of the storm troopers, the Morès group became known for its brutal street fighting, the disorders it caused during Jewish celebrations, and the manner in which it terrorized any opposition at an antisemitic meeting." [25] It was impossible to tell exactly how many Parisians approved or disapproved of such tactics.

The same year that Morès formed his fighting unit Drumont received a personal blow that severely strained his friendship with Daudet. In the 7 January 1891 issue of Le Figaro there appeared an article which cut Drumont to the quick. Its author, Philippe Gille, did not mention him by name but he left little doubt that France's leading antisemite was the topic of his piece. The article in question was actually a review of a recent play, L'Obstacle, by Alphonse Daudet, which told the tale of a young man whose marriage engagement was broken by rumors to the effect that his father had really died from a form of hereditary syphilis.

It seems that Daudet, in explaining the plot to the journalist, had inadvertently revealed some intimate details surrounding Drumont's private life of ten years before. He never expected, so he said afterward, that the journalist would be so indiscreet as to put this information into print. Daudet, according to Gille, said that Drumont was not aware of his fiancée's reasons for ending their engagement and that in a state of despondency he instead married his mistress, Louise Gaète. Although Drumont and Daudet eventually patched up their friendship, at the time the aggrieved party was ready to fight a duel for the sake of honor. [26]

Drumont had been deeply hurt by what he felt was his friend's betrayal of confidence. He had, after all, taken a large house at Soisy-sous-Etoiles to be near Daudet's property and family at Champrosay. His country home had a magnificent garden which sloped down to the banks of the Seine and this dwelling was unique in that the side which faced the road had no openings. Drumont liked to call it "the house with no windows" and found it suited the reclusive side of his temperament. Some of friends expressed concern over his desire to be cut off from the world. Apart from these few acquaintances whom he received at table, his only close associates were his domineering main, "la terrible Marie," and his horse named Bob which he often rode through the forest at Sénart.

His personal misfortunes were compounded by public disappointments. Six years after the initial success of his major book the antisemitic movement was stalled in France. It had established itself on the national political landscape to a degree believed to be modest by its adherents and even by many of its adversaries. It did not seem to be growing. This lack of movement was reflected in the melancholy titles Drumont gave to his political exposés. This desperation and groping for issues were evident in his volume *Le Secret de Fourmies* (1892) which deals with the violent clash between workers and soldiers on May Day of the previous year.

This bloody encounter left nine dead and several wounded. But all that Drumont could say of its cause in 200 pages was that the sub-prefect where the tragedy took place was a Jew named Ferdinand Isaac. This alone in his opinion could explain governmental policy to the working class and this was supposed to be symptomatic of all that was wrong with France. Drumont posed as a friend of the people and as a progressive posture this was not an unusual image for many politicians of this era. What made Drumont different was that he also claimed to be a loyal son of the church and at the same time he castigated what he labeled the "Catholic eunuchs" of the conservative party for not speaking out about the bloody encounter which had taken place at Fourmies.

Drumont was often annoyed that Catholic working class circles did not devote as much attention to the Jewish question as he would have liked and expected. His main preoccupation was with "the horde of German Jews" in France. "When he comes from Cologne and his name is Eugene Mayer, the Jew thinks it's fine that Camille Dreyfus goes to the synagogue with his deputy insignia on...If he comes from Hamburg and his name is Joseph Reinach, the Jew disguises himself as a French office to inform Germany that our cavalry is not up to par." These three proper names of Mayer, Reinach, and Dreyfus frequently appeared in his articles, were often pilloried by Drumont and would soon figure in most important episode of his career.

Whatever lack of forward movement Drumont might have felt was soon erased by the prospect of a new venture, the founding of his own newspaper. Books had been suitable in propagating his message, but to stimulate and sustain political momentum a newspaper would be a more effective tool which could hammer away at issues of daily concern. Drumont's was not to be the first antisemitic journal to be published in France. There had been others, usually short-lived and not published in Paris. The prospect of his own sheet appearing in the capital was too tempting for him to overlook. Journalism was the profession he knew best and fate was about to be kind to him.

His chance for a fresh comeback arrived in the person of J.B. Gérin, the director of the *Semaine Financière,* an influential publication which was consulted by leading bankers and investors. Not exactly the sort of backer for what claimed to be a socialist faction and even less likely as the promoter of an antisemitic newspaper. Less than a year earlier

Gérin had published a journal which defended Jews, particularly against attacks from the likes of Drumont. It seems that Gérin received no encouragement from these beneficiaries of his solicitude, and he then turned to their enemies in a moment of need.

In order to have some outstanding debts paid off, Gérin arranged for Drumont to be the editor of his own newspaper which was to be printed on presses acquired by Gérin as part of a liquidation transaction. Gérin was supposed to handle the financial page and money matters and Drumont's task was to assemble a staff. His terms were solid and generous. Gérin put up 300,000 francs, accorded Drumont an annual salary of 25,000 and appointed a certain Monsieur Wiallard to be the on the spot financial director of the entire operation. One of Drumont's associates, Jules Guérin, speculated that Wiallard because of his occasional association with Jews, was a crypto-Semite.

For the time being Drumont was in a state of euphoria. Jean Drault recalled the excitement in antisemitic circles at the prospect of putting out a Parisian daily: "The following day I ran to the Rue de l'Université. There I saw Drumont all radiant, rubbing his delicate, fine hands together and laughing a bit satanically---'Boisandré told you?' he cried out. 'Yes, we're off!...Right in the middle of town, 14, Boulevard Montmartre! First floor above the mezzanine a balcony with a window for the paper's title, *La Libre Parole*. A nice title, eh?'' [27]

Drumont later recalled that it was one of his dearest friends, Madame Alphonse Daudet, who suggested the title while she happened to be singing a Spanish song to him one evening at Daudet's country home. He was captivated by the violent Iberian melody and took from the lyrics the name of what would soon become one of France's more influential papers.[28]     Everything about the title, *La Libre Parole,* seemed fitting: It also held overtones from the line found in the gospel of Saint John, "the truth shall make you free." And the journal's motto, "La France aux Français," was chosen to appeal to nationalist tastes.  However attractve the new enterprise may have seemed to others perhaps this suggestion made by Madame Daudet caused her husband to harbor a certain uneasiness about Drumont's presence because rumor had it that the latter was a trifle interested in the former's wife. In any event the two writers by this time appeared to have made up after their row of the previous year, and they both looked forward to the maiden issue of the new journal.

The staff that Drumont assembled was made up of some capable and curious young men. The three main rooms where they were to work had just been freshly painted and furnished, and on every wall there hung a crucifix. Jean Drault remembered the "three copy boys, the leader of whom wore sargent major gold braid, were dressed in royal blue livery with buttons as big as pre-war hundred *sous* coins, which bore in relief the initials L.P. One would swear that they'd stepped out of a book." [29]

One member of the new regular staff, Jacques de Biez, did not last long on the job. This lieutenant of Drumont had earlier run off to London to marry a novice from a convent in Poitou. De Biez apparently told her that he was the journal's real director and when she persisted in loitering about the office he decided to quit before the truth became evident. De Biez was swiftly replaced by Georges Duval who also left after quarreling with Drumont. He was an experienced journalist and his colleagues were amazed by the monocle he wore which made his face twitch in a most extraordinary way. Most of the new staff, however, stayed on despite their master's terrible temper.

No one was more faithful or to be of longer service than Jean Drault, the pen name of Alfred-Achille Olivier Gendrot, who before his death in 1951, had passed through and worked in almost every phase of French antisemitism. He started his writing career composing humorous accounts about army life. On the staff of *La Libre Parole* Raphaël Viau, another colleague, remembered this journalist who always chewed the ends of h is moustache and was seemingly lost in a perpetual fog.

Viau himself was a star-struck young worshipper of Drumont. Coming down from Nantes to this citadel of antisemitism seemed to him "a bit like Mecca to the Moslems."[30] He never forgot his first meeting with his idol, "his two arms raised to heaven screaming his indignation against the misdeeds of Israel, numerous, he said as all the grains of sand in the deserts of Judea: 'Ah! these Jews! these Jews!' He used to pronounce: *ces Jüefs! ces Jüefs!* his lips violently pushed out as if to make a wild, sudden ferocious contact with the whole Jewish race, and swallow them whole in one powerful breath. And I found it very beautiful, beautiful like something out of the past, this fierce and unshakable hatred."[31]

In his memoirs Viau has left some marvellous portraits of the heteroclite crew with which he worked. After the departure of Jacques de Biez the only exponent remaining of that weird band of Celtic racism was Gaston Méry. He was a tall blond fellow, always smiling, and his novel *Jean Révolte* bore the subtitle *Le Méridional, voilà l'ennemi.* He hated southern politicians and preached a holy war to the Celts against what he termed Mediterranean mongols whom he felt were destroying France's racial purity. Viau recalled that "Méry often complained of terrible migraines in a soft voice. In order to write he would sometimes cover his head with a handkerchief without explaining why. During moments of distraction he devoured the works of Papus and incredible amounts of brochures on spiritism and occultism." Papus was the pen name of Gerard Encausse, the author of some of the leading works on the hermetic sciences, and was known in his time as "the Balzac of occultism." His influence over Méry and many others was enormous and it presumably led Drumont's accomplice to found his own occultist journal, *L'Echo du Merveilleux.*"

Other members of the staff included Adrien Papillaud whose assignment was the National Assembly. His job was to gather political information and turn it into articles "more violent than literary." "He used to read aloud these pieces, lacking any courtesy, gave out two or three laughs which went on like fanfares, and he left as he arrived like Mephisto." Others who wrote for the journal were Gyp, the celebrated lady novelist, Benjamin Gadebert, a would-be playwright, Albert Rogat, Félicien Pascal, Plista, Millot, de Pradal de Lamase, and Commandant Biot who wrote on military matters, not to mention many others who helped make *La Libre Parole* into one of Paris' more effective papers and the meeting place for antisemites of all persuasions.

The staff usually rubbed shoulders with members of the Antisemitic League, members of the Jockey Club, priests, and old communards, who all met and passed through these offices. The most colorful visitor was the Marquis de Morès who often showed up followed by his frightful strong arm men. One of them was named Vallée, who dressed like a carpenter and claimed to be the inventor of the "blade to cut a Yid a day." Morès and his friends had the habit of arriving at the offices at night blowing hunting horns full blast which they dubbed "the death cry of the Jews."

There was one person in this gathering, however, whom Drumont would regret ever having seen. To his embarrassment and that of his staff it turned out that the journal's financial overseer was in fact a Jew named Crémieux-Wiallard. When rival journalists got hold of this tidbit they made Drumont an object of ridicule. Drumont was mortified but he determined that Crémieux-Wiallard had in fact converted and could produce his baptismal certificate. Still Drumont did not wish to reveal this news himself for fear of losing subscribers and he swore that "he would get rid of that dirty Jew who got himself in among us as soon as possible." [32]

Drumont professed to defend Wiallard and the sincerity of his conversion. One of Drumont's associates, Guérin, later accused Drumont of harboring the convert at the behest of Gérin because they were all allegedly involved in some blackmailing scheme and assorted skullduggery. The following year Gérin was arrested for abuse of client confidence. [33] It was not an uncommon practice for newspapermen to resort to blackmail selected victims. Despite or perhaps because of such practices the journal prospered under Gérin's financial wizardry and Drumont's considerable talent in the field of journalism. Wiallard was eventually replaced by a young fellow named Devos, the nephew of Drumont's maid who nagged her master until he yielded and gave her kin a job.

The new journal got off to an auspicious start. In its official maiden issue, which appeared on 20 April 1892, Drumont presented to the world the familiar format that would be a familiar sight in France for several decades. This was the age of the popular press, mass circulation news-papers, and yellow journalism, all features which identified *La Libre Parole* as a true child of its age. And from Henri Rochefort Drumont also learned some of the techniques of the gutter press. In his first editorial Drumont offered a philosophical discourse on the Jewish question, its international implications, and how it was ruining France. To be precise, he presented details on how Jews were supposed to pull the strings and make Europe dance. "Rothschild intervenes on orders from Germany, to defeat the Russian loan; Isaac tries out Lebel rifles on Frenchmen; Dreyfus sends poisoned wheat to those Russians dying of hunger..." Not the same figure who would be later be arrested for spying but the same name implanted in readers' minds in the first issue of France's leading antisemitic newspaper.

## Notes

[1] Paul Devaux, *Joseph et Mardochée: symboles du monopole et du proxénétisme juifs* (Paris: Union des Bibliophiles, 1887), p.7.

[2] Jacques de Biez, *La Question juive* (Paris: Marpon, 1886).

[3] Georges de Pascal, *La Juiverie* (Paris: Bleriot, 1887), p 81. the Reverend de Pascal devoted a good deal of attention to this character: "M. Dreyfus, before becoming a deputy, was a member of the Paris Municipal Coun-cil. He is a Jew of about forty years of age, quite adept in politics and bu-siness...Although he is a radical deputy, M. Dreyfus does not lead an egalitarian life; he has a whole entourage and luxury like M. Clemenceau and the majority of our radicals who have a fortune or earn money and whom the radical masses imagine live on dry bread and pure water in order to come to the aid of what they call the workers and the wretched. Radicalism is quite simply a political option like any other...The poli-tico-financier type of M. Dreyfus is common in Paris; actually this type is neither a financier nor a politician; he is a bold, active, avid character, but one who never goes after anything small, who remains a bastard, and that is why I call him politico-financier because he nibbles off of poli-tics and finances." pp.81-83.

[4] Drumont, *La Fin d'un monde,* p. 109.

[5] Ibid., pp. 226-227.

[6] Ibid., iv. See also Joseph Harris, *The Tallest Tower* (Boston: Houghton Mifflin, 1975).

[7] In his fragmented correspondence Félix Nadar appeared to be decidedly ambivalent about Drumont's work. In a letter dated 15 April 1888 he ex-pressed his indignation at Taxil's attacks against the clergy and denounce all vilification against unpopular religious groups. See Félix Nadar,

Notebook 24988, letters number 255, 256, Félix Nadar correspondence Bibliothèque Nationale, Paris, Salles de Manuscrits. In subsequent letters Nadar thanked Drumont for sending him a copy of *La Fin d'un monde* which he felt he "needed because I had trouble with your first book." Letter dated 21 May 1889. In a letter dated 8 August 1897 he thanked Drumont for continuing to send him copies of his newspaper.

[8] Francesco Nitti, *Catholic Socialism* (London: George Allen, 1911), p.200.

[9] Raphaël Viau, *Vingt ans d'antisémitisme* (Paris: Fasquelle, 1910), p.11.

[10] Jean Drault, *Drumont,* pp.40-46. German racists also propounded the assertion that Christ was not Jewish but really an Aryan.

[11] See Michael Burns, *Rural Society and French Politics,* (Princeton: Princeton University Press, 1984), and Alexandre Zévaès, *Au temps du boulangisme* (Paris: Gallimard, 1930).

[12] Viau, *Vingt ans d'antisémitisme,* pp.13-14.

[13] Donald Dresden, *The Marquis de Morès* (Norman: University of Oklahoma Press, 1970). See also Byrnes, op. cit., pp. 227-250.

[14] Drumont, *La Dernière bataille,* xv.

[15] Ibid., p. 193.

[16] Viau, *Vingt ans d'antisémitisme,* p. 15.

[17] Quoted by Byrnes, p. 239.

[18] Drumont, *Le Testament d'un antisémite,* p.400.

[19] See ibid., pp. 399-439.

[20] Léo Taxil, *M. Drumont, étude psychologique* (Paris: Létouzey, 1890), p.8. Taxil's satirical portrait is similar to this modern description of psychotic behavior: "A phobic patient may say: 'I cannot cross the street. I am afraid of the bus. I agree that my fears are out of proportion, but still I cannot cross the street. However, I am prepared to examine my fear.' A neurotic character will say: 'I do not cross the street because, unlike the idiots who risk their lives and get killed, I enjoy staying home!.....The psychotic, however, says dogmatically: 'The bus drivers are after me and I must hide at home. You should examine them, not me!'' Quoted by Ludwig Eidelberg, editor in chief, *Encyclopedia of Psychoanalysis* (New York: The Free Press, 1968), p.352.

[21] Taxil, *M. Drumont.*, p.180.

[22] Drumont, *Le Testament d'un antisémite,* pp.245-246.

[23] Quoted by Byrnes, op. cit., p. 49.

[24] Jehuda Reinharz, *Fatherland or Promised Land* (Ann Arbor, University of Michigan Press, 1975), p. 16.

[25] Byrnes, op. cit., p. 241.

[26] See Emmanuel Beau de Loménie, *Edouard Drumont,* p.71 and Léon Daudet, *Quand vivait mon père,* p. 42.

[27] Jean Drault, *Drumont,* p. 83.

[28] Drumont, *Souvenirs,* p. 156.

[29] See Drault, *Drumont,* p.88

[30] Viau, op. cit., p.27.

[31] Ibid., p.33

[32] Jules Guérin, *Les Trafiquants de l'antisémitisme,* p.38.

[33] Ibid., p. 35.

5
## Panama

> *There is a Paris journalist who wrote*
> *three pro-canal articles for 1,000*
> *francs each. By the time he had*
> *finished the third article he had*
> *sold himself on it so thoroughly that*
> *he had invested all his savings in it*
> *and lost everything he had.*
> —Clemenceau

Apart from the novelty of an antisemitic daily based in Paris, *La Libre Parole* did not manage initially to capture the attention which its editor believed it deserved. Throughout the summer of 1892 Drumont would have to be content with exploiting topics which finally enabled him to break a story about government corruption and restore his former popularity. This chapter is concerned with studying Drumont's talent for grafting his antisemitic philosophy onto the tradition of journalistic muckraking. Whereas *La France juive* had been mainly devoted to his views on the Jewish question, *La Libre Parole* was able to make the transition linking it to the broader concerns of national affairs. This extended range of Drumont's talent permitted him to increase his credibility, and his new-found stature as a fearless journalist helped prepare the way to the Dreyfus affair.

It would not be until the end of 1892 that *La Libre Parole* came into its own. It then played a major role in exposing what came to be known as the Panama affair thanks to its vigorous campaign against the malfeasance caused by the directors of the Panama canal enterprise.

What ultimately led Drumont to publicize the scandalous operations of the Panama company were his articles against Jews in general and Rothschild in particular. His new journal wasted little time in aiming at big targets. To him the great Jewish financier stood for all the evils of capitalism and Semitic influence. Rothschild always remained Drumont's favorite bugbear. By concentrating attacks on this symbolic and conspicuous figure he exposed the strong and weak sides of his campaign. Such articles were designed to have appeal to the working class and its struggle against the upper middle class. Rothschild may have been the most famous of contemporary money figures, but he was one among others. And the nature of his dealings left him a bit remote from the immediate effects of the social question. Rothschild was, strictly speaking, a financier not a banker; he dealt directly with governments. Those areas in which workers' interests were immediately affected--the factory system--were not conspicuously controlled by Jews. Hence for all its symbolic value attacks on Rothschild from a racist position were blunted in some but not all working class circles.

This did not prevent Drumont from pressing the issue. On 13 May

1892 he decried the plan to review the privilege of the Bank of France which was controlled by Rothschild. In particular he accused the project's sponsor, the eminent deputy, Auguste Burdeau, of having taken a bribe to insure its favorable passage. Publicly challenged, the politician reacted and sued for defamation. During the trial that followed Drumont had difficulty proving his charges. Burdeau's lawyers, Waldeck-Rousseau, pressed Drumont to admit that he had nothing more than rumors to print. Thus Drumont was found guilty for libel, was sentenced to three months in prison and was obliged to print in his own paper the story of the trial. He also had to pay a fine of 1,000 francs and the cost of eighty retractions in eight newspapers in Paris and the provinces. The total price of this adventure came to 100,000 francs. Jean Drault recalled two years later, when Burdeau died that his funeral cortege passed beneath the windows of *La Libre Parole,* that the marchers, shaking their fists, cried out 'Murderers! Murderers!' They were admitting that *La Libre Parole* was a bit responsible for killing Burdeau. It should have killed It should have killed others.''[1]

This confrontation was Drumont's baptism of fire in the world of newspapers. The trial does not seem to have done much damage to his reputation. Indeed it probably helped him somewhat in certain quarters where he was viewed as a martyr who dared to challenge the most powerful man in the government and society. As a result of his trial and conviction Drumont was hailed in some socialist circles. An anonymous piece in the 16 June 1892 issue of *La Revendication,* the official organ of the trade union movement, bears witness to his new found support in working-class circles: "But M. Drumont, having to suffer today because of the campaign he is waging against big finance--of which we are the victims--we owe him our deepest sympathy." The author goes on to disavow certain features of Drumont's program and adds: "We have gathered to salute this man the defender of all exploited people, the intrepid adversary of all exploiters..."

Another controversial adventure was also taking shape for Drumont in the month of May. It was his chief goal to drive Jews out of French llife. Two areas on which he concentrated were high finance and the military with appeal for the former directed at socialists and for the latter at nationalists. With a series of articles, "Jews in the Army," Pradal de Lamase, a former pontifical zouave, specifically singled out individual Jews for condemnation, accusing them of being "the spy who shamelessly traffics in the secrets of national defense...with the Cahens, the Dreyfuses, and all their other coreligionists." Pradel de Lamase charged that they were seizing sensitive positions in the military in order to sell military secrets to Germany.

In his third article of the series appearing on 26 May, Pradel de Lamase attacked Théodore Reinach. The latter, he claimed, "had for barrack companions (either in the 13th or 12th artillery), a Lehman, a Lévy, a Cerf, a Dietsch, a Hersch, a Dreyfus...'' It is interesting to remark that Alfred Dreyfus was a member of the 14th artillery. Given such precise details as early as 1892, it was understandable that Drumont's readers expected to discover a treacherous artillery officer named Dreyfus.

As a result of these articles Drumont was challenged to a duel by Captain Crémieux-Foa of the 8th Dragoons which were stationed at Meaux, He was a member of an old wealthy family and took it upon himself to uphold the honor of the Jewish servicemen and fellow officers who were insulted. Never one himself to shrink from a fight, Drumont accepted and both combatants were lightly wounded during their duel in the forest of Saint Germain. Drumont was in top form that day. The Marquis de Morès, acting as a witness, remarked upon observing his torso: "I never saw so much hair on a chest. He's as hairy as a bear."[2]

This duel settled nothing and only led to two others of greater significance. Since the articles which sparked the controversy were signed by Pradel de Lamase, he and Cremieux-Foa also fought a duel with pistols which resulted in no injuries. What is intriguing about these combats was that one of the seconds for Crémieux-Foa was Count Charles-Marie Ferdinand Walsin Esterhazy. This shady nobleman was eager to pose as a friend of the Jews with the hope of some financial compensation for services rendered. The articles denouncing Jews in the army claimed to mention information received from an anonymous officer. Esterhazy made a great show of protest over this point by demanding that the unknown informer be unmasked and dismissed from the army. However as historian David Lewis remarks: "There may have been a weird irony in Esterhazy's indignation. It is not unlikely that this anonymous officer behind Lamase's article--the officer whom Esterhazy wanted to be expelled from the army--was Esterhazy himself."[3] Mysterious details such as these have kept generations of scholars and historians interested in the Dreyfus affair.

It was the third duel provoked by this point of honor which caused the greatest consternation. The other second of Crémieux-Foa, Captain Armand Mayer, was encouraged by Esterhazy, and because of a quarrel over news leaks about the duel to the press he found himself facing the expert sword of Morès. They met at ten o'clock on the morning of 25 June on the Ile de la Grande Jatte in the Seine, just north of Paris. This encounter with swords started out briskly. During one of his lunges, Mayer received Morès' weapon which pierced his lung and stopped at the spinal column. The fatal damage was not at first apparent, but after Mayer was taken to the Gros Caillou hospital, he died at 5:30 in the afternoon that same day.[4]

The death of Captain Mayer produced a massive uproar. Many thought that the campaign to vilify Jews had become excessive. A French officer had been insulted and killed because of his religious background. As a result of this outcry *La Libre Parole* was shaken but undaunted. Its circulation continued to rise despite or perhaps because of the adverse publicity. The day following Mayer's death Drumont professed grief: "Our emotion is profound in the presence of a victim of a point of honor and we respectfully salute his coffin."

Twenty-four hours later Drumont had regained his composure and wrote that Mayer had really deserved his fate by his mere presence in the army. By way of explanation he described Guèrin, one of Morès' seconds as a "gentle soul, like most antisemites, who only become violent because they are exasperated by the cold and cunning ferocity by which the Semites crush us." But public indignation over the tragic death was enormous. Several thousand concerned Frenchmen followed Mayer's funeral procession through the streets of Paris. In the National Assembly Freycinet, the Minister of War, declared that "the army does not distinguish between Jews, Protestants and Catholics." The full Chamber applauded this statement denouncing the crime of sowing discontent in the army.

Morès was arrested and held for five days in the Mazas prison. On 2 July 1892 *La Libre Parole* published two confidential letters sent out by General Saussier, the military governor of Paris, to his colleagues demanding to know the name of the officer behind the inflammatory article which had appeared in Drumont's journal and consequently provoked the duel leading to the death of Mayer. Morès went on trial on 29 August along with the seconds involved in the fatal duel. Ironically, Morès' lawyer was Edgar Demange, one of France's leading attorneys who later took up the cause of Dreyfus.

During the tumultuous trial a series of witnesses kept emotions at the boiling point. Esterhazy was summoned to offer testimony about Mayer's character and family life, an occasion which he used to gain favorable publicity about himself. Even Léo Taxil was to offer his opinion about the political ends of antisemitism. He claimed to have heard Guérin at a public meeting advocate "the massacre en masse of the Hebrews." Mores was brilliantly defended and cleverly depicted not as a reactionary but as "a man of tomorrow, a man of the future, whose ideas are not yet very well balanced because he is young..." The defendant was fortunate in that he had a trial by jury. He was acquitted and released to a waiting throng of well wishers who hailed him as their tribune "in the apotheosis of a veritable popular uprising." [5]

Because the Minister of War, Freycinet, denounced those who were causing dissension in the army, he was the object of Drumont's pen: "Jewry....has made its fief out of the Ministry of War; it's at home there, and nothing can dislodge it." Despite the increased sales, *La Libre Parole* had been shaken by the bad publicity and attempted to prove that its philosophy was well based in Christian tradition. As if to detract from the effects of Morès' murder trial it published long, lurid accounts of ritual murder accusations. When the head rabbi of France, Zadoc-Kahn, protested and quoted papal disclaimers fo such calumnies, Drumont simply pooh-poohed the denials and reminded his readers of the church's long-standing animosity towards jews and Judaism.

This reliance on Christian tradition was momentarily shaken by a sensational interview on the subject given by Pope Leo XIII to the famous journalist Severine. Thanks to the intercession of Catholic friends. Severine decided to speak directly to the Pope on the Jewish question. She went to Rome and wrote in *Le Figaro* what appeared to be a papal condemnation of antisemitism.

Drumont and his sympathisers throughout Europe were momentarily dismayed. They went to great lengths to offset the effect of Séverine's journalistic coup. Drumont stressed that whatever the Holy Father might have said it was not a pronouncement *ex cathedra*, thus not binding as dogma on the faithful What he really meant was that no one should pay attention to what the vicar of Christ had said on this particular occasion. Drumont spoke with some authority of his own. As Europe's most vociferous Jew baiter he was accorded the title of "the pope of antisemitism" by fellow journalists.

The series of articles which followed shed light on the ambiguous stand taken by the church and the duplicity of Drumont on this question. When the Pope seemed to decry antisemitism Drumont discounted his word, but when the head of the Catholic church seemed to back away from his statements the journalist then upheld the importance of papal authority. Any crisis of faith for antisemites was subsequently averted when papal spokesmen publicly qualified the remarks which the Pope had made to Severine. Drumont was relieved to print on 11 August this notice taken from the London *Daily Chronicle*: "His Holiness is not satisfied with the article published by Mme Séverine in *Le Figaro*...in substance, the statements on antisemitism have been faithfully reproduced. The Holy Father, while condemning violent means, upholds the antisemitic movement as long as it is carried out in a legal fashion, as in Germany for example...." [6]

In order to assume that Catholics had not been led astray by sentimentaity, Drumont published this excerpt from the Vatican newspaper, *L'Osservatore Romano* of 23 August 1892:

"They (the Jews) had better watch out what they are doing, the insatiable and proud leaders of the Judeo-Masonic tyranny in our time, as the people's patience might be over as soon as God stops putting up with them. Then there will be excesses, disorders, even horrible crimes, but who will be responsible?...."

For her article Drumont bore Séverine no grudge. He emphasized that she was merely a woman journalist with "more feeling than thought," incapable of understanding the deep philosophical roots of antisemitism. She was wrong, he believed, to interpret his philosophy from the strictly religious point of view. Here is the first question he would ask her: "Why is it that the Moslems, who surely do not blame the Jews for crucifying Jesus Christ, since they adore Mohammed, detest the children of Israel as much as the Christians of the Middle Ages, and that today's anti-semites are largely freethinkers?"

Drumont did not seem in fact to be concerned with her answers. He and Séverine had become very good friends. Their mutual affection was deep enough for her to keep her apartment on the fourth floor above the newspaper offices and for a certain length of time she came to share his ideology concerning the Jewish question. But by the time of the Drey-fus affair she would break with Drumont's violent antisemitism and go her own way. In the meantime she had found a home at *La Libre Parole*.

In the first year of its existence the major reporting in this newspaper was specifically and overwhelmingly anti-Jewish in tone and substance. Other journals were also anti-semitic when the occasion arose but Dru-mont's sheet made this field its special province. The journal seems to have been popular among various social groups, particularly among large numbers of Catholics and poorly educated parish priests. Judging by its staff the readership must have been more extensive. In short it had special appeal to those who existed on the margins of society, to those who felt displaced by the rapidly changing society around them. Above all it appealed to those who sought and thought they had found an ex-planation for the ills of contemporary French society.

Catholic bishops could not be expected to approve of Drumont's pro-claimed independence and strong criticism of the hierarchy's political positions. The newspaper was designed to be read whole and it culti-vated the underdog mentality and the conspiratorial view of history. One observer recalled that *La Libre Parole* was read by "curates, commu-nards, and concierges," In short, it enjoyed a mixed clientele.

Readership was not limited only to these ranks. The journal's racy, hardhitting style and muckraking was to have a widespread appeal particularly in 1892 as revelations about the Panama affair began slowly to intrigue the general public. Drumont claimed to have found the an-swers to pressing national problems. In his memoirs Daniel Halévy, for example, recalls how his friend Degas was worried "by the debasing of French morality...Drumont, a powerful pamphleteer, offered an ex-planation of this decline and Degas listened to his daily article as docilely as he had listened to the tales of Dumas *père*. He soon became a passionate reader of Drumont, but because of my father's Jewish origin he was always very careful not to show us his intense antisemitism." [7] That friendship like many others would in fact end when the Dreyfus affair reached the peak of fury on the national scene.

Any item showing the Jews in a bad light was grist for Drumont's mill. One of his favorite themes was *la traite des blanches*--"white slavery." He never missed a chance to bring up this lurid subject--which had some basis in reality---and to link it to the Jews. On 5 November, for example he published an article bearing huge headlines which dealt with the trial in Lemberg of twenty-eight Jews who had been condemned for trafficking in human flesh. This piece concluded that no one should be astonished by this monstrous scandal and claimed that the Talmud permitted Jews to treat Gentiles like animals.

Some did participate in white slavery during that period of massive emigration to the New World. In fact Jewish women were also pressed into this service. Like many members of other ethnic groups these criminals provided women to the millions of uprooted men who had traveled abroad and left their families behind in Europe. The story of Jewish participation in this trade was highly exaggerated by the yellow press. It was sensational and made very good copy. The prefect of the Paris police, Alfred Morain, stated, however, that "in proportion to the number of cases of this kind which really occur the topic of the white-slave traffic occupies far too much space in certain newspapers." [8] In Drumont's journal such tales were offered as a supplement to the ritual murder craze which was also prevalent at the end of the century throughout Europe. This was one of the most durable inflammatory themes which continued to appear in Drumont's newspaper long after his death. In any event, the theme of white slavery must have helped prepare readers to accept Jewish involvement in the growing Panama scandals as an example of Jewish profiteering in the New World at the expense of innocent Christians.

On the matter of the ritual murder accusations the German-speaking world provided Drumont with a fertile source of information. Despite his professed hatred for things German, Drumont always gave favorable reports of antisemitic activities in those lands. In the summer of 1892 his reporter Achille Plista, for example, covered an antisemitic rally in Bavaria and had the pleasure of delivering a speech before the audience of well-wishers. Declared Plista: "The emancipation of the Jews in Europe is the work, or better still, the sin of France. France will be the first country to put them back in their place. And since it is a fact of universal history that the initiative of all great movements came from France, her example will be followed by everyone once again."

During his tour of German-speaking lands Plista was enchanted to make the acquaintance in Vienna of the popular antisemitic deputy and

Christian socialist, Doctor Karl Lueger, who told him: "I have no need to tell you how carefully I have read the works of Drumont." He further commented to his guest that Germany like France up to now had resisted "that Jewish poison" but with the coming of capitalism the struggle must be waged more fiercely. It is instructive to recall that for the young Adolf Hitler, Lueger was "the last great German to be born in Austria."[9] After his death Drumont's disciples would point with pride to this praise as proof that France was supposed to have antedated Germany in the development of the anti-Jewish revolution. During his lifetime Drumont was seen as the French counterpart to Lueger, but the differences separating the two were significant. Lueger did use anti-Jewish language in his campaigns as political rhetoric, but on a personal level he did not really hate Jews. Jew hatred was central to Drumont's politics and character and as such his views point towards the vicious antisemitism of the twentieth century.

By the time Plista was conducting his tour of antisemitic areas Drumont has already put into action his plan to have Jews removed from public life. By the middle of the year he was astute enough to capitalize on one of France's growing major political-financial scandals--the Panama affair. He did not uncover the corruption involved but at a critical stage of its unfolding he effectively exposed in detail the depths to which the political system had fallen. It is important to recall that scandals of this type would plague the Third Republic and weaken its authority right up to its demise in 1940. The word Panama used to mean for Americans the triumph of National Endeavor, but for Frenchmen of 1892 the name of that isthmus stood for corrupt politics of the worst type. For the latter it was doubly important for it also served as the prelude to the Dreyfus affair. In both these cases Drumont's journal played an outstanding role.

The Panama scandals have often been studied before but almost no works deal with the crucial role played by Drumont. The rest of this chapter examines the manner by which Drumont exploited Panama and helped create the impression that it was a gigantic swindle operated by Jews. Drumont like most Frenchmen realized that for centuries men had dreamt of cutting a canal across Panama. In the nineteenth century that dream almost came true. The logical choice for such an undertaking was Ferdinand de Lesseps, dubbed by Gambetta as "the great Frenchman" because of his success in completing the Suez canal. De Lesseps himself was too old to supervise the actual details of such a vast operation, but he had not lost the faith of the public and he entrusted the Panama enterprise to his son Charles. This would be the first of a series of misjudgments on his part. The same qualities which had led de Lesseps to tackle the job also led to his downfall and that of many others.

Unfortunately for his supporters de Lesseps was not an economist, an engineer or a very good organizer. At an advanced age he was a booster and his main task was to create enthusiasm for his ventures in order to sell the shares that would finance construction of the canal. Charles de Lesseps was the real director of the operation. He was honest and relied on his father's advice and vast prestige, and thus he laid the groundwork for disaster.

At the very beginning of this venture, in the summer of 1879, the Universal Panama Interoceanic Canal Company had put its shares on sale in Europe and America. But because of investor reluctance only 60,000 of the 80,000 shares were bought up by the public and these mainly in France. In order to boost sales Charles de Lesseps thought it wise to seek the services of a banker named Marc Lévy-Crémieux, who was commissioned to form an underwriting syndicate and to buy support from the press. The scheme worked at first and the company was successfully launched. It is interesting to note that initially the influential newspaper, *Le Petit Journal,* had denounced the excavation scheme but later offered lavish praise for its success. The education of the press was the specialty of Lévy-Crémieux. Two years later, however, this same journal would stand in the forefront in denouncing Dreyfus.

When the canal venture collapsed and Charles de Lesseps had stand trial the director tried to play the innocent in explaining his company's policy of bribes and its association to Lévy-Crémieux and assistants. To these exculpations Judge Samuel Perivier retorted: "You gave them the dirty job which you preferred not to do yourself but provided them with the means of doing."[10] In the company's initial stages such business practices were not uncommon among members of the entrepreneurial world. Buying part of the press to advocate a particular scheme was seen by interested parties as just another means of publicity. Many newspapers were not immune to this lucrative, shady practice and this included the journal founded by Drumont. But in the case of Panama and the problems it incurred such devious practices became a temptation which was difficult to resist when the initial venture encountered troubles.

The digging of the canal had not begun till early 1882. The following year de Lesseps reiterated that the target date for completion would be 1888. But unforeseen circumstances would soon force him and the company to abandon this goal. De Lesseps was oblivious to outside criticism. He failed to reckon with local insurrection, unhealthy climate, and above all he remained rigid in his belief that his canal would be a sea-level canal despite the different sea levels of the Atlantic and Pacific oceans.

When this discrepancy could no longer be ignored it was decided that new plans were needed in order to install a system of locks. De Lesseps then called on the services of Alexandre Eiffel. Cost overruns then obliged the company to sell more and more stock, and to insure success de Lesseps was resolved to set his sights higher and to use his influence in Parliament. What had started off as a rather questionable tactic then turned considerably more shady. It would be later viewed by the public as corruption on a large scale. And Drumont was to strive to make this view prevail.

The Panama Canal Company had repeatedly borrowed money from the public. After more appeals for funds, the company in 1885 sought permission to secure a public lottery loan with the assistance of the National Assembly. De Lesseps was becoming desparate. According to one observer, Allain-Targe, he threatened that "if the Republic refuses what the Empire has authorized, I shall be obliged to lay responsibility on all concerned. I have behind me the active press." [11]

After a government investigation of the project various changes were stipulated, mainly concerning the system of canal locks, and the work once again moved forward. However even the support of Charles Baihaut, the Minister of Public Works, was not able to keep the venture afloat indefinitely. More loans were sought and obtained but never enough to complete the work. Finally by the end of 1888 the last loan had been raised but it proved to be insufficient despite the public promotion campaign which had been renewed by the two de Lesseps throughout the country.

Several thousand small stockholder, many of modest means, had invested their life savings in this venture. By the fifth time de Lesseps passed the hat the project's initial glow had dimmed considerably in the public eye. Those who hated him resorted to drastic measures to defeat his last bond issue. They declared, for instance, that he had just died and they then dumped Panama shares onto the market in order to depress the price. When these enemies in Parliament defeated the motion which he sponsored to form a new company there was nowhere left to turn for the "great Frenchman." In early February 1889, the Civil Tribunal of the Seine approved the dissolution of the company and appointed a liquidator. In May 1890 a parliamentary committee which had been sent to Panama asserted that the excavation project would need eight more years and almost one billion additional francs to reach completion.

After the final collapse of the project shock waves swept through France and public reaction was predictable. It felt swindled and to a large extent it was a justified feeling. Lifetime savings were destroyed, credit ruined and suicides ensued. What had begun as a dream for easy profit had turned into a nightmare. That the company suspended operations amidst rumors of scandal during the centennial year of the French revolution and the Boulanger crisis led many on the Right and Left to question the nature of their governmental system. The state promised to initiate a series of investigations to clear up the circumstances of the collapse. More than 100,000 stockholders signed petitions demanding action of some sort, mainly in the hope of refloating the company in order to recoup some of the enormous financial losses.

There were also those who demanded that charges be brought against the company's officials. On this score the government dragged its feet understandably, because many members of Parliament were implicated. Thus the scandal did not erupt immediately in all its sordid details. In place of facts rumors and gossip were all the public had to rely on. But on this occasion even rumor had its place. Under its pressure the inner circle responsible for the debacle cracked wide open, and the catalyst which lanced the boil was Drumont.

The Panama scandal was to be Drumont's finest hour. At last his social philosophy was put into action and seemed to be substantiated. Even a broken clock must be right two times a day. Drumont had been denouncing Jews for so long that he was bound to stumble across some involved in a dubious operation. He was no less merciless towards those Gentiles whom he accused of being their lackeys.

From the beginning of his career Drumont had always hated Ferdinand de Lesseps. In 1886 he had accused Freemasonry of "naturally playing a big role in the launching of that problematic Panama business..." His animosity was probably sparked by those clerical circles which never forgave de Lesseps' attitude on the Roman question in 1849. In 1890 Drumont had devoted a large section of his book, *La Dernière bataille*, to berating the Panama fiasco. One historian of the canal, Ian Cameron, described this work as "a scurrilous and sensational attack on the *Compagnie Universelle* in general and Ferdinand de Lesseps in particular... his book is wildly exaggerated and reads today like the composition of a hysterical schoolboy." [12]

In 1890 this volume was not viewed in such a negative light. Whatever the faults of Drumont's book he was fortunate enough to have written a powerful and timely broadside attacking the obvious corruption surrounding the scandal. Drumont played upon public consternation and impatience over the government's inability to provide explanations. In his view..."it (the government) is always on your back. It forbids parents to have their children raised as they see fit....it is always around whenever it is a question of offending feelings, but it never intervenes when it is a question of protecting a French interest." [13]

With regard to the Panama affair Drumont maintained that the government had been corrupted by a dishonest press. He also claimed that Paris alone had 1573 "journals, reviews, and periodical publications," and that none was able to uncover the truth behind the widespread corruption. To be sure, not all these journalists had been bribed, he asserted; what had happened, however, was a classic case of manipulation by the press which had lasted for the previous eight years.

Drumont explained this conspiracy of silence as a Jewish plot to promote the Panama venture. He even went so far as to speculate that perhaps the scandal was originally a gigantic fraud designed to cheat hundreds of thousands of humble French stockholders out of their funds. Given the lack of progress and the vast sums already spent, he reasoned that the possibility of a massive hoax could not be excluded. He vigorously asserted that Ferdinand de Lesseps was himself a tool in a Jewish publicity campaign to deceive Frenchmen: "Jews experience a bizarre intellectual joy in attesting their power by creating false glory; they are happy when they've represented a traitor as an eminent patriot..." [14] De Lesseps was supposed to be placed into this category and Drumont called him a liar who deserved to be shot.

In this version of the Panama venture de Lesseps was held responsible for all its failures. Here Drumont devoted much space in his book and journal to lurid descriptions of the excavation site and the poor working conditions. Even in death he declared there was no justice for what he claimed were 30,000 dead workers whose cadavers were unceremoniously disposed of by being thrown into ditches and fetid swamps. For Drumont "this, moreover, does not interest the French public; having fallen into a state of intellectual debility, it only sees what is in the newspapers. Thirty thousand human beings dying in a far corner of the world just to facilitate financial transactions, the thing doesn't exist for the reader; on the other hand he is full of emotion when he learns that some Jew named Loewy has arrived from Vienna in a coach to visit the Exhibition." [15]

The arrival of such a personality was nothing less than the forerunner of a massive invasion of Christian Europe, particularly France. According to Drumont, "as soon as they've cleaned up a bit, these Galician Jews, who are now shaking their lice from their greasy caftans, will come to occupy positions in Vienna, there to become *Pressjude* (sic), Press Jews. Journalists from Frankfort and Vienna already brilliantly represented here, will enter into the Parisian press, and there'll be no way for a Christian to keep abreast of opinion." [16] This was Drumont's explanation for the lack of critical coverage of the Panama affair. However, unable to cite specific names in this regard he claimed he had "...already explained that the part of responsibility of the journalist as an individual was entirely minimal in this gigantic *humburg* (sic). It is the general picture which must be studied."

The portrait that he gave of his profession was touching. In Drumont's view journalists from the Left bank were fine fellows, "obscure heroes of the press," who were underpaid, especially those who wrote for Catholic newspapers which offered only three francs per page. Journalists from the Right bank, he averred, fared no better but for different reasons. They were reputed to be more independent, more honorable but because of poor working conditions and uncertain family situations one could see them dragging their children around the streets from café to café at all hours of the night.

Under such circumstances morals were easily corrupted because, observed Drumont, "society is a brothel, and you have to give in to the rules of a brothel." [17] Drumont said that he often encountered such colleagues and asked them how they could write the lies which appeared under their names in/ the press. By way of a reply he was informed: "I write that stuff for the scumbags who govern us because I am in need but I don't believe a word of it...You know that I am more antisemitic than you..." Drumont would then inquire as to why the journalist did not give up such a dishonorable occupation and he was told that "when you don't want to run on foot or race after tramways like a dog in the gutter, you can't be disagreeable with Israel." [18]

If such scenarios were to be believed the corruption of the press and by analogy the decadence of society were understandable. "It is thus frightening to think that thanks to the unique power of money wheeler-dealers can make themselves absolute masters of opinion, to exert an irresistible pressure which robs people of their free will." [19] So awesome was this force in forming public opinion that "Panama was truly an effort at suggestion by the press, and victims fell little by little into a sort of magnetic state which prevented them from thinking, reasoning and defending themselves." [20]

Drumont expressed sympathy for those Gentile correspondents who he felt had to prostitute themselves and for the hundreds of thousands of small stockholders who had allowed themselves to be duped. One source of blame he identified to be the court system. Magistrates, who should have investigated the Panama company, were reputed to be as corrupt as the politicians who were persuaded by de Lesseps and associates to protect and further their dubious enterprise.

By denigrating the court system Drumont dealt one more blow against the institutions of the Third Republic. The corrupting agent of society in this instance, proclaimed Drumont, was to be found among the Jews. Thus it is not surprising that Drumont should once again lay the blame squarely at the feet of Rothschild. This accusation was to be expected by Drumont's readers. But in also attacking the role of Cornelius Herz he was closer to the mark. He then provided his audience with a brief sketch of Herz and his business activities, especially those in America where the expatriate Frenchman started his extraordinary career. Why, Drumont demanded to know, did not the Americans also invest in Panama? He reasoned that either they knew Herz's schemes too well or they saw little merit in the Panama canal.

The role that Herz was to play in these events was that of the middleman between the company and public officials. He received his instructions from the head of the corporation. For Drumont de Lesseps was "the great corrupter." In this capacity the noted entrepreneur had checks distributed to those legislators who were considered helpful to his cause. More than one hundred out of some nine hundred politicians were implicated and ultimately accused of receiving payment, so many in fact that Drumont conjured up this graphic scene: "A fine spectacle was to be seen: checks formed in a column and marching on the Palais-Boubon."[21]

Though he exaggerated the scope of the payoffs, the editor of *La Libre Parole* was essentially correct in calling attention to the abuses involved.

From the beginning till the end of the Panama scandal Drumont was proud to take the credit for his role in exposing malfeasance. He always insisted that what others saw as merely another example of swindling in the capitalist system was in effect the symptom of a much greater malaise. "The Panama affair is a microcosm in which you see in action everything which has a social role."[22] As an ideologue Drumont was concerned with uncovering the basic causes of corruption, and as a polemicist he excoriated the shortsightedness of his countrymen who refused to accept his interpretation of events. He recalled how Rothschild had previously escaped popular wrath, but on this occasion "the victims of Panama went further and *Le Gaulois* informs us: 'before dispersing, the stockholders who had assembled on the Rue Caumartin, voted a message of congratulations to Monsieur de Lesseps.'"[23] Such fatuousness was an example of France's hopeless condition.

Exasperated by conduct of this sort, Drumont swore that he had done his best to warn his fellow citizens: "I've been writing and asking everyone for information, now I'm leaving this heap of documents alone and I'm going to stroll for a few days in the forest where I'll amuse myself by striking the traplines set by Cahen d'Anvers to catch pheasants."[24]

At the time he wrote his book Drumont confessed that he lacked conclusive proof to prove his allegations. He was saddened to write: "It is clearly impossible to produce a document thus labeled: 'I, the undersigned, deputy from said department, recognize that on said day, at said hour, I received said sum in order to sell my vote."[25] When he expressed these sentiments in *La Dernière bataille* he had no such proof, but because of his patience perseverance would soon be rewarded.

For all his faults and bias on this occasion Drumont was on the right track. He was convinced that there was a bigger story lurking beneath the surface, and he was quite correct. What then befell Drumont was a journalist's dream come true. Having established a reputation as one of the leading voices among the anti-de Lesseps forces, he received the services of Ferdinand Martin, a disgruntled banker who had worked for the Panama project but felt that he had not been rewarded enough for his efforts. He went to Drumont seeking vengeance and offering information.

On 6 September 1892 *La Libre Parole* began publishing Martin's articles, "The Hidden Side of Panama," under the pseudonym "Micros." It was a bombshell. While most of the press was thrashing about in the dark, this was the first time that names and facts were brought to light regarding those who were responsible for the scandal. Up to this moment Drumont had to be content with reporting and repeating such trivia about which jewish businessman owned what hotel in Panama. This was pretty much the same thin stuff that was featured in his articles on French military involvement in Indo-China.

But the article by "Micros" was of a different order. This was visible information that no government could afford to ignore or coverup. The article charged Freycinet, the Minister of War, Rouvier, the Minister of Finance, and many others of accepting bribes from Jewish businessmen like Lévy-Crémieux, Baron de Reinach and Léopold Arton. Baron Jacques de Reinach was born in Frankfort into a banker's family. He was truly cosmopolitan, knew several languages, had many high level contacts, and made his headquarters in Paris. Arton, whose name had been Léopold Aaron, was an unprincipled, well-traveled adventurer, and was associated with various bankruptcies. In Brazil he converted to Catholicism for the sake of an advantageous marriage, and once he returned to Paris he founded a Catholic bank in the Place Vendôme. He was also involved in an outfit known as the Dynamite Society, which was founded to sell explosives to the Panama operation.

Arton's real function was that of an intermediary to arrange bribes between the Panama company and well-placed figures in the government. The fact that he had replaced Cornelius Herz was the event that helped expose the entire scandal. Herz had threatened to publicise all of Reinach's activities and swore that only a large sum of money would maintain his silence. For years the Baron paid but by the time *La Libre Parole* began to attack certain implicated individuals, including Reinach himself, the Baron panicked, went to Drumont and promised more information if the editor promised not to use his name in print.

This was to be Drumont's second great coup. The series of "Micros" articles had just finished, and the vindictive Martin had nothing left to divulge. But his muckraking pieces and the intimidation they caused bore results. It was then that Reinach proposed his offer to inform on his associates, according to Drumont. On 3 November 1892 Drumont finally began to serve his three month sentence for defaming Burdeau and for which he had been earlier convicted. The government had postponed his imprisonment but now found that by imposing sentence just when his journal was the most sought-after paper in Paris it gave the appearance of incarcerating a genuine hero of the people.

According to Viau, Drumont's staff feigned sadness at the sight of their master on his way to jail. They could not, of course, conceal their pride in his work but they were somewhat relieved to be rid of their irascible overseer for a few months. Nevertheless Drumont must have chuckled to himself as he entered the Sainte-Pélagie prison. He had left behind a series of journalistic time bombs set to go off in the government's face while he was behind bars.

This tactic must have endeared Drumont to his fellow inmates. Sainte-Pélagie was the prison for political offenders. In his memoirs Drumont fondly recalled carrying his food tray on his way to the room that would be his home for three months. It was spacious and called the "Big Tomb,' but it was a tomb "with a stove, cigars and all you'd need for writing."[26] From its windows he had a good view of Paris, especially of the Jardin des Plantes directly across the street.

Prison fare did not bother him. Whatever he might have lacked was brought by his "faithful and good maid Marie. For three months, under frost and snow, she would cross Paris and pass under the eyes of the dumbfounded turnkey, bringing to a man, who is happy with a good roast beef, a piece of fruit, what would feed an army corps." This maid did not think much of her master's companions: "What nasty people, sir, these anarchists are! They say they're capable of anything."

In fact Drumont claimed that he was honored to be in such company and to have walked within the walls in the steps of so many illustrious predecessors. Although he decried anarchism in deed and principle, he was rather fascinated by the anarchist prisoners, especially by their tales of woe of vengeance against society. All in all, Drumont was amused by his prison experience: "The stay at Sainte-Pélagie left me the impression of one of those hotels in the Latin Quarter where they sing all day."[27]

Thinking about all that he had done, Drumont began "to chuckle and dance a jig in the Big Tomb." There, cut off physically from society, he bombarded the outside world with a series of scathing editorials which he signed with the pseudonym "Silvio Pellico." Nineteenth century readers recognized this as the name of the great Italian journalist-patriot whose country was inspired by his memoirs about imprisonment for political offenses.

From his cell Drumont appeared to be holding court with the rest of France which eagerly awaited his latest broadside. Through his journal he voiced concern about all sorts of questions from French soldiers fighting "in the pest holes of Dahomey against monkey-faced niggers" to famous personalities caught up in the political intrigues of Paris. But these topics were trivial compared to the big stories: "What enobles the journalist's work is the lofty thought which dominates and inspires him," he wrote. And what kept all the eyes of France and Europe fixed on Drumont was the daily ration of sensational revelations about Panama.

While he was still in prison his main informant, Baron de Reinach, apparently committed suicide. Earlier on 8 November, the police tried to serve him with a summons to appear at the trial of the Panama company directors. The baron felt obliged to return to Paris ten days ahead of schedule. In the meantime he had been trying to arrange affairs, to reach an agreement with Cornelius Herz, the most notorius figure in the entire scandal. After quarreling with his nephew Joseph Reinach for not having blocked the official inquiries, he returned home and retired for the evening. The following day on Sunday morning his valet found him dead in bed in his sumptuous home on the Rue Murillo. The sudden death seemed too opportune and no immediate autopsy was performed, thus the public was left to conclude that he had committed suicide in order to avoid more humiliation. Others in the press hinted that he might have been murdered by the sinister forces which were supposed to control French political and economic life.

After the consternation subsided over the baron's untimely death, Reinach's name was replaced in the press by that of the surviving mystery man, Cornelius Herz. His complete role in the scandals has never been fully revealed. But he seemed to have exercised undue influence over Reinach to the extent that he was able to blackmail him for exorbitant amounts of money.

Herz's life seemed like something out of a detective story. He was born in France in 1845 of German-Jewish parents, and in 1849 his family emigrated to the United States where he attended the finest schools. After graduation Herz returned to Europe and served in the Franco-Prussian war where his medical knowledge earned him the post of assistant surgeon-major. Upon return to the New World he tried his luck in Chicago and San Francisco where he posed as a man of influence and contacts. The *San Francisco Evening Bulletin* described him as a person who "told of marvelous cures abroad and talked of kings, queens, and princes as if they were his favorite friends." [28]

Herz had established an imposing reputation for himself and acquired a sizable fortune in San Francisco. He had many inventions to his credit and was considered a genius in electricity and its use in combatting disease. He was bold enough to claim that some of Edison's works wer really his own. After borrowing a large sum of money from friends and associates, Herz quietly left San Francico and settled in Paris. There he built up a following and made it his business to acquaint himself with the top men of influence in politics and finance. One of the people he cultivated was Georges Clemenceau, who once declared: "In case of death I want my children raised under the direction of M. Cornelius Herz." [29] As a result of such blind trust Clemenceau's reputation suffered greatly from association with the master swindler, and he was not able again to make headway in politics till after the turn of the century.

In 1886 Herz became the first American citizen to receive the Grand Cross of the Legion of Honor for his services during the Franco-Prussian war. According to the *New York Times:* "Dr. Cornelius Herz, the eminent electrician, is the only American who has ever made Grand Officer." [30]

By then the hustler had been hobnobbing with the mightiest international figures. He was sharper and much more unscrupulous than his associates. It was finally revealed that he had bled 10,000,000 francs from Reinach by threatening to make known a letter of the Baron's exposing his liaison between Panama and Parliament. It was when Reinach, through Clemenceau, tried to have Herz stop certain scandal sheets that the Baron was forced to take his own life. Herz never stood trial; he fled to England where he was to die a sick man six years later. Of his career the *San Francisco Examiner* commented: "Dr. Herz's brilliant attainments brought him into contact with many prominent people in this city, and everyone he met had cause to remember him. He found it an easy matter to raise funds by his various schemes, and always forgot to return the money he raised." [31] For many years to come Drumont and other journalists rarely tired in reporting the details of his fantastic career.

With Reinach dead and Herz out of the country *La Libre Parole* kept the stunned nation reeling with the new revelations and allegations of polictical and financial intrigues. By the end of November it was printing the names of politicians and journalists who had taken bribes to support the Panama company. Because these tainted funds were transmitted by check, a new word, *chequard,* to describe those implicated, was introduced into the French political vocabulary. Drumont's journal also printed incriminating evidence in the form of a letter from Reinach to various deputies like Antonin Proust who was forced to resign his chairmanship for the French delegation to the Chicago World Exhibition scheduled to be held the next year. Due to Drumont's campaign other politicians sufferd similar fates.

During these hectic months *La Libre Parole* briefly became France's most important journal. Its printing went far above the 200,000 mark and its editor, who had been imprisoned by the regime he was attacking, became the toast of Paris. Praise was forthcoming from alls ides. Paul Bourget's new novel, *Cosmopolis,* reflected society as Drumont saw it, a world which had exchanged its traditional values for those of a degenerate, international bourgeoisie. The arch nationalist writer Maurice Barrès, a great admirer of Drumont, later dedicated to him his novel *Leurs Figures* which was a fictional account of the Panama affair. In the eyes of Drumont and a good deal of France the antisemitic view of society must have seemed vindicated. On 30 November he offered his readers a quotation from one of his favorite philosophers, Thomas Carlyle, concerning the collapse of society. Going one step further than his British mentor he comments: "The Jewish microbe has been a frightful dissolvement for this politically minded middle class." He continued to fulminate that if the little people did not pay closer attention to his philosophy there would be more disasters ahead for France.

The success of *La Libre Parole* campaign was seen by Drumont as proof of the value of antisemitism. He gave high praise to "the triumph of antisemitism abroad," especially in Germany where the Catholic party was beginning to cooperate with anti-Jewish politicians. In particular he devoted much attention to the ongoing trial of Hermann Ahlwardt. This petty embezzler and school teacher had charged on one notorious occasion that a Jew named Loewe had delivered a shipment of defective rifles to the German army. He argued that this was proof of a Franco-Jewish plot to ruin Germany's military might. [32] The accusation was false and Ahlwardt received a five month prison term, but he also received enough voter support to send him subsequently to the Reichstag. This would be a lesson which Drumont would turn to his own profit on the French electoral scene.

Given his rabid nationalism, one might have expected Drumont to praise Loewe. But hatred of Jews always took precedence over his professed hatred of Germans. Actually there seemed to be little scorn directed towards the latter for Drumont commented in his editorial of 11 December: "What is truly beautiful and worth admiring is the attitude of those German Catholics and conservatives." Unlike their counterparts in France he praised with a bit of exaggeration their support of the anti-Jewish cause across the Rhine, and he exhorted his fellow believers to follow their example.

The campaign sparked by Panama continued to bear fruit. The government was reorganized to the minimal satisfaction of most concerned. The German Ambassador in Paris, Count Münster, commented: "The Loubet-Ribot Ministry, which had fallen into the Panama Canal, has just been resuscitated under the form of a Ribot-Loubet Ministry." The scandal scattered victims in its wake. During a violent confrontation in the Chamber, Paul Déroulède accused Clemenceau of receiving 400,000 francs from Herz, claiming that Herz was a spy and that Clemenceau was his accomplice. Clemenceau retorted: "Monsieur Déroulède, you have lied!" The affronts were resolved on a field of honor where both men exchanged six shots in a pistol duel at a distance of twenty five meters. General Saussier was supposed to be the arbiter of this confrontation but he declined the offer. Clemenceau may have saved his honor on this occasion but the cloud of suspicion continued to hang over his political reputation.

On 7 January 1893, the trial of the Panama Company directors began in Paris. The following month sentences were pronounced. Ferdinand and Charles de Lesseps were fined 3,000 francs apiece and given five years imprisonment. By the middle of the year they had appealed the verdict and the Supreme Court reversed the lower court's sentencing. The elder de Lesseps retired to his country home, but his son, unable or unwilling to pay damages had to spend time in exile in England before arranging his return with the authorities.

Riding on the waves of popularity, Drumont failed to make political capital from his activities against the republicans. If he had been more adept at partisan intrigues, he might have surpassed his journalist's instincts and effectively led a movement to overthrow the system of government that allowed such a scandal to occur. Direct political confrontation was not in Drumont's personal style. For all his impassioned eloquence he mainly fancied himself an intellectual and preferred to limit himself to agitation in the press. It is true that he would try his hand in the political arena with mixed results, but ultimately he believed and acted as if direct activism would have to be undertaken by others who shared his ideology.

Although it was impossible at the time to view the Panama controversy dispassionately, subsequent investigation has been able to shed more light on just what happened during the scandals. It was natural for an aroused public to assume that the Panama venture collapsed because their vast investments had been used for bribery and corruption of government officials. But an examination of total company expenditures shows that most of the funds were actually used for the purposes designated and that the excavations themselves proceeded as best as possible given the unforeseen obstacles and managerial incompetence which had arisen.[33]

Factions on the political extremes profited from the scandal. To the Left Panama was proof of the inherent corruption of the republican center regime. Drumont gave voice to both these judgments and added that the scandal was a sign of Jewish control and manipulation as exemplified by the activities of the prominent figures which he helped to expose. Historian Robert Byrnes, however, observes that "Herz, Arton, and Reinach had become involved long after the major damage had been done."[34]

The last point seemed academic at the time of Drumont's campaign. The worst error committed by the Republicans was to allow Drumont's paper to reveal how badly things were handled by the Panama officials and to identify their middlemen. Failure and reluctance to investigate promptly--or to cover up successfully--the entire operation left the field clear for Drumont and reinforced the credibility of his journal and program to drive Jews out of national life.

Evidence of the effect of Drumont's campaign could be observed in the contemporary press. The former communard and radical deputy, Arthur Ranc, for example, denounced antisemitism in *Le Matin* of 12 September 1892 but added: "There are, however, Israelites who are the shame of their race. These are the upstarts made my money who deny the Revolution." Among the worst offenders he placed Rothschild. And an anonymous writer observed about Drumont in *L'Illustration* of 31 December: "Now he does battle against Judea, demolishes high finance, and preaches the extermination of the Hebrews and the social-Catholic liquidation of the Rothschilds, all this in the name of Christian charity."

Although Drumont distorted many features of the Panama scandal, the general public felt he deserved the honor for having led the way to expose and topple corrupt elements within the government. Whether they all shared his radical antisemitism was beside the point. Through his vigorous muckraking campaign the credibility of *La Libre Parole* was established. Drumont had provoked the powers that be to acknowledge widespread corruption within the regime. The same journalistic tactics would again be used within two years to arouse support for the conviction of Alfred Dreyfus. How Drumont and his staff managed to do this highlights the strength and importance of the press on governmental affairs. Without the kind of press that was typified by *La Libre Parole* there might not have been a Dreyfus affair. The following chapter will examine the role which his journal played in provoking and publicizing that scandal for which Panama served as a prelude.

## Notes

1   Drault, *Drumont*, p.112. According to Alfred Mourlon the government had considered denigrating Drumont's growing popularity in prison by having a former police official reveal the editor's role as an informer during the period of the Empire. In Mourlon's opinion the scheme failed when the plot was revealed to Drumont. See Alfred Mourlon, *La Mâchoire d'Ane*, vol. I, no. 3, 1 November 1896, p.3.

2   Viau, *Vingt ans d'antisémitisme*, p.25

3   David Lewis, *Prisoners of Honor*, (New York: William Morrow, 1973), p.72.

4   See Ernest Crémieux-Foa, *La Campagne antisémite. Les duels, Les responsabilités* (Paris:1892)

5   Drault, *Drumont*, p.122.

6   See also Eduardo Soderini, *The Pontificate of Leo XIII* (London: Burns Oates & Washburne, 1934), vol. I, pp.136-138.

7   Daniel Halévy, *My Friend Degas* (Middletown: Wesleyan University Press, 1964), p.98

8   Alfred Morain, *The Underworld of Paris* (New York: Blue Ribbon Books, 1931), p.255. See also Ernest Bell, *Fighting the Traffic in Young Gilrs* (New York: 1910), and F. Trocasse, *L'Autriche juive* (Paris: A. Pierret, n.d.), p.154.

9   Joachim Fest, *Hitler* (New York: Harcourt Brace Jovanovitch, 1974), p.42. See also John W. Boyer, *Political Radicalism in Late Imperial Vienna* (Chicago: Univ. of Chicago Press, 1981)

132

10 Maron Simon, *The Panama Affair,* (New York: Scribner's, 1971) p.148

11 Adrien Dansette, *Les Affaires de Panama* (Paris: Perrin, 1934) p.27

12 Ian Cameron, *The Impossible Dream* (London: Hodder and Stoughton 1971), p.98

13 Edouard Drumont, *La Dernière Bataille,* p.328

14 Ibid., p.338

15 Ibid., p.352

16 Ibid., p.405

17 Ibid., p.403

18 Ibid., p.404

19 Ibid., p.410

20 Ibid., p.421

21 Ibid., p.427

   Ibid., p.454

23 Ibid., p.455

24 Ibid., pp.428-429

25 Ibid., p.449.

26 Edouard Drumont, *De l'or, de la boue, du sang* (Paris: Flammarion, 1896) p.34

27 Ibid., pp.52-53

28 Quoted by Maron Simon, op. cit., p.187

29 Ibid., p.190

30 Quoted by Maron Simon, op. cit., p. 114.

31 Ibid., p. 228

32 See P.G.J. Pulzer, *The Rise of Political Antisemitism in Germany and Austria* (New York: John Wiley, 1964), p.112.

[33] See André Siegfried, *Suez and Panama* (New York: Harcourt, Brace, 1940), p.280 and Rolt Hammond and C.J. Lewin, *The Panama Canal* (London: Frederick Muller, 1966).

[34] Byrnes, *Antisemitism in Modern France,* p.333. See also Jean Bouvier, *Les Deux scandales de Panama,* Collection Les Archives (Paris: Juillard, 1964).

6

## The Dreyfus Affair

> The greatest bane inflicted
> on France by the Revolution
> was the newspaper.
>
> - - Rivarol

As a result of the Panama affair Drumont had established his reputation as one of the leading journalists of France. His newspaper now deserved credibility. He always insisted that what would become known as the Dreyfus affair was a direct outgrowth of Panama with all that was entailed by government corruption and treachery. The purpose of this chapter is threefold: it attempts to examine the role, if any, which Drumont may have played in the inception of the Dreyfus affair, to recount its reporting in his newspaper, and to analyze its effect on his political career and public opinion. The well known details of the affair need no extensive retelling here except insofar as they bear upon the objectives of this study.[1]

One of Drumont's favorite complaints against the Jews was their presence in the government and military. January 1893 saw the appointment of Alfred Dreyfus as a trainee to the General Staff of the army. He was the first Jewish officer to be so honored. He was highly intelligent, ambitious, and reserved, all character traits which would be cast in a suspicious light by those who did not appreciate his appointment. Since he was jewish some of his colleagues were destined to be apprehensive because of the influence of the jingoist press. As historian David Lewis commented: "Who could be sure Drumont was not preparing an article about 'The Jew on the General Staff.' "[2]

In the first months of 1893 Drumont was serving a prison sentence convicted of having defamed the government for its role in the Panama affair. For the time being his journal was content to emphasize what it viewed as the vindictiveness of the republican regime and the popularity of its celebrated editor it had chosen to punish for revealing the truth. Concern over the presence of Jews in the army was soon to become another variation of Drumont's mission to unmask dangers confronting the French nation.

After leaving prison Drumont tried in vain to profit politically from the role he had recently played in uncovering government wrongdoing. On the advice of various supporters he ran for a seat in the Chamber of Deputies from the constituency of Amiens. In spite of a spirited campaign he lost heavily with 3,717 votes to his Radical socialist opponent named Fiquet who received 11,614. Drumont claimed he was defeated by "Jewish gold'' but the more sober analysis of his collaborators suggested that political antisemitism had limited appeal at the polls. Drumont may have been popular as a journalist but his political philosophy still could not then be transformed into votes in the Spring of 1893. By the end of the decade, however, at the height of the Dreyfus affair, he would finally manage to have himself and supporters elected to the Chamber of Deputies.

One factor in Drumont's political campaign which must have disconcerted his audience and contributed to his defeat was his curious brand of populism. He always claimed to be a friend of the working class and a sympathizer of "non-Jewish" socialism. What separated Drumont from other Catholic candidates who claimed to favor the working people, a figure like Albert de Mun, for example, was his independence from clerical parties and his extremely violent language. After his defeat at Amiens he looked into the future and proclaimed: "All Frenchmen, sickened by the continuing scandals...will soon say: the Jew, the Jew, the Jew! At the hands of the inevitable catastrophe you will pay for everyone, you'll be blamed for all the evil of these past fifteen years...You're guilty in fact, Jews, and yet the punishment will still be more terrible than what you fairly deserve..."

Throughout the 1890s he blamed Jews for every conceivable form of social unrest. If anarchists and socialists resorted to violence, it was, reassured Drumont, the fault of the Jews for having driven them to desperation. *La Libre Parole* of this period was full of apologetic articles in this vein. In a significant editorial dated 23 November 1893 he went so far to enlist to his cause the thought of Karl Marx on the Jewish question by suggesting that "the French would thus do well to seek in the critical part of Marx's work weapons with which to rid themselves of the Judeo-Masonic regime." This line of reasoning, coupled with attacks against Pope Leo XIII, must not have been appealing to more conservative elements who might have been expected to help form some of Drumont's natural constituency.

During the first half of 1894 *La Libre Parole* regularly featured articles which highlighted the threat of espionage within France. Earlier in the decade the military attache of the American embassy, for example, was convicted of passing information to German intelligence and expelled from France.[3] German officers and an Italian general had also been apprehended for spying. Armed with such material Drumont consistently emphasized this theme in countless editorials and articles.

In view of the qualified apologetics by which he tried to exonerate or at least explain sympathetically the question of anarchism the gradually declining readership of *La Libre Parole* was not surprising. Two years after the sensational revelations of Panama Drumont found it increasingly difficult to uncover scandalous material with which to electrify the public. On 24 June 1894 Sadi-Carnot, the president of the republic, was assassinated by an anarchist. Drumont had never appreciated his presidency nor that of his successor, Casimir-Périer. Once again Drumont deplored the act of assassination but tried to explain it in terms of an act of desperation. As he extended the range of his recriminations and attacked old supporters, journals, and politicians, his newspaper, by mid-year, was faced with mounting financial problems. Drumont had irritated so many public figures with his scathing articles that he feared law suits and unexpectedly he went into voluntary exile in Brussels.

From exile Drumont continued to rail against the establishment. Ironically, Drumont was absent from Paris during those months when that combination of circumstances was forming which by autumn of that year would result in the arrest of Captain Alfred Dreyfus. In most of the histories on the subject there is no unanimity concerning the factors which led to his incarceration. Some historians have taken Drumont's absence as proof that he had nothing to do with the arrest of Dreyfus.[4] However, other students of the affair more familiar with certain circumstantial details involving the initial phase have suggested that there may have been a link between Drumont's newspaper and those individuals who first identified Dreyfus as the traitor on the General Staff.[5]

Whatever the nature and extent of Drumont's involvement might have been, one fact is indisputable. His newspaper had made a practice of nettling the government and army over the question of allowing Jews to be present at high level positions. By mid 1894 the Minister of War, Auguste Mercier, was clearly the man in the middle of this score. A series of questionable professional decisions on his part had weakened his position in the cabinet and he was routinely attacked by ultranationalist newspapers. Historian Guy Chapman observes that: "he was assailed with violent abuse by the Left and all the mischief-making press, in particular Rochefort and Drumont." [6] While other journals criticized Mercier's military judgment Drumont repeated these charges in ways that impugned his loyalty and he also accused him of being particularly indulgent towards Jews. [7] The minister of war and his subordinates could not fail to be sensitive to this line of criticism. On 15 October, the very day of the arrest of Captain Dreyfus, La Libre Parole excoriated Mercier for turning aside the conviction of a Jewish army doctor and he was accused of protecting traitors.

Suspicion seems to have fallen on Dreyfus because his handwriting resembled that of a document which had been retrieved from the office of the military attaché in the German embassy in Paris. The document, known as the bordereau, mainly dealth with information having to do with the artillery. When photographs of this evidence were circulated to determine its origin no one was at first able to identify its author. However when it was shown to officers Albert d'Aboville and Pierre-Elie Fabre, it was their opinion that the author must have been someone on the General Staff. Fabre and d'Aboville were anti-Jewish and the latter was connected with Jules Octave Biot, the military correspondent of *La Libre Parole*. After deliberation the two officers suggested that the bordereau's script bore a resemblance to that of Captain Dreyfus.

After consulting graphologists of dubious qualifications the army decided to arrest Dreyfus.[8] During those two crucial weeks between the arrest and its public disclosure the army investigators desperately tried to uncover additonal evidence. Apart from the two officers mentioned above no one, with the possible exception of Colonel Sandherr, the head of the Intelligence section, seemed to have wished to insist on the guilt of Dreyfus. The army investigators worked feverishly to bolster the case in order to forestall any negative publicity. Guy Chapman was correct for the most part in asserting: "The antisemitic shadow over the case came, not from the army, but from the press."[9] What he neglected to state was the connection of army staff with contacts to this press.

After two weeks of secret incarceration it was a matter of time until the news began to circulate and become known to the public. The information was communicated to various journals. Drumont's sheet was not the first to reveal the prisoner's name. It would seem probable that figures within the widening circles of military investigators informed sympathetic journals. Although Drumont was still in Brussels, he was in daily telephone communication with his staff and his associate Raphaël Viau asserts he knew about the details of the story.[10] In the *Libre Parole* of 29 October 1894 correspondent Adrien Papillaud printed this notice:

### A Question

Is it true that recently a rather important arrest has been made by order of the military authority? The individual arrested is supposed to be accused of espionage. If this news is true, why is the military authority keeping absolutely silent?
An answer is demanded.

A. Papillaud

Other newspapers featured similar pieces. The 1 November issue of *La Patrie* wrote of a "Jewish officer attached to the ministry of War" and *Le Soir* first revealed his name. In its 1 November edition *La Libre Parole* announced in large headlines: "High Treason. Arrest of the Jew Officer A. Dreyfus." A long article by Biot, the military correspondent, declared: "We have one consolation and that is that it is not a real Frenchman who committed such a crime!"[11]

News of the sensational arrest was briefly eclipsed by reports of the death of Tsar Alexander III. He was considered France's major ally in view of Russia's support for France's anti-German coalition.[12] A few days alter Drumont and other journalists were again providing details on the case with claims that Dreyfus had given a complete confession. In his first article on the case from exile Drumont asserted that the accused soldier was part of a "great Jewish plot which would deliver us bound hand and foot to the enemy."

At the highest levels of the military establishment on-going investigations tried to amass more evidence to build the case against Dreyfus. [13] Drumont repeatedly charged that the government was not serious in its prosecution out of fear of various figures who were allegedly compromised in the Panama affair. This charge was one of Drumont's favorite themes which he constantly repeated till the end of the century. By invoking this earlier scandal from which he derived much credit he hoped the public would extend its confidence to his journal during the present affair. Drumont also took credit for being in alrge measure responsible for unmasking treason and corruption in military circles. He was so moved by self-satisfaction that he revived the title of the series of investigative pieces, "The Jews in the Army" in order to emphasize the point of the precarious state of national security.

Throughout this initial period of the affair *La Libre Parole* continued to cast doubt on the integrity of Mercier and his handling of the case. But by the beginning of December Drumont had completely altered his editorial policy and the Minister of War was hailed as a great patriot. One possible explanation of the *bordereau*, in behalf of Mercier. According to members of Drumont's staff Esterhazy had contact with their editor and he may have convinced Drumont that Mercier and others on the military staff were seriously pressing the case against Dreyfus. [14]

The trial began on Wednesday 19 December and it was closed to the public. National security interests were cited as the main reason for secrecy. The general public was thus unable to follow all the deliberations. Even Dreyfus' lawyer was unaware of certain items of secret evidence which had been brought to the attention of the judges who consequently found the accused guilty and sentenced him to life imprisonment. Many journals expressed regrets that the condemned officer was spared capital punishment. Drumont took great satisfaction in the trial's outcome and viewed it as a vindication of all that he had preached over the past decade.

Writing in *La Libre Parole*, correspondent André de Boisandré reflected the antisemitic impression of the trial by depicting Dreyfus "as the modern incarnation of the traitor of all times." On the last day of the year Dreyfus' appeal for review was rejected by the court. Another member of Drumont's staff, Georges Nangis, summed up the recent events and pronounced: "The year has been good for antisemitism and for France." In the first edition of the journal for 1895 Drumont basked in the glow o self congratulations and predicted a concerted effort to drive all Jews out of France.

On 5 January 1895 Dreyfus was forced to participate in a memorable ceremony of public degradation. Many writers and journalists have recorded that scene and commented on the prisoner's strident expression of innocence. Convinced antisemites and many patriots overcame initial impression of Dreyfus' protests and Gaston Méry commented for Drumont's journal:"In the magnificent setting of this military parade the degradation was not for an individual fault, it was the whole race whose name was shamed." On this note Drumont's life work seemed vindicated.

Drumont could not fail to regard these events as a personal success. After Casimir-Périer resigned as president of France his successor, Félix Faure, granted amnesty for political offenders and Drumont, among others, was allowed to return to Paris. He was received as a conquering hero by thousands of his followers who arranged a triumphal parade through the streets of the capital. They recognized in Drumont the intrepid journalist whose social ideas and journal had been responsible, in their opinion, for creating a climate of public opinion which permitted the arrest and conviction of a Jewish officer. Drumont's readers had been well prepared by his previous activities. In the previous chapter it was observed that even the name Dreyfus had been mentioned in connection with various scandals allegedly involving Jews. It was not surprising, therefore, to his readership that someone bearing this name should eventually be accused of one of the many crimes which Drumont imputed to his people.

Most historians of the affair are agreed on the general role in which *La Libre Parole* played in inflaming public opinion. [15] It was part of the jingoist, untranationalist tradition of French journalism and it was made more effective for its role in the Panama affair and its violent antisemitism. What is also intriguing is the possibility of this journal's particular role in the singling out of Dreyfus in the first place. Did Drumont or his staff have a direct hand in the process of accusation? There are some indications which invite this hypothesis, but it must be stressed that there is neither any hard evidence to sustain the charge of complicity.

Over the next few years Drumont's newspaper would be involved in light skirmishes with rivals over the question of a revision of the Dreyfus trial. The ultranationalist press made on occasion mention of the affair to remind readers of the dangers, domestic and foreign, that confronted France. The family of Alfred Dreyfus also tried, albeit with scant success, to keep public interest aroused by the plight of its son. Apart from the family almost no Jews were concerned with speaking out in his behalf. Despite this lack of support and interest Drumont continued to claim that a vast international Jewish conspiracy was at work to subvert the government and the army regarding this question.

Lack of Jewish support for Dreyfus can be attributed to two factors: confidence in the court martial proceedings and fear of antagonizing anti-

semitic militants. French Jews, like the rest of the country, had no opportunity to know the facts or to doubt the army's integrity at that stage.
Rather than make the trial and its revision a Jewish cause they not un-
reasonably preferred to rely on the civil rights guaranteed by the republic.
Fear of public opinion, particularly negative reactions from Drumont
and his supporters, also prompted them not to bring up the subject
in public.

From various perspectives the Dreyfus case may be seen as a struggle
which was caused, reflected and ultimately was resolved by the press.
Newspapers were formidable weapons to control and guide public opinion. At the lowest ebb of its fortune the Dreyfus family attempted to a-
rouse public interest in its cause by having published the false report of
the escape of Alfred Dreyfus from Devils' Island. On 11 September 1896
*La Libre Parole* announced the sensational news, taken from the British
press, that the escape had occurred just as it had often predicted. [16]
When it was revealed that the report was false Drumont insisted it was at
least proof that Jews had not accepted the court verdict as final.

From the viewpoint of the Dreyfus family the fabricated story did provoke a little a little helpful sympathy. As a result of the publicity Bernard-
Lazare, a radical journalist of Jewish background and anarchist leanings,
published the first of many books on the subject. It aroused scant attention at the time but it indicated that the case was not forgotten and that its
verdict was not universally accepted. [17]

Other newspapers began to show renewed interest. On 10 November
*Le Matin* published a facsimile photograph of the *bordereau* which it
bought from one of the handwriting experts, Teysonnières, whose testimony helped convict Dreyfus. For the first time the general public had
a chance to speculate on the quality of evidence submitted at the trial.

Drumont's journal was vehement in its denunciation of such speculation. For a brief spell, however, it was unusually restrained following
publication of the *bordereau*. It is possible that Esterhazy, the document's author, prevailed upon Drumont not to draw more attention to
it. It is known that Esterhazy had contacts with Drumont and his paper.
However any corroborating evidence regarding this association may have
been eliminated from Esterhazy's correspondence from this period.
One leading historian of the affair, Marcel Thomas, gives several indications of that link which could have been pursued by a diligent investi-
gator at the time. Thomas also notes that key times bearing on this connection appear to have been removed from the collection of Esterhazy's
letters. Thus the true extent and nature of the Esterhazy-Drumont link
may never be known. [18]

By mid 1896 Esterhazy's activities had attracted the attention of some figures in the military intelligence community. Major Marie-Georges Picquart learned that Esterhazy's handwriting was identical to that of the *bordereau* which had been attributed to Dreyfus. The counter-intelligence expert examined other evidence used in the court martial which was supposed to have been destroyed. When he brought these findings to the attention of his superiors, he was strongly advised to let matters rest. Picquart refused to acquiesce and in November he was reassigned away from Paris, the center of revisionist activities.

The high command privy to these matters was concerned. It was during this time that Henry concocted the famous forgery bearing his name which was to be known as the *faux Henry*. Its exposure as a fraud would later reveal the depths of deception to which the army resorted in order to keep Dreyfus in prison. To strengthen the original verdict Henry continued to add distorted evidence to the Dreyfus file. Picquart, sensing his precarious position, informed his lawyer, Louis Leblois, who, contrary to his instructions, revealed the following year what he knew to the prominent senator, Scheurer-Kestner, a friend of the Dreyfus family.

Whatever Drumont knew of these developments he did not allude to them in the first half of 1897. Since they had not been made public it did not serve his purpose to draw attention to them. Esterhazy continued to frequent the offices of *La Libre Parole* and he tried in vain to have Drumont donate funds to him. By this time Esterhazy appeared to be a liability to the army and probably to Drumont as well.

On 29 October Gaston Méry interviewed Scheurer-Kestner and demanded he produce the proof of Dreyfus' "innocence." The senator refused to do so at that time and Méry branded him as the key figure in a "Jew-loving, Huguenot cabal" seeking to destroy the army and the nation. After this date the affair and the possibility of revision was the subject of wide commentary in the press at large.

Drumont deplored the growing national debate. In his editorial of 2 November he gave full vent to his indignation and predicted: "When the moment comes, the break will be clean. We'll throw them aside, these intruders, without a shadow of regret." A few days later he voiced a desire to see Dreyfus dead: "I do not believe that outside the Synagogue there would be many tears in France if an 'intelligent bullet' suppressed a cursed being who....has been the disgrace and scourge of his country." Drumont concluded later that "our race will have an avenger, it always had one and the history of Israel is replete with these usurpations--insolence and merciless tyrannies always followed by punishments as frightful as they are derserved." It can be observed that during the course of the affair the violent tone of Drumont's articles and journal progressively increased with growing public debate on the merits of the case. Language such as this tended to set the stage for widespread riots which soon would cause considerable damage and some loss of Jewish lives.

The controversy surrounding Scheurer-Kestner's public stand aroused considerable comment. It was then revealed that the handwriting of the *bordereau* closely resembled that of Esterhazy. What had been confined to a small circle of individuals suddenly became public knowledge. On 15 November *La Libre Parole* printed a long article attacking Matthieu Dreyfus, the prisoner's brother, which was signed "Dixi." The article was brought to Drumont by Esterhazy, however it is unclear whether he was its author. The piece asserted that someone highly placed in the Ministry of War had been a co-conspirator of Dreyfus and that the letter had copied the writing style of another officer in order to divert attention. The piece was an obvious ploy to prepare public opinion for the charges where were to be lodged against Esterhazy.[19]

The reputation of Esterhazy was greatly tarnished by the publication of his love letters to his mistress, Madame de Boulancy. The scandal was enormous. The letters were quite old and had no relevance to the case of Dreyfus, Drumont was adament in indicating, but they seemed to show the public the officer's venal personality and pro-German feelings.[20] In these amorous missives he displayed deep contempt for France and hig praise for Germany, and their effect was to strengthen the suspicion that he was quite capable of the treason which had been imputed to Dreyfus. Esterhazy was understandably upset by these sensational revelations but the army believed it had no choice except to clear his name in court.

By January 1898 the degree of public divisiveness over the Dreyfus affair was increasing at an alarming pace. Vocal demonstrations also formed to march throughout Paris and other cities. The street in front of Drumont's office was apopular rallying point for anti-Jewish and ultra-nationalist militants. Mobs of students formed in front of the National Assembly to mock and condemn Scheurer-Kestner. The anti-Dreyfus groups were roundly encouraged by the nationalist press, especially *La Libre Parole,* among others. Gaston Méry, for example, denounced the Dreyfusard politician as "a senile idiot who half-presides over the Senate and presides over the Syndicate like a cooked apple and a turd." [21] Abusive language of this sort was not uncommon in the press of this period but appearing in the midst of a growing national crisis its effect was indendiary.

It was during this period that Emile Zola became interested in the affair. The highpoint of his involvement would not be evident until the publication of his famous open letter, but in the meantime he was the object of some of Drumont's most vituperative statements. The editor of *La Libre Parole* rightly sensed that the call for revision was gathering support and he feared that Zola's name and polemical skills would hasten the process.

Anyone who expressed the slightest doubt about the court martial of

144

Dreyfus was accused by Drumont in endless articles of being in the pay of Jews. In his first editorial of 1898 he took delight in increasing public resistance to the "cynicism, effrontery, the *houptza* (sic) of that Jewish gang dishonoring the army and disturbing the country..." Drumont continued to repeat the charge that all opponents were in the pay of Jews and Germans.

Nine days after this piece the court martial of Esterhazy began. Most observers were confident that the verdict would establish his innocense, and the judges dismissed any connection between him and the Dreyfus case. In the streets Esterhazy was hailed as "the martyr the Jews" and groups of rioting students roamed through Montmartre and the Latin Quarter attacking those they perceived to be enemies of the ultranationalist cause.

*La Libre Parole* acclaimed the acquittal of Esterhazy as a victory for antisemitism. Art students burned an effigy of Matthieu Dreyfus in the Place Blanche while a large crowd shouted "Burn Dreyfus! The dirty Jews! The dirty Jews!" After his trial Esterhazy visited the offices of *La Libre Parole* to thank personally Drumont for his support and steadfastness. In ultranationalist and antisemitic circles there was a feeling of certainty that the call for revision had definitely been thwarted.

Except perhaps for Drumont these forces on the Right had not appreciated the determination of Emile Zola. On 12 January 1898 he launched a polemical bomb in the shape of an open letter to the government powers responsible for handling the Dreyfus and Esterhazy cases. The article appearing in Clemenceau's journal, *L'Aurore,* had the effect of again stirring up the political passions of the entire nation. Drumont had always hated Zola and in response to his explosive open letter he published one of his own addressed to President Faure on 14 January in which he accused the novelist of being an "agent of a foreign power." The fact that Zola's letter had been printed in Clemenceau's newspaper, Drumont asserted, was proof of a conspiracy emanating from the same circles which had been involved in the Panama scandal and had been exposed by *La Libre Parole* a few years earlier.

The climate of violence increased throughout France and much of it was fanned by the inflammatory rhetoric of Drumont's journal. In several cities gangs of demonstrators, thugs, and students attacked and looted shops owned by Jews.[22] In Algiers riots led by Drumont's friend and ally, Max Régis, repeatedly stormed the Jewish quarter for four days while the police stood by passively. In antisemitic circles militants were certain that these examples of public disorder would increase and herald the beginning of the revolution they had preached over the previous decade.

On 19 January Drumont accused the government of not revealing all its evidence relating to the conviction of Dreyfus. Stung by such criticism, the governement obliged its opponents and resolved to try Zola for challenging its authority. The trial of the accused novelist and activist was to begin on 7 February and it attracted even more attention at home and abroad. Larger crowds than those which had attended Esterhazy's trial took to the streets and created an atmosphere of tension and political uncertainly. The temper of the mobs was aroused by the press, particularly *La Libre Parole* which treated Zola as "foreigner's son, a Venetian pornographer," as a lackey of the Jews and enemy of Christianity, who "in his dung-mouthed, excrement-eating, madness goes so far as to give a filthy character the name that hundreds of millions of human beings pronounce only with veneration and tenderness." It was Drumont's tactic to besmirch his name to such an extent that Zola would be doomed to punishment at the hands of the state court.

On 23 February Zola and Perrenx, the editor of *l'Aurore,* were found guilty. After appealing the verdict he was again found guilty and he fled France to choose exile in Great Britain. In his absence Clemenceau's journal continued to harrass Drumont and the agrieved editor demanded satisfaction by means of a remedy that had become traditional in such disputes. They fought a duel on 26 February and both figures emerged unscathed.

Injury stemmed from other activities of Drumont. In the midst of national controversy his journal preached the most virulent forms of violence against Jews. As a result in France and Algeria ultranationalist crowds set upon Jews, their establishments, and synagogues in a orgy of destruction. Drumont was so pleased by these results and by his support in Algeria that he decided once again to try his hand in politics. On this occasion he resolved to run for office in that colony where the European populace was even more sympathetic to his views than fellow countrymen at home. He and his followers were convinced that if the antisemitic revolution had to start somewhere it seemed most likely that it would be in Algeria from which it would spread to the metropolitan area. Although the object of their wrath was different it is relevant to observe that this was the same logic which extreme rightist elements would employ gain against the republic in 1962. In both cases the extremists thought they could count on the fear of status deprivation among the European settlers to further their aims in the metropolitan area. In both cases, however, the tradition of democracy was strong enough to prevail but not before submitting to powerful waves of assault from the dedicated forces on the far Right.

Drumont was partially correct in his assessment of the Algerian situation. In February 1898 he and many other Frenchmen were convinced that the affair had once more been definitely laid to rest. He also believed that this apparent victory was the right moment to relaunch his political career. With support from Max Régis in Algiers he was easily persuaded to seek a seat in parliament from a constituency in North Africa. [23] In

Algeria the precarious status of the settlers was a relevant factor in stimulating anti-Jewish sentiment. In this territory large concentrations of Europeans lived among a much larger Moslem population. It was feared that if the latter ever got the upper hand the French citizens would be dispelled. To distract attention from their ruling class status the colonists tried, for the most part with scant success, to direct Arab animosity toward the relatively large Jewish Algerian community.

In early April Drumont arrived in Algiers and was enthusiastically greeted by Régis and his supporters. There he waged a well-organized campaign and on 8 May he won by receiving five times as many votes as his rival. After victory he was accompanied to parliament by other deputies elected on the antisemitic ticket where they formed a block that pressed for enactment of anti-Jewish legislation. Drumont was overwhelmed by the election and on 27 June he proclaimed with confidence that "antisemitism will be the revolution of tomorrow."

The prophecies were premature. What Drumont espoused with regard to the Jews had to wait more than four decades before becoming a reality in France. The importance of his activities, however, cannot be underestimated for it is the purpose of this study to show in its last part how Drumont initiated the tradition that would bear its evil fruit during the occupation years of the Second World War.

For all his satisfaction in being elected it soon became evident that Drumont was not well suited to representing antisemitism in a parliamentary democracy. Its methods were not his and he was temperamentally unable to abide by the rules of conventional politics. Election returns for the rest of the country indicated that militant antisemitic candidates did rather well at the polls but their numbers remained too limited to change the course of the nation's direction on the matter of the Jewish question. In terms of public performance Drumont was a poor speaker, and in his way as a private man he rapidly grew impatient with the system. His term in the Chamber was not noteworthy and Drumont was not unhappy in his decision to forgo reelection in the future.

By the middle of 1898 Drumont and the rest of france were convinced that the Dreyfus case was forever closed. However the appointment of Cavaignac, the new Minister of War, was to have the unintended effect of plunging the nation once again into crisis. In his desire to clear the decks for army reform Cavaignac ordered the loose ends of the Dreyfus case to be re-examined. He was personally certain of Dreyfus' guilt. During the process of reevaluating the pieces of evidence it was discovered that one of the more important items, to be known as the *faux Henry*, was indeed a forgery.[24]

Cavaignac was an honorable soldier and he had not been privy to all the secret manoeuvres in the case. Because of this sensational discovery

France found itself again in turmoil. After Major Henry was asked to explain the forgery he was arrested and later found with his throat slit in his prison cell. According to Drumont Jewish agents had gained access to the prison and silenced this officer who was hailed as a hero by the forces opposed to revision of the Dreyfus Case.

Following Henry's apparent suicide Esterhazy fled the country. Drumont wrote by way of justification that he was impelled to exile not out of guilt but out of fear of suffering the same fate as Henry. The editor of *La Libre Parole* denied that Esterhazy had been his friend and that there was nothing suspicious about his connection with the journal. [25] He argued instead that Henry and Esterhazy were both victims of an insidious Jewish cabal. On 9 September he violently denounced what was termed "the Syndicate" by the anti-Dreyfusard forces: "The Jew has not changed: he is still the same cursed creature that we have had to slaughter and hang...because he has always betrayed and robbed the people who gave him hospitality, because he has always organized Dreyfus' affairs." Such rhetoric was not untypical of just Drumont's journal: many others voiced similar violent sentiments and contributed to the climate of hatred which increased steadily as the controversy unfolded and expanded. What set *La Libre Parole* apart from the other anti-Dreyfusard journals was the relentless, obsessive character of its ideological position. It was a newspaper which never changed its attitude toward Jews up to the moment of its demise in 1939.

Foreign policy matters also contributed to the climate of apprehension in France. While the affair flared up again there arose an incident in Africa which pitted French and British prestige against one another. An attempt by a Captain Marchand to invade the Sudan was checked at Fashoda by the British. The failure of French expedition was viewed by France as a national humiliation and it increased the rancor of xenophobia at home. [26] This too was imputed by Drumont to the Jews.

In order to thwart the anticipated drive for revision Drumont attempted to turn public sympathy by sponsoring a subscription list for Henry's widow. Throughout the month of September 130,000 francs were donated and accompanied by violent comments which exemplified the depths of political and racist passions aroused by the revisionist campaign. To prove their patriotism even some Jews volunteered to donate to the subscription list sponsored by antisemites. [27]

In early 1899 opposing forces had been jolted by news of the sensational death of President Faure. On 10 February he had suffered a stroke in the arms of his mistress at the Elysée Palace. Throughout the rest of the year Drumont repeated the charge that the woman involved had been sent by Jews to murder the president who had been opposed to the revisionists. His successor, Emile Loubet, was frequently vilified for not harboring such sentiments.

Because of these suspicions Loubet became the target of the radical Right which attempted in the person of Paul Déroulède to stage a coup d'état. Drumont, too, had little regard for the new regime and his journal rarely missed a chance to denounce what he called "la république juive." In spite of his expressions of sympathy and understanding he rightly thought Déroulède was incapable of overthrowing the government.[28]

Drumont shared the same lack of confidence in a former member of his antisemitic association, Jules Guérin who also tried and failed to topple the government. Guérin was one of the bullyboys of the Marquis de Morès and he believed in violent measures as a form of revolutionary activity. He tried to lure writers away from Drumont's staff to work for his own journal and organization which had its headquarters in the Rue de Chabrol. By the end of the summer Guérin and his followers had converted their offices into an armed camp and for forty days they defied the government after which they were forced to surrender. He was no more successful than Déroulède but both leaders of the radical Right demonstrated how far they were prepared to go to challenge the authority of the state on the question of a new trial for Dreyfus.[29]

When Drumont resumed his seat in the Chamber of Deputies he used it to denounce the renewed drive for revision. In early June the government decided to allow Dreyfus to return to stand trial again. Drumont and his colleagues expected the second trial to reaffirm the initial conviction, however his hope was now expressed with explicit violence in his editorial of 3 July. "If circumstances dictated that I were invested with authority permitting me to save my country, I'd drag the big Jews and their accomplices to a court martial which would have them shot...."

When the second Dreyfus trial started on 7 August 1899 Drumont's vitriolic prose increased in volume and maintained a steady level of abuse for the duration of the extraordinary court proceedings. In the end when the condemnation of Dreyfus was reconfirmed on 9 September Drumont and other journalists saw it as the triumph of the army and nation and another defeat for the Jews. But their mood of victory dissipated following the decision of President Loubet on 19 September to grant a pardon to Dreyfus. It was obvious to all concerned that no military court, in spite of evidence to the contrary, would have the courage to reverse its previous judgment, and the fact that technically, Dreyfus was not declared innocent but pardoned instead was a theme Drumont and his successors never ceased to repeat for the remaining long life of the journal.

The most significant result of the affair was the increased ideological polarization of French politics. In electoral terms the country did not seem to change substantially. But the interminable wrangling and divisiveness left their marks on the political consciousness. The liberals and leftists emerged with a heightened sense of mission and purpose. The rightists and ultranationalists were determined not to forget what they perceived to be the abdication of the government to these forces. Because of the unusually raucous and bitter polimics andtisemitism became more wide-spread during these years of controversy, and this development in public sensibility can be considered to be the major result of Drumont's involve-ment in the Dreyfus affair. Whether or not he or his journal had directly participated in the initial identification of Dreyfus as the traitor on the General Staff, the evidence pointing to this hypothesis must, according to the research of Boussel, Guillemin, and Thomas, remain circumstan-cial and conjectural. What does not remain in doubt is the demonstra-ted force of antisemitic propaganda and Drumont's abillty to influence public opinion during the Panama and Dreyfus affairs.

Most contemporary observers of France at the turn of the century be-lieved that antisemitism in that land had been dealt a defeat from which it could not recover. Its chief partisans, like Drumont, though seemingly routed, vowed to continue their struggle well into the twentieth century.

## Notes

1 The literature on the case is extensive. See Leon Lispchutz, *Biblio-graphie thématique et analytique de l'affaire Dreyfus,* (Paris: Fas-quelle, 1970) and my "A Bibliographical Overview of the Dreyfus Affair," *Jewish Social Studies,* vol. XL, no. 1, (Winter 1978), 25-40.

2 See David Lewis, *Prisoners of Honor,* p.21 and Georges Clemenceau, *Contre la justice* (Paris: Stock, 1900), pp.14-19.

3 On contemporary espionage, see Guy Chapman, *The Dreyfus Case,* (New York: Reynal, 1955), pp. 37-44.

4 See William C. McCully, *Drumont and Dreyfus,* unpublished doctoral thesis,

5 On antisemitic influence in initially identifying Dreyfus as guilty, see Henri Guillemin, *L'enigme Esterhazy,* (Paris: Gallimard, 1962), pp. 11-27; for the opposing viewpoint, see Douglas Johnson, *France and the Dreyfus Affair,* (New York: Walker, 1966), p. 37.

6 See Chapman, p.65.

7 See *La Libre Parole,* 17 August 1894.

8 On the role of graphologists, see Chapman, p.75, Johnson, p.24, and Lewis, pp. 20, 21.

9 Chapman, p.66.

10 Viau, *Vingt ans d'antisémitisme,* p.90. On other aspects of spy-mania, see Alan Mitchell. "La Mentalité xénophobe: contre-espion-

nage et racines de l'affaire Dreyfus, *"Revue d'histoire moderne et contemporaire* 29 (July 1982): 489-99.

11   For the general journalistic reaction to the case, see Patrice Boussel, *L'Affaire Dreyfus et la presse* (Paris, Colin, 1960).

12   Drumont consistently followed a pro-Russian policy and his journal always published anti-Jewish articles taken from the Russian press.

13   For recent light on this investigation, see André Ehrhardt, *A travers l'affaire Dreyfus: Henry et Valcarlos,* (Paris: Klincksieck, 1977).

14   On the Drumont-Esterhazy connection, see Marcel Thomas, *L'Affaire sans Dreyfus* (Paris: Arthème Fayard, 1971), pp.174-178, Drault, *Drumont,* p.226-228.

15   See *Boussel,* pp.10-27.

16   For a detailed examination of the so-called escape incident, see Chapman, pp.126-131.

17   On the role of Bernard-Lazare, see Nelly Wilson, *Bernard-Lazare: Antisemitism and the Problem of Jewish Identity in Late Nineteenth Century France* (Cambridge: Cambridge University Press, 1978).

18   Thomas, pp. 168-176.

19   See Viau, p.164.

20   In the rest of this unpublished correspondence Drumont repeatedly underscores the urgency of the Esterhazy trial for the nation and the antisemitic cause. See dossier 24901, nos. 83, 84, 85. Département des manuscrits, Bibliothèque Nationale, Paris.

21   *La Libre Parole,* 8 Dec. 1897.

22   See Steven Wilson, "The Antisemitic Riots of 1898 in France," *Historical Journal,* vol. XVI, (1973), 789-806, and *Ideology and Experience,* pp. 106-124.

23   On the spectacular career of Max Régis, see Viau, p.179, Charles-Roberft Ageron, *Les Algériens musulmans et la France* (Paris: Presses Universitaires de France, 1968), vol. I, pp, 603, 604, 607, and Louis Bernard, *Conséquences de l'antisémitisme: troubles d'Algérie et de Nice* (Paris: 1899). By most press accounts Drumont's stay in Algeria was well received. See in particular Drumont's own scrapbook of photographs in Harvard's Houghton Library, "Extraordinaire recueil composé à l'intention d'Edouard Drumont pour

lui être offert par ses électeurs et admirateurs d'Algérie.'' Lee Friedman Fund. *PFC9 D8262 Z898d 16.

24  For a detailed examination of this forgery, see Chapman, pp.133-135, and Ehrhardt, pp. 15-46.

25  See Johnson, pp.203-206.

26  On the repercussions of the Fashoda incident, see Jacques Chaste-net, *Histoire de la troisième république, la république triomphante* (Paris: Hachette, 1955), vol. III, pp.153-158, 363.

27  On the widow Henry subscription list, see Pierre Quillard, *Le Monument Henry* (Paris: Stock, 1899), and Steven Wilson, *Ideology and Experience,* pp. 125-166.

28  See Zeev Sternhell, *La Droite révolutionnaire, 1885-1914, les origines françaises du fascisme* (Paris: Seuil, 1978), p.104.

29  For Guérin's account of the Fort Chabrol incident, see his *Les Trafiquants de l'antisémitisme* (Paris: Juven, 1905).

The Phoney Peace

> Only lice were exterminated
> at Auschwitz.
> --Darquier de Pellepoix

In the wake of the Dreyfus affair the fortunes of Drumont and his journal began to decline. The antisemitic movement suffered a setback because of its vehement opposition to the Dreyfusard revisionist campaign. After Dreyfus was officially vindicated the appeal of Drumont's polemics diminished in the eyes of the general public. The ideological thrust of reactionary political movements passed to newer groups such as Action Française and after the turn of the century France was more concerned with the growing threat from Germany.

The appeal of antisemitism, however, remained in some quarters. The remarkable fact of Drumont's legacy in the twentieth century is is durability long after his death. The purpose of this chapter, therefore, is to examine the activities of Drumont until the First World War, the fortunes of his journal and successors between the wars and to establish the link between them and the rise of fascism in France and anti-Jewish collaborationism during the German occupation.

In *La Revue Indépendente* of January 1900 Maurice Le Blond gave this description of Drumont's newspaper: "among the most dangerous and most baneful journals it would be fair to place in the front rank *La Libre Parole.*" Le Blond went on to chart the political success which Drumont had enjoyed among the French settlers in Algeria and his less successful efforts to arouse anti-Jewish sentiments among the Moslem population. Regarding the latter Drumont had scant effect but Walter Laqueur reports he was more appreciated in other parts of the Arab world. "Anti-Jewish feeling was spread by the churches in Palestine. Eliyahu Sapir wrote in 1899 that the main blame was the Catholic church and in particular the Jesuits, but he also mentioned the impact of the French antisemitic publicist Drumont." [1]

Drumont's influence was also discernible in the composition of *The Protocols of the Elders of Zion.* This forged document had been composed in Paris and written originally in French by someone during the Dreyfus affair and it was destined to become the major tract in the international repertory of antisemitic propaganda. According to its chief historian, Norman Cohn, it drew "particularly on the writings of Des Mousseaux, Chabauty, Meurin and Drumont." [2] The idea of an international Jewish conspiracy was a major theme running through Drumont's writings and his incessant propaganda on this score helped pave the way for its massive popularity following the First World War.

The influence of the antisemitic political block in France continued to decline during these years. Drumont grew progressively impatient with the tradition of parliamentary democracy. On 14 June 1901 he verbally denounced two colleagues on the floor and refusing to restrain himself, he was expelled and forbidden to return to his seat for one month. Many segments of the public, too, were convinced that the movement he led was on the wane.[3] Despite his efforts to found a new group, Le Comité National Antijuif, his fortunes sank further and on 27 April 1902 Drumont lost his last election in Algeria and was obliged to relinquish his seat in the Chamber which had failed to serve him as a springboard for his movement.

The emergence of rival movements also challenged the authority hitherto monopolized by Drumont. His former associate, Jules Guérin, had completely broken with *La Libre Parole* and founded his own journal to which were attracted others like Raphaël Viau. In his memoirs Viau records that Drumont's journal attracted a diminishing number of supporters following his defeat.[4] To bolster flagging interest Drumont continued to voice with diminishing returns the basic themes which had brought him notoriety and fame in the past. In response to the great pogrom at Kishinev in 1903, for example, he gloated and predicted on 26 June more of the same threatening: "the day when the Jews and Protestants fall from power, they won't find it surprising that they are reminded then of today's persecutions in order to justify future reprisals."

The rise of Maurra's Action Française also drained away support. Drumont had little confidence in the ability of monarchism to draw popular strength, and although he and Maurras shared many common enemies, they disagreed on the type of political program to save France. An example of the fresh appeal which Maurras represented was illustrated by Léon Daudet, who had started with Drumont, and gradually come to appreciate the vigor of the monarchist cause and ultimately became a leadingwriter for *Action Française*.[5] In order to challenge the appeal of Maurras Drumont tried to reemphazise the particular populist tendencies proclaimed by his followers by affiliating himself with *Le Mouvement Jaune*, founded by Pierre Biétry in response to the demands of workers who were dissatisfied with mainline socialist unions. Biétry, who also followed an antisemitic line, was wary of Drumont's attempts to infiltrate his particular union and his efforts came to naught.[6]

The fact that Drumont consistently tried to link socialism and antisemitismism proof, in the judgment of Zeev Sternhell, of the French origins of fascist idology. Although some factions of the socialist movement denounced the link between racism and populism, others took pride in the compatibility of Drumont's idology with that of the proletarian struggle. In the prestigious journal, *Le Mouvement Socialiste*, of July 1906, Robert Louzon declared: "Like Drumont, we think for our part that clericalism exists, that semitism exists. Semitism and clericalism constitute the two poles of the great bourgeois solidarity, and it is this struggle for influence which more and more is tending to become the dominant note of the internal history of the bourgeoisie." [7]

Like the socialists Drumont also shared a sense of anti-clericalism. His variety was much more limited in scope and was largely confined to criticizing the church hierarchy for its accomadation to the ruling elite which he claimed was dominated by Jews. Whatever quarrels Drumont may have had with the French bishops they disappeared in 1905 during the bitter struggle which resulted in the separation of church and state. The aid that Drumont brought to the church party was deeply appreciated to the extent that his past utterances against them could be forgiven. The triumph of the anticlerical forces confirmed in Drumont's mind the victory of the Dreyfuards and the enemies of Christianity whom he identified as the Jews. Catholicism had been forcibly and legally displaced from its status of France's official church and the resulting bitterness among the faithful was a theme to which Drumont never tired to return. [8]

Many of Drumont's associates began to die off, and in his memoirs Viau recalled that these years constituted "the swan song of the antisemitic movement" as far as Drumont was concerned. In 1908 the distinguished writer and close friend, Francois Coppée, died and in August so did Boisandré, followed shortly by the death of Guérin. The next year witnessed the passing of Papillaud and Méry. Drumont sensed that his own time was running short and this intimation of impending mortality is reflected in an unpublished letter date 11 August 1909 from Félix Nadar who implored: "Judge, my good Drumont, the sad state to which your old friend has been reduced." Drumont shared this sense of anxiety in the face of death.

Drumont's own health was poor and he made plans to arrange his remaining years. To this end he set into motion plans to have himself elected to the French Academy. He justified his candidacy and qualifications in his memoirs: "I have no vanity; I have a rather cerebral pride which is sufficient unto itself. I am convinced that my work, the current of which I have in reality created, will not pass unnoticed in the movement of ideas of the twentieth century." [9] Drumont's bid for membership was defeated by a novelist he despised, Marcel Prévost, author of such books as *Scorpion* and *Les Demi-Vierges*.

The year 1910 was an important date for Drumont. His home and library were one of the many victims of the great flood which ravaged Paris. Characteristically, he blamed the inundation on Jewish lumber merchants whom he charged had upset the ecological balance by harvesting excessive amounts of timber up the Seine during the flood season.

His talents and voice did not go unappreciated in all circles during his final years. Following a favorable review of Charles Péguy's *Le Mys-*

*tère de la Charité de Jeanne d'Arc,* the disappointed Dreyfusard and socialist, without embracing antisemitism, however, found time to praise those elements in Drumont's social philosophy which he shared as well such as love for traditional France, and independent practice of Catholocism, and interest in the social question. [10] Drumont was flattered by Péguy's praise.

Because of his concern for the social question and the working class. Drumont continued to attract the attention of socially-minded Catholics. In 1910 he sold *La Libre Parole* to a group of liberal Catholics led by Joseph Denais. He had previously spurned requests to sell to Action Française because he judged its monarchism to be archaic and unappealing to the working class. Drumont was allowed to write for the journal under the new management but old colleagues such as Drault were upset by the increasingly clerical tone of the newspaper which had been absent at the height of its influence and popularity. [11]

The reconstituted staff brought new talent to the journal, one of whom was to become Drumont's wife. She was Madame Fugairon, Denais' editorial secretary, and it was decided after three years that in view of the journal's increased Catholic viewpoint it would be proper for them to marry accoring to church rites. In the *Réveil de Royan* of 11 December 1913 it was noted that "the scandal of M. Edouard Drumont's civil marriage...has been regularized in a Catholic manner."

Drumont needed a wife to look after him in those years of declining health. The outbreak of war in 1914 caused him to denounce those forces he consistently blamed for manipulating the fate of Europe. On 1 August in *La Libre Parole* he accused "cosmopolitan Jewry" for "spreading hatred with its gold...the French should throw them overboard" in order to drive "the parasitic, exploiting sons of Israel" to Berlin. The threat of Paris by the German army caused Drumont to abandon the capital and take up residence in the country where he composed his memoirs. [12] In the interest of national unity during wartime writers like Drumont were prevailed upon by the French government not to exacerbate racial hostility on the home front. Due to this limitation he had very little to say during these years. His health also deteriorated rapidly to such an extent that he was obliged to return to Paris for treatment at a special clinic. There on 3 February 1917 he collapsed during dinner with his doctor and died almost immediately. He was seventy-three years old.

His funeral took place at the church of Saint-Ferdinand des Ternes and was attended by approximately one hundred mourners. He did not die unforgotten. From this death till the rest of his own life, Arthur Meyer sent his widow a small sum of money. Meyer, the Jew turned Catholic and antisemite who had inadvertently helped to launch Drumont's career three decades before, remained faithful to the end to the latter's world view. [13]

In his editorial eulogy Denais vowed to continue the master's mission: "We shall have to constructive work in the fertile fields of that social Catholicism which has assured the success and crowned the victory of the antisemites of Vienna and of lower Austria." Jean Drault, overcome with grief, added in his article of tribute that Drumont "has created work which will live." Press reaction to the demise of Drumont ranged from the polite to the praiseworthy. *Le Figaro* observed that thanks to him In *Action Française* Daudet reminisced: "Drumont taught us to understand our time." And despite their differences Charles Maurras added: "we all began to work in his light." His colleague Albert Monniot hailed him as a "demolisher" and "exterminator" of social prasites and predicted his name would be loudly cheered in the future. [14]

In *L'Oeuvre Française* of 15 February 1917 Drault chided "the stupid socialists" who accused Drumont of sowing hatred against Jews by reminding" that the sole invention of antisemitism is the Jew himself, as Bernard-Lazare loudly declared." In *Le Gaulois* of 5 February Georges Drouilly cautiously observed that "now is not the time to argue whether Drumont was right or wrong in making himself the champion and spokesman of an undeniably passionate cause which no thinker would dare say was entirely false."

Drumont was dead but his legacy would continue. It has been observed that this particular synthesis of socialism, antisemitism, and Catholicism contributed to the foundation of fascist ideology in France. It is the task of the rest of this chapter to show how that matrix of ideas became reality during the interwar years and the period of German occupation.

The most remarkable observation concerning the declining fortune of *La Libre Parole* was the durability of antisemitism in France. Two principal explanations are possible for this phenomenon. Much of the antisemitic movement, it must be remembered, had been eclipsed by the Dreyfusard victory and the national preoccupation with Germany. It should also be noted that the antisemitic cause was taken up by other formations on the extreme Right such as Action Française. Thus for three decades after the official end of the Dreyfus affair antisemitic forces incubated in France only to flourish again in time of crises after the great depression and the rise of fascism. The writers associated with *La Libre Parole,* despite its diminished status, were active in extreme political circles for one half century after Drumont's death.

For the duration of the First World War press criticism of Jews was reduced to the minimum. On occasion, however, *La Libre Parole* had to be suspended as press historian Claude Bellanger put it, "for having stirred religious controversies" during wartime. [15] On the question of Zionism in *La Libre Parole* had changed its editorial position. It should be remembered that Drumont occasionally voiced qualified support for Theodor Herzl. Like the leader of Zionism he had urged Jews to leave

Europe. However by 1917 the journal denounced Zionism and espoused the nascent Arab nationalism in Palestine once it had passed into the British sphere of influence. These articles were often accompanied by violent denunciations of Jews in Poland and Russia. In short the new editorial policy suggests that *La Libre Parole* did not wish Jews to have any rights anywhere. [16]

With the end of the war and the consolidation Bolshevik power in Russia *La Libre Parole* featured numerous articles denouncing and exagerrating the role of Jews in revolutionary activities. On 29 November 1918 Albert Monniot with reference to Jews demanded that the French government "liberate our territory of all this vermin." He described local socialists and Jews as "the vermin of the world at its task of putrefaction." In many lands apprehension toward Jews was aroused by their participation in revolutionary causes. On this point historian S. Eittinger comments: "In short, never before in European history had so many Jews played such an active part in political life and filled such influential roles during the first few years after the Russian revolution." [17] This observation rapidly became one of the more potent weapons of antisemitic propaganda in the postwar years. In response to this perceived provocation *La Libre Parole* had the distinction of publishing in 1920 the first complete French translation of *The Protocols of the Elders of Zion*.

By 1923 *La Libre Parole* was exhausted. Some of its liabilities were assumed by associates of Action Française. This development is notewrothy because when the journal reappeared in 1928 it was to be staffed by dissident members of Maurras' group. In these last issues praise of fascism became quite noticeable. Not only Mussolini but also Hitler came in for early and lavish adulation. The journal devoted extensive coverage to the Hitler-Ludendorff trial and 26 February 1924 it published a large photograph of Hitler on its front page. Two days later readers viewed Hitler's own words recorded in his trial testimony on the origins of his antisemitic world view. These articles are significant in that it was suggested that the long-standing feud between France and Germany could be evaluated in favor of a common front against "Judeo-Bolshevism," The exploitation of this brand of cooperation would prove to be highly significant in paving the way for collaborationism less than one decade later.

Shortly after the appearance of these pro-fascist articles *La Libre Parole* ceased to exist as a daily newspaper. It interrupted publication on 22 May and reappeared for the last time as such on 7 June 1924. Its last edition denounced the French court system for permitting the revision of the Dreyfus case. Members of the old staff were saddened by its demise and Drault lamented: "*La Libre Parole* is no longer here to beat the drum and attract people." [18]

The disappearance of Drumont's journal was relatively brief. After ceasing publication in 1924 it reappeared four years later when domestic political conditions began to change and created a demand for its revival. Its rebirth was stimulated by the crisis that beset Maurras' Action Française after its condemnation by the Vatican in 1926. Papal denunciation forced some of its militant younger adherents to move into other channels of rightwing activities.

One of the young rightists who helped restore the journal was Jacques Ploncard d'Assac, born in 1910 and destined to become one of France's more articulate spokesmen of the extreme Right. In April 1928 he decided to reedit *La Libre Parole*. He had already been the director of a review, *La Lutte Anti-Juive et Anti-Maçonnique*, where he had gained experience. On 1 July Drumont's old journal reappeared bearing the familiar masthead. Ploncard did not have sufficient resources to publish a daily sheet and it was destined to remain more of a monthly propaganda review than a newspaper.

The reborn journal was plagued by internecine struggles.[19] It remained faithful to its founder's mission and in the 15 October issue it pledged to support his widow: "I extend my hand to Monsigneur Dubois, the archbishop of Paris...because Catholics cannot abandon the widow of he who wore out his brain in defending them." The journal also drew upon inspiration from abroad. Its new director wrote on 1 January 1929: "We'll soon be able to take that beautiful step forward, and we'll act so we can extend courtesies to *Der Stürmer*, the Bavarian antisemitic organ which weekly sends us news of its programs and successes. What the Bavarians have done, the French will carry it even farther."

The nazi link was to be forged more tightly by another editor, Henry Coston. He remained its principal administrator until it was banned on the eve of the Second World War. Like Ploncard, Coston had been born in 1910 and had been a militant in Action Française. At an early age he discovered and cherished Drumont's writings and became in his own right one of France's more intrepid and durable antisemites. Coston provides the concrete link between fascist ideology and fascist reality.

After Ploncard relinquished control of *La Libre Parole*, Coston, along with René Plisson became it directors. The first issue of the new series, appearing on 1 October 1930, carried an excerpt from Drumont's works and critical articles on his career. It also made a special appeal to rescue his memory from "the overwhelming silence" imposed on public opinion by his enemies.

This plea was answered in 1931 by the great Catholic novelist, Georges Bernanos, who published *La Grande peur des bien-pensants*, a lengthy biography on Drumont and meditation on his social and religious thought. Bernanos had demonstrated with Maurras' street fighters, *les camelots du roi*, and although he came to adopt reservations about Hitler's brand of antisemitism, he shared Drumont's hatred of Jews. The general public might have been surprised by the publication of this work, but Coston was aware of its inception as early as 1 June 1929 when in reference to Bernanos he wrote: "His father used to get angry when he read newspapers. He also read the books of Drumont which early fell under the gaze of the young man." [20] Whatever Bernanos ultimately though of the nazis his comments on Drumont and Jews were eagerly publicized by Coston and Ploncard who shared no reservations about the nature of national socialism.

By the early 1930s fascistic and rightist groups in France began to grow in strength and numbers. The repercussions of the great depression in the United States were deeply felt in Europe and helped precipitate the crisis which ultimately brought Hitler to power. Up to this time Mussolini alone had seemed enough for an example for rightist elements but the arrival of Hitler signaled a decisive turning point and spurred greater hopes in these same circles. Few groups were more eager to voice support and emulate nazism than those associated with *La Libre Parole*.

It is impossible to review here the rise of fascism in France between the wars. [21] Fascism made the claim to be radically different by virtue of its professed concern for the social question and its mass appeal. On this score Drumont as a self-proclaimed national socialist was regarded by his admirers as an ideological precursor. On occasion Drumont had generally charged that Jews were behind most of Europe's problems. For the most part he treated them as agents of Germany working against France.

After Hitler's coming to power the charge of Jewish complicity with Germany made no sense. At *La Libre Parole* under the leadership of Henry Coston the accusation was modified to state that Jews were agents of the Soviet Union in league against France and Germany. Here is an example of the pro-German viewpoint which frequently appeared in the journal founded by Drumont: "The Versailles treaty for the German nationalist is the work of the detested Frenchmen. France is, moreover, for the national socialist, a corrupt country infiltrated by niggers and Jews...Are the Hitlerites entirely wrong?" [22]
Franco-German cooperation, Coston argued, was the path to follow to regain national greatness and protection of the Aryan race.

Coston was sufficiently inspired by nazism to found his own fascist group. By the end of 1933 his image appeared in propaganda brochure photographs dressed in a black shirt and crossbelt as the self-appointed leader of the *Franciste* movement, the mission of which was to come to the defense of "Aryan-Christian civilization." This small group is not to be confused by another which bore the same name and had been founded by Marcel Bucard, a former seminarian who had taken to politics. The two groups were bitter rivals and in the February 1934 number of *La Libre*

*Parole* Coston cautioned: "Don't be confused! There are two *Francismes!*" Both these political formations were inspired by and received some funds from Germany and Italy.

Competing political factions on the Right were able to defer rivalry for a brief period in the face of the Stavisky scandals. During that winter the Third Republic was shaken by the worst public disorders since the Dreyfus affair. Toward the end of 1933 it had been revealed that a high society gangster named Alexandre Stavisky had bribed important government officials. Stavisky had been born in Russia, and although he had been converted to Catholicism at an early age by his father the fact that his background had been Jewish was stressed by the rightist press. After his sudden death under controversial circumstances he was buried in Père Lachaise cemetery at a short distance from the gravesite of Edouard Drumont.

What aggravated the scandal was the notorious demonstration of 6 February 1934 in Paris. On that date several thousand rightist militants marched on the National Assembly and clashed with police in the Place de la Concorde. The confrontation left twenty dead and almost one thousand wounded. [23] The bloody riots signaled a turning point for the Right and its propaganda network. In reporting this event few journals were more vitriolic than *La Libre Parole*. It rushed into print a special edition featuring a cartoon that depisted a grotesque Jew shouting to the police: "Shoot them, those dirty Frenchmen!" In an attempt to restore public order the government seized the 30,000 special copies of Coston's newspaper.

One of the riot victims deserves special mention in passing. A luckless adventurer named Louis Darquier, who added the pretentious name of de Pellepoix to his own, had found himself swept along with the mob surging down the Rue de Rivoli toward the battle site from which he emerged with sustained injuries. After a rapid recovery he appointed himself "President of the Association of the Wounded of the Sixth of February." With this title he entered politics. At the same time he knew little about the political uses of antisemitism, but Henry Coston was to teach him that it could be employed for an electoral campaign. He then won a seat on the Paris Municipal Council and became one of France's more ferocious and vociferous Jew baiters. For his conspicuous services to the antisemitic cause Darquier was later selected to be commissioner for Jewish Affairs during the occupation years in which capacity he helped despoil and allowed tens of thousands of French Jews to be sent off to the death camps. [24]

Collaboration with Germany had started long before the Second World War. [25] Coston's faction was one that cooperated on the most intimate terms with Germany's foreign propaganda agencies. In April 1934 he reported the results of an inquiry which concluded that under Hitler Germany did not necessarily have to follow a policy of enmity toward France. Coston travelled to Germany to hold interviews with the highest nazi officials. In July *La Libre Parole* reported "...the peoples of Western civilization will always be grateful to Hitler's Germany for initiating this work of purification by rejecting from its bosom this stiffling, foreign, poisoned body and for beginning the new holy war against the Jewish infidels who strive to annihilate us."

Coston's journalism was highly appreciated by the nazis. To assure that he kept delivering their message he was sent by them that winter to cover a famous trial to be held in Berne dealing with the authorship and propagation of *The Protocols.* In May 1935 the Swiss courts found its publishers and distributors guilty of spreading racist lies..[26] Coston's services were noted by the nazis and their *Weltdienst* organization which subsidized sympathetic journalists. Its director received this report from his Swiss representative: "Coston is mentally of an almost incredible agility. He is certainly a true national socialist, but is, nevertheless, I think, not completely honest and certainly not free of exaggerated personal ambition. Even his external appearance is that of a young man somewhat pleased with himself who loves to be painted in the pose of a Führer."' [27]

Coston's intimate ties with nazi propaganda agencies were exposed in the journal, *Le Droit de Vivre,* which was published by L.I.C.A. the Ligue Internationale contre l'Antisémitisme. This organization had been founded by Bernhard Lecache, the son-in-law of Séverine. Drumont's old friend and associate. For this reason alone Coston and Lecache became embroiled in a journalistic vendetta which spanned the rest of the decade. In retaliation for this exposure Coston declared in April 1935 he would run for office out of the Jewish third arrondissement in Paris. His main purpose was to sow disorder and to put up posters announcing his platform replete with slogans like the following: "Purge Paris of Kikedom. Give bread and work to French workers first....to foreigners next if any are left." [28]

In 1936 Drumont's old colleagues and successors celebrated the 50th anniversary of *La France juive* and on 15 May hailed its author as an "Aryan revolutionary..." an inner demon gave him the strength to pursue the task. Coston felt obliged to continue the mission and in 1937 he decided to go to Algeria for the purpose of political agitation. There he was fined by a court in Blida for publishing violent articles which were deemed dangerous to public order. Later a Jew was killed by one of his bodyguards.

Antisemitic activities increased throughout Europe. Some of the results of the Stavisky affair, the civil war in Spain, and the Popular Front was the heightened sense of menace pervading the forces of the Right in France.The fact that a socialist Jew, Léon Blum, could be elected with some communist support incited extreme rightists to believe that France had been displaced in the European scheme of things and was subservient to the interests of the Soviet Union. To those who wished to counter this perceived threat links and sympathy with nazi Germany were increasingly attractive.

Upon his return to France from Algeria Coston in March 1937 sent congratulations to Darquier de Pellepoix who had coined a phrase which echoed the racism of Proudhon and had attracted public attention: "We must in all urgency solve the Jewish question. Either we must expell the Jews or we must massacre them."[29] During the nazi occupation Darquier was to have it both ways. Coston echoed this call for extermination in a thinly veiled article which pleaded for Germany to do the job: "If we were the victims of poisoning, would we call for help from the one who administered the poison to us? Certainly not. We would call our friends' doctor who would do the impossible to pull us through and might just succeed. It's quite logical. Instead of seeking the good offices of the poisoners or his accomplices, strangle them both."

The use of medical terms not uncommon with reference to the campaign to destroy the Jews. The power of its appeal can be gauged by its effect on a writer like Louis-Ferdinand Céline. In 1937 he published *Bagatelles pour un massacre,* the first of three violent tracts steeped in antisemitism. His commitment was unequivocal: "I became an antisemite and not just a little bit, to laugh about, but ferociously, to my very depths, enough to blow up all the kikes."[30] Scholars, critics, and admirers still debate the significance and origin of his hatred of Jews, but Céline was forthright in identifying his sources: "All Aryans must have read Drumont....Darquier de Pellepoix...H. Coston..."[31] Léon Daudet thought that compared with Céline, Drumont's books "seemed like a glass of orange blossom water." With evident satisfaction Coston remarked in his journal of 17 June 1937: "In its mysterious ways the work of Drumont is reentering French politics today."

In some sectors Drumont's spirit had never left. One of the better known antisemitic writers of the older generation was Urbain Gouhier. He contributed to the reborn *Libre Parole* and in September 1939 one of his articles was delivered at the nazi *Weltdienst* annual congress: "It is the task of 'World Service', "he wrote," to organize resistance against the Jews simultaneously at all points of the planet...Germany has been saved...we men of 'World Service' constitute the international police against the Jews, the poisoners of morality of the white race."[32] In response to the *Weltdienst* directives journalists like Gouhier and Coston increased their efforts to present a pro-nazi viewpoint of world affairs.

Their efforts were particularly appreciated and effective in spreading the war scare on behalf of German propaganda during the Czechoslovak crisis. Apprehension over possible war was a legitimate concern for

France, but the effect of pro-nazi journalism was to demoralize France to permit Germany a free hand in central Europe. For Coston the question was simple: "The fatherland is in danger! Which one? Theirs or ours? France or Judea...Frenchmen, will you be stupid enough to play the Jews' game?" [33] Much of France and Great Britain were content to yield to Germany's demands at the Munich conference, and the effect of defeatist propaganda played no small part in the manipulation of public opinion.

After the dismemberment of Czechoslovakia it was the turn of Poland. In France authorities realized the effect that the radical press on the Left and the Right had a negative influence on the formulation of its policies. With increased pressure on Poland the French government took drastic measures to curb this source of journalistic dissention and subversion. On 20 March 1939 it proclaimed the Marchandeau decree which prohibited radical newspapers from appearing, especially those which did not conceal their foreign contacts and sympathies. *La Libre Parole* was included on the censor's list and it never appeared again as a regular newspaper or a propaganda sheet.

It is important to review briefly the evolution of *La Libre Parole* during the years following the death of Drumont. After the sale of the journal in 1910 to a group of Catholic leftists it had retained elements of its traditional antisemitism contained in an expanded format which stressed broader treatment and coverage of public issues. It had changed from a journal of opinion to something more akin to a journal of information albeit with a Catholic orientation. After 1917 until 1924 its antisemitism was considered subordinate and part of its expanded religious flavor. After 1928 till its disappearance in 1939 *La Libre Parole* returned to the strident antisemitism of its founder. During this period it was little more than a propaganda sheet of a small though active fascist group centered around the energetic leadership of Henry Coston.. [34]

It might be thought reasonable that this study of Drumont's career and legacy should conclude with the final suppression of his newspaper. But it would be the supreme irony to note that just when *La Libre Parole* disappeared Drumont's program for racist politics was about to become law in France. Before the fall of France in 1940 legal discrimination against Jews was being considered in high circles with chauvinist inclinations. In his controversial book, *Pleins pouvoirs,* about the collapse of the Third Republic, playwright Jean Giraudoux could write: "We fully agree with Hitler in proclaiming that a policy only attains its higher form if it is racial..." [35] Strident French xenophobia under the Vichy regime would prove to be a willing accomplice with Germany's racist program for eliminating Jews from national life. The fact that many of Drumont's direct successors advocated this course of action warrants a brief investigation of their wartime activities during the years of nazi occupation.

In May 1940 the phoney war was over and France was utterly defeated on the field of battle. The search for scapegoats to explain the debacle was not slow in coming. On the far Right joy was not concealed at the demise of the republic. That it took German help to achieve this end made the nazis appear to be national liberators. Robert Brasillach, chief editor of *Je Suis Partout,* expressed this view of thanks and cooperation: "We French collaborators have all more less slept with Germany and the meaning of this concubinage will remain sweet to us." [36]

The exhilaration of Céline's disciple, Lucien Rebatet, was also explicit: "Defeat 'paid' better than victory! It toppled ignoble parliamentarianism. A military triumph might never have given us this good luck. All about me I was gloating over the decomposed heads of Jews." [37]

While most of France did not express such violent sentiments, many came to regrd Jews as the cause of its misfortune in the wake of its political and military debacle. The war and defeat resulted in a massive status deprivation and following the collapse antisemitism became on of the means to explain the country's swift decline on the European scene. Large sectors of the general public had been in varying degrees conditoned by the rightist press during the previous decades to look upon Jews as foreigners who wished France to fight Germany for their own sake. This negative evaluation enabled the Vichy regime to enact anti-Jewish laws before the Germans requested it and without much protest from the country as a whole. Much of the credit for this perception of Jews goes to the press on the radical Right, and *La Libre Parole* had been among the more strident vehicles in pressing for persecution of Jews.

At the beginning of the nazi occupation it was official policy not to alarm Jews unduly and provoke foreign opinion about the effect of the new antisemitic legislation.. [38] Consequently, it was perceived in extremist fascist circles that the national revolution proclaimed by Pétain was less than energetic. This state of affairs was especially irksome for the groups of journalists from the old staff of *La Libre Parole.* After the capitulation of France and the reappearance of the press Henry Coston believed he would have little difficulty in reissuing Drumont's old newspaper. Accordingly, a new edition was prepared and ready for press but plans were aborted by German occupation authorities without any explanation. [39]

Coston and his former associates however, were not without a sense of mission or an outlet for their talents. He and others were assigned by the Vichy government to become part of a documentation center for anti-Masonic affairs with the intention of exposing and eliminating from national life the influence of this organization. While working for this agency Coston often contributed to its publication, *Les Documents Maçoniques.* In its pages there appeared numerous articles which blamed an alleged alliance of Jews and Freemasons for having obtained the pardon of Dreyfus and for weakening France throughout the years following the conclusion of the affair. Coston's activities were not limited to this periodical alone. As the status of the Jews grew more precarious more newspapers printed pieces asserting that they deserved whatever fate was about to befall them. Coston soon became a contributor to this line of journalism.

When the press began to reappear in June 1940 Jean Drault found himself as the director of *La France au Travail,* a journal which was destined to become in time one of the more anti-Jewish publications. Its column were opened to Coston who in the issue of 3 November urged more drastic measures to be taken against Jews: "So the long-awaited yellow posters have finally appeared...not on all those shops that deserve them...at least not yet. Patience. While waiting for the happy days when all Jewish merchants hang out their little sign, go pay them a visit." In this vein Drault reprinted the following excerpt from Céline's *L'Ecole des cadavres* in the issue of 20 December: "We'll put such a scare into the Yids that they'll evaporate from the planet. Don't even have to touch them. We'll just singe them a little...on the arse...it'll be like waking up from a nightmare. They'll be gone for good." And in the 22 February 1941 issue writer Charles Dieudonné sternly warned against the marriage of Aryans with Jews and urged "the purging of the race as an essential condition of the national revolution."[40]

Later that year Dieudonné expressed joy at the sight of Jews being driven from the city of Orléans: "The outrage done to Joan of Arc was being washed away...whose memory will be celebrated without having to suffer the presence of the Jews." In the same newspaper two days later Coston celebrated at long last "the cleaning up of the capital" in an article which undoubtedly reflected the sentiments of many of his contemporaries who witnessed the same scenes on 15 May 1941:

> The solution of the Jewish question is well under way. Yesterday morning almost 5,000 ghetto Jews were arrested by French police and sent to concentration (and work) camps in the region of Orléans. To be sure, we would have preferred ourselves that police vigor would have first come down on those old Hebrew tribes which only yesterday constituted the general staff of those famous two hundred families. But one has to begin somewhere...Isn't the main point to purge Paris and France of the hundreds of thousands of parasites who claim to live at our expense? They're at the head of the line on the buses at the Austerlitz station from which five special trains are to take them to their new residence.

As the anti-Jewish drive increased within France more tributes to Drumont's legacy were publicly acknowledged. The expulsion of the Jews was seen to be the fulfillment of his vision "to exterminate" the Semites from French soil. On the 50th anniversary of the founding of *La Libre*

*Parole* his devotees put out a special issue of the review, *La France Européene*, on 20 April 1942 which recapitulated the fortunes of his journal from 1929 till 1939. Jean Drault recalled that Drumont's paper first came out when Hitler was only three years old. He thus reasoned that Frenchmen should have no qualms about those who challenged the nationalist credentials and roots of antisemitism in their land. The anniversary was celebrated by a great banquet held at the Hotel de l'Ecu de France near the Gare de l'Est and was attended by many prominent antisemites including Celine. [41]

The same tribute was echoed in *Le Cahier Jaune,* a review with close nazi ties, by André Chaumet in the February 1942 issue who admonished those who "think an anti-Jewish struggle is but a pale copy of the German. Don't the nazis know that pure Frenchmen of France, and Darquier is one of them, had nothing to learn from anyone in that regard?" Darquier de Pellepoix, it should be recalled, learned the political advantages of anti-semitism from Henry Coston. There was great joy among anti-semites in June when Darquier assumed control of the Commissariat of Jewish Affairs, the government agency which was charged with driving the Jews out of France. [42]

Throughout this period Drumont, the father of French antisemitism, was hailed in numerous publications as an ideological precursor of the French state as conceived and administered by Vichy. In the October 1942 number of *Le Cahier Jaune* his grateful widow wrote to André Chaumet: "In your letter I learned that the bust of my husband, Edouard Drumont, presides over the anti-Jewish propaganda you are making across France, the France defeated by the Jews!!...I read your articles with emotion and find in you and the collaborators of *Le Cahier Jaune* the ardor of fighters for the right cause..Drumont would have been proud of you."

More tributes were forthcoming in preparation for the centenary of Drumont's birth. In "one of the most obscene antisemitic and anti-allied papers published in Paris throughout the tragic years of German rule, *"Au Pilori* of 3 March 1944 Drault evoked the public ceremony held before Drumont's former residence in the Landrieu passage and he praised its celebrated inhabitant as the prophet who "foresaw the evil from which France almost died." [43] And in the 28 April issue of *Je Suis Partout* Jean Saillefest quoted at length the words of Drumont in praise of Germany's treatment of the Jewish question, suggesting that he would have approved of what was currently befalling his avowed enemies.

In the May 1944 issue of *La Chronique de Paris* several articles were devoted to his memory in that month of his centennial celebration. Hundreds of admirers assembled on 3 May at his graveside, a group which included many young men in uniform "who will go to fight the Jewish Bolsheviks." Above all, concluded the writer Henri Poulain, he would be remembered in the words of Léon Daudet as "the winner of future victories" and "Drumont deserves the title of precursor of that French revival and his memory must live among us like a supernatural presence."

The most poignant testimony was perhaps to be found in *Le Réveil du Peuple* of 10 May in a piece called "We Miss Drumont," a long synopsis of the antisemitic movement in France, which concluded by comparing his mind to that of contemporary successes: "Drumont's work was to make the instinct of preservation explode in people's souls. And the work of Hitler was to furnish it with weapons, to bring to it as a champion that Titan: the Germanic warrior." This quotation and many other similar in content are significant in several respects. After the war many apologists and not a few scholars attempted to put distance between the spirit of Drumont and Hitler, between French and German antisemitism. There were differences to be sure, but as these uninhibited testimonies of praise demonstrate such reserve was absent during the years when Drumont's (and Hitler's) deepest wish was coming true regarding the murder of Europe's Jews.

Shortly before the end of German and Vichyite rule in France Henry Coston on 20 June 1944 brought out a special facsimile edition commemorating *La Libre Parole,* replete with photographs and articles inspired by Drumont's legacy. Perhaps the most fitting tribute was composed by Lucien Rebatet on 28 July in *Je Suis Partout* "I admire Hitler. We admire Hitler. In the struggle against all the outdated crappy trivia of the nineteenth century Hitler had numerous predecessors, analysts, dialectitians, more brilliant and more agile than he among whom Drumont was to be found. Such enthusiastic comparisons go far in explaining why Drumont's name, though not the antisemitic spirit, was obscured during the postwar years.

At the time of France's complete liberation it became evident that the Vichy regime had one of the more unsavory records in Europe regarding the expulsion and ultimate deaths of many of its Jews. The cause of this aspect of the war years remains the subject of controversy for the country as a whole and for the Right in particular. [44] It could be strongly argued that such policies would not have occured if Germany had not occupied France. Yet it is equally true that before the war certain political formations on the Right advocated the deportation which was carried out under nazi auspices and with some French cooperation. And even at their lowest ebb groupings such as Coston's and those associated with it, among others, were able to make their voices heard in order to press for such an anti-Jewish policy.

As in the time of Drumont anti-Jewish sentiment was manifested in two discernible areas: a militant antisemitic minority helped to spread a general anti-Jewish antipathy among a much larger number of fellow citizens, who while not hating Jews probably had little contact hence little concern for them either. Even in defeat and disgrace virulent anti-semitism, considerably diminished after the Liberation, did not completely disappear.

## Notes

1  Walter Laqueur, *A History of Zionism* (New York: Holt Rinehart and Winston, 1972), p. 212. See also Yehoshafat Harkabi, *Arab Attitudes to Israel* (Jerusalem: Israel Universities Press, 1972), pp.223, 300, 493, and Neville J. Mandel, *The Arabs and Zionism before World War I* (Berkeley: University of California Press, 1976), p.55

2  Norman Cohn, *Warrant for Genocide* (New York: Harper & Row, 1979), p.57 Since Drumont s death it was revealed that his and several other Parisian journals received special funds for favorable publicity from the Tsarist police. It is not clear whether this clandestine connection envolved collaboration on *The Protocols*. See Arthur Raffalovitch, *L'Abominable vénalité de la presse francaise* (Paris: Librairie du Travail, 1931).

3  In the 15 March 1901 issue of *La Revue Blanche* Gustave Kahn could write: "It is not the French Jews at all who are inspired by Germany; it is truly the antisemites who believed that Ahlwardt was giving the signal of a new era and hastened to imitate the Germans. That did not last long in Germany and there is no reason for that sickness to last any longer among us."

4  Viau, *Vingt ans d'antisémitisme, p.* 313.

5  On the differences between Drumont and Maurras, see Maurice Barres and Charles Maurras, *La République ou le roi* (Paris: Plon, 1970). See also Eugen Weber, *Action Française* (Stanford: Stanford University Press, 1962) and *The Nationalist Revival in France, 1905-1914* (Berkeley: University of California Press, 1968).

6  On Drumont's attempt to infiltrate Biétry's movement, see Sternhell, *La Droite révolutionnaire,* p. 271-277. Like Drumont, Bietry enthusiastically praised the recent pogroms in Russia. Solidarity between the workers of both lands was expressed by slogans such as "Go forward, Russian brothers, sow their (the Jews') bones across the fields."

7  Ibid., p. 326

8  See Maurice Larkin,      *Church and State after the Dreyfus Affair* (New York: Barnes and Noble, 1974). Larkin quotes this recollection of Drumont by Vincent Bailly, the editor of *La Croix* who took plea-

sure in his saying: "If you ever get tired in the middle of a speech, shout 'Down with the Freemasons!' and that will give you time to spit. Shout 'Death to the Jews!' and that will give you time to go out for a pee.' " p.86.

9   Drumont, *Sur le chemin de la vie*, p.209.

10   Edouard Drumont, *"La Jeanne d'Arc* un acien Dreyfusard," *La Libre Parole,* 14 March 1910. See also Eric Cahem, *Péguy et le nationalisme français* (Paris: Cahier de l'Amitie Charles Péguy, 1972) pp. 155-158.

11   Joseph Denais had previously been employed at *Le Peuple Francais* which had been founded by the activist abbe democrate, *Garnier.* See also Stephen Wilson, "Catholic Populism in France at the time of the Dreyfus affair: *The Union Nationale." Journal of Contemporary History,*    vol. 10, No. 4., October 1975, pp. 667-701.

12   Madame Edouard Drumont, *A French Mother in War Time* (new York: Longman, Green, 1916), p.141.

14   For detailed press reactions to the death of Drumont, see *La Libre Parole,* 6 and 7 February 1917.

15   Belanger, *Histoire générale de la presse française,* vol. III, p.434.

16   See my "Antisemites on Zionism: The Case of Herzl and Drumont" *Midstream,* vol. XXV, no. 2, February 1979, 18-27.

17   S. Ettinger, "New Trends in the Development of the Jewish People after the First World War," *A History of the Jewish People* (Cambridge: Harvard University Press, 1976), p. 944.

18   *La Vieille France,* 2 May 1924, p.24.

19   See *La Libre Parole,* 1 December 1928

20   To gauge the depths of Bernanos anti-Jewish hatred, see his virulent article, "Fantasie sur l'histoire de demain," *Almanach d'Action Française,* 1928, pp. 171-185. See also Henri Guillemin, *Regards sur Bernanos* (Paris: Gallimard, 1976), Joseph Jurt, *Les Attitudes politiques de Georges Bernanos* (Fribourg: Editions Universitaires, 1968), pp.17-36, 118-121, NS *Georges Bernanos,* Max Milner, ed. (Paris: Plon, 1972), pp.68-96.

21   See J. Plumyène and R. Lasierra, *Les fascismes français* (Paris: Seuil, 1963), Philippe Machefer, *Ligues et fascismes en France:*

*1919-1939*(Paris: Presses Universitaires de France, and Bertram M. Gordon, *Collaborationism in France during the Second World War* (Ithaca: Cornell Univeristy Press, 1980).

22  *La Libre Parole,* 30 August 1933. On this journal's opinions see its issues of May 1932 and 15 December 1937.

23  On these political crises see Alexander Werth, *France in Ferment* (New York: Harper and Brother, 1935), Maurice Chavardès, *Le 6 Février 1934: la république en danger* (Paris: Calmann-Levy, 1966), Laurent Bonnevay, *Les Journées sanglantes de février 1934* (Paris: Flammarion, 1935), and Jean Grandmougin, *Histoire vivante du front populaire* (Paris: Albin-Michel, 1966).

24  See J.C.Fernand-Laurent, *Gallic Charter* (Boston: Little, Brown, 1944, pp.123-127. Despite its socialist rhetoric *La Libre Parole* and its supporters attracted support from leading conservative and reactionary figures. One of these personalities was Duke Joseph Pozzo di Borgo who helped found and lead the *Croix de Feu* and was an associate of François Coty during his anti-communist campaign. Pozzo di Borgo was also the president of the *Institut-Anti-Marxiste de Paris* and a benefactor of *La Libre Parole.* See *Dictionnaire de la politique francaise,* Henry Coston, dir. (Paris: Lectures Françaises, 1967), vol. I, pp. 877-878.

25  See Max Gallo, *Cinquième colonne: 1930-1940* (Paris: Plon 1970).

26  See Cohn, *Warrant for Genocide,* p. 230. Evidence of nazi interest in Drumont and French antisemitism is reflected in Walter Frank's *Nationalismus und Demokratie im Frankreich des Dritten Republik* (Hamburg: Hanseatische Verlaganstalt, 1933).

27  Quoted by Louis Bondy, *Racketeers of Hatred* (London: Newman Wolsey, 1946), p. 248. See also Jean Drault, *Histoire de l'antisémitisme* (Paris: Editions C. -L., 1942).

28  *La Libre Parole* often reprinted items of antisemitic interest from abroad. On 28 September 1935 it carried, for example, a speech by Julius Streicher who justified the abolition of political parties for one major reason: "the Jew is not born to fight. He seeks instruments and finds them in the person of political party leaders. While there still exist political parties in all foreign lands, we have destroyed them in Germany so that the Jew will not find among us the instrument by which he divides in order to dominate better. We know that the French and English are ready to extend a hand to Germany, but we know also that there are forces which try to prevent this in the interests of Jewry."

29  Bondy, *Racketeers of Hatred*, p. 191.

30  Quoted by Bettina Knapp, *Céline,: Man of Hate* (University: University of Alabama Press, 1974), p. 115.

31  Louis-Ferdinand Céline, *Bagatelles pour un massacre* (Paris: Denoël 1937), pp. 318-319.

32  Louis-Ferdinand Céline, *L'Ecole des cadavres* (Paris: Denoël, 1938), p.35.

33  *La Libre Parole*, 1 June 1938.

34  See Charles A. Micaud, *The French Right and Nazi Germany: 1933-1939: A Study of Public Opinion* (New York: The Duke University Press, 1943).

35  Jean Giraudoux, *Pleins pouvoirs* (Paris: Gallimard, 1939), p.76 My translation. On the new government's Jewish policy, see Michael R. Marrus and Robert O. Paxton, *Vichy et les juifs,* (Paris: Calmann-Lévy, 1981).

36  Quoted by Jacques Polonski, *La Presse et la propagande et l'opinion publique sous l'occupation* (Paris: Edition du Centre, 1946), pp. 79-80. See also Michèle Cotta, *La Collaboration* (Paris: Colin, 1964), and Henry Coston; *Paris, journaux et hommes politiques. Lectures Françaises,* December, 1960.

37  Lucien Rebatet, *Les Décombres* (Paris:Denoël, 1942), p.467.

38  See Lucy Dawidowicz, *The War Against the Jews: 1933-1945* (New York: Holt, Rinehart and Winston, 1975), pp.359-363, Robert Paxton, *Parades and Politics at Vichy* (Princeton: Princeton University Press, 1966), *Vichy France* (New York: Knopf, 1972), and Michael Marrus and Robert Paxton, *Vichy France and the Jews* (New York: Basic Books, 1981).

39  See Saint-Paulien, *Histoire de la collaboration* (Paris: L'Esprit Nouveau, 1964), p.263.

40  For a detailed analysis of Darquier's activities, see Joseph Billig, *Le Commissariat général aux questions juives* (Paris: Editions du Centre, 1955-1960), 3 vols.

41  Personal correspondence from Henry Coston, dated 5 May 1973.

42  See Pierrard, *Juifs et catholiques français.* pp.295-301 and Jacques Duquesne, *Les Catholiques français sous l'occupation* (Paris: Grasset,

1966).

43  Bondy, *Racketeers of Hatred*, p. 197. See also Joseph-Marie Rouault, *La Vision de Drumont* (Paris: Mercure de France, 1944).

44  For a self assessment of the extreme Right in France, see François Duprat, *Les Mouvements d'extrême droite en France depuis 1944* (Paris: Editions Albatros, 1972). See also Jean Laloum, *La France antisémite de Darquier de Pellepoix* (Paris: Editions Syros, 1979).

Conclusion

Antisemitism is the socialism
of fools.

--August Bebel

It has been observed and argued throughout this study that antisemitism in France often is exacerbated during crises of national status deprivation. Antisemitism by itself is not necessarily capable of being translated into a widespread violent movement without the accompanying crisis on the political and social levels. The constancy of this assertion is borne out no less after the Second World War than before the conflict. It is beyond the scope of this study to examine every aspect of antisemitism in postwar France. It is possible, nevertheless, to trace and to discern that persistent tradition of racism which has come to be associated with Drumont. In order to conclude this study a review of Drumont's legacy during this period is called for to understand some of the mutations and the persistence, however diminished, of Judeophobia in his homeland.

After the Liberation in 1945 Drumont's style of antisemitism had been discredited through association with the policies of Vichy and the Reich. In the opinion of his faithful admirer, Georges Bernanos, Hitler had given antisemitism a bad name. Drumont's influence, however, did not entirely disappear. His successors who had collaborated like Coston and Ploncard chose temporary exile or a modified, more subdued form of rightist and anti-Jewish activism. The virulent militant variety would not be tolerated by public opinion. Coston, for example, founded a successful publishing house and journal, *Lectures Françaises,* to promulgate these views in a different format.

Public criticism of Jews in France was in great measure muted or nonexistent and did not reemerge until after the Six-Day War of 1967. General de Gaulle no less than his rivals on the extreme Right had always been concerned with the question of France's loss of status as a great international power. After the end of the colonial wars he embarked on a campaign to strengthen France's global image, and the Arab-Israeli war in 1967 afforded him the opportunity of supporting the Arab lands at the expense of France's former ally, Israel.

The General's anti-Israeli policy was broad enough to include all Jews as was made clear by his famous press conference of 27 November 1967 in which he referred to Jews on the whole as being "self-assured and domineering" who "provoked ill-feeling" against themselves. In his book on the subject the respected political analyst, Raymond Aron, remarked: "We all recognize the style and the adjectives as being those of Edouard Drumont..." [1]

De Gaulle's comments and policies provoked a heated international controversy. According to Aron and many others it would have been misleading to accuse de Gaulle personally of antisemitism. His actions, many reasoned, were solely prompted by foreign policy considerations. In the analysis of the pioneer scholar on French proto-fascism, Zeev Sternhell, the anti-zionist stance of left-wing Gaullism is nonetheless strongly reminiscent of the anti-Jewish ideology adopted by French rightist political movements which on occasion try to put forward a progressive, populist face. [2] In this context it should be remembered that *La Libre Parole* had once advocated support of Zionism earlier in the century until it seemed to clash with French foreign policy in the Near East. In both instances Jews in France were often accused of disloyalty to national destiny and world peace.

Whatever de Gaulle's personal and public attitudes towards Jews may have been, his pejorative utterances and anti-Israeli policy unleashed a bitter debate. What was not in doubt was the aftershock of his new policy. The domestic effects of this policy were not without serious repercussions. One result of the general's remarks against Jews and the ensuing national uproar was to blur the lines between anti-Zionsim and anti-semitism in the minds of some French. According to Léon Poliakov anti-Zionism in the post-war world often though not always necessarily became a pretext for antisemitism. [3] Because of the acrimony and controversy less distinction was made between Jews and Israelis.

This confusion of categories was translated into the political and social arenas. Because the country as a whole had made a remarkable recovery in the post-war world the average Frenchman could afford to be more tolerant towards stangers. But certain provincial sectors of traditional French society experienced new forms of social and cultural malaise. This is not the place to review post-war French history, but it is significant to note that the presence of millions of foreign workers aroused xenophobic tendencies which were reflected in some elements of the rightist press in articles reminiscent of those which *La Libre Parole* and chauvinist journalism had made popular three generations earlier. This same anxiety had been exploited by Drumont in the 1880s and was repeated by his ideological heirs in the 1960s. In provincial cities rapid change in traditional life styles produced the anguish of anomie and cultural disintegration which Paris had experienced one century earlier.

One result of increased criticism of Jews was expressed in several provincial cities in a series of bizarre events which came to be labled "the rumors of Orléans," after the city of their origin. [4] De Gaulle's controversial remarks, the events of May 1968, anti-Zionism on the Right as well as on the Left, and a sense of social upheaval provoked a wave of hysteria which revived old charges of Jewish control of the white slavery trade. It should be recalled that this charge was one of many which Drumont was fond of publicizing. In 1969 large numbers of French Jews, questioned by the Right and some of the Left, once again felt themselves vulnerable to the ill will of many fellow citizens. Dozens of provincial cities were swept up in a frenzy of Jew hatred in the form of boycotts, threats, and slander, recalling the anti-Jewish violence that flashed across France at the time of the Dreyfus affair. Almost one century after Drumont's initial triumpsh his ghost had not yet been completely laid to rest.

Although classical antisemitism usually is manifested on the Right, certain elements on the Left, recent scholarship on the subject demonstrates, are not immune to the use of anti-Jewish hostility for opportunistic political purposes.[5] Drumont, at the height of his popularity, was capable of fusing antisemitism and Catholic populism, drawing upon conservative and certain independent socialist ideologies for his strength and appeal. Drumont's avowed championship of the proletariat led him to receive qualified praise in some French socialist circles. In these quarters antisemitism could be viewed, before the Dreyfus affair, to be at worst a form of socialism which overemphasized the Jewish question. This professed concern for the working class on certain levels of the radical Right became a cornerstone in the edifice of French fascism.

Marxian socialism formally repudiated classic antisemitism when it became a conspicuous feature of the Right. But on the matter of political enemies and propaganda tactics Drumont's antisemitism and various socialist revolutionary movements had one important factor in common: they shared a similar demonology. A comparative study, for example, of their respective iconological propaganda traditions would bear out this assertion. What the bourgeoisie was to many socialists the Jews were to the antisemites. Indeed if one were to substitute the word Jew for bourgois in samples of their vulgar propaganda this similarity would become evident. These words of a French radical from 1848 typify this particular extremist position found on the far Left of the early socialist tradition: "We demand the extermination of property and capitalists....the prescription of bankers, the rich, the merchants, the bourgeois...."[6] This type of radical rhetoric came easily to Drumont's lips.

It is important to recall that some socialists and many of Drumont's followers claimed to be the heirs of the Jacobin terrorist revolutionary tradition. To be sure, not most socialists nor all antisemites went to these extremes, but whenever France felt itself to be declining such homicidal instincts were not uncommon. In 1894 a Catholic observer, Louis Bernard, castigated Drumont for the violence he incited and the author commented on the journalist's populist appeal: "This is what explains the tenderness of Mr. Drumont for communists and anarchists, because he sees in these men the only soldiers capable of carrying out the war of extermination he has undertaken against the Jews."[7] This early fusion of radicalism and antisemitism contributed to the formation of the protofascist experience in France.

That Drumont could appeal at times to his land's revolutionary tradition is not surprising. In France it is a tradition that has been claimed by many factions along the political spectrum. Drumont consistently spurned the traditionalist monarchist conservatives, treating them as political fossils whose time had passed. Students of European fascism and anti-semitism have frequently come to recognize that the movements in question at the heights of their effectiveness were modernist in their thrust and appeal. To label them merely retrograde and reactionary is to overlook their inner dynamism and seductiveness. [8] Drumont was greatly supported by large numbers of Catholics and he was also welcomed by some independent socialists to such a degree that his movement may be classified by what Zeev Sternhell and other scholars term proto-fascism. [9] Drumont was active during this incubation period and his thought helped contribute to its subsequent development in France. This has been ideologically and historically demonstrated by the careers of Coston, Ploncard, and associates during the years between the world wars.

Like the nazis after the defeat of the First World War Drumont and his followers became influential after the defeat of the war of 1870. His heirs and kindred spirits enjoyed similar success after the defeat of 1940. Hannah Arendt has drawn attention to the similarities between his brand of national socialism and the immensely more successful and notorious variety which came to power in Germany. Historian Jacob Katz also recognized this link when he observed: "Anti-Semitic propaganda was everywhere linked up with social criticism....Drumont is outstanding in this respect...he outdid his contemporary anti-Semites of other countries. His vehement rhetoric is reminiscent of the Nazi propaganda in the Weimar Republic..." [10]

In both cases Jews were blamed for every imaginable ill of their respective countries. National discontent was displaced upon the Jews. Drumont, to be sure, cannot be considered the equivalent of Hitler. the former's movement, however, differed mainly in degree of success from the latter's, having developed decades before the enormous blood-letting and brutalization of peoples during the First World War. In both instances the liberal political order was the target of their attacks, and just as Weimar succumbed so did the Third Republic also run out of friends one decade later. In Germany and France the liberal republics were assaulted by the political extremes. That tradition developed by Drumont proved to be one of the more effective and durable instruments in contributing to the weakening of parliamentary democracy in France.

The means by which Drumont achieved his limited success was the press. He spent most of his life in the area of endeavor. It was his fortune to have been active at a time when the influence of newspapers was at its height. What he learned in this field enabled him to write his best-selling books and to produce his highly effective journal. In its time La Libre Parole was one of the best written journals and reached on occasion the pinnacles of influence. The field of journalism was to remain the preferred profession for Drumont's disciples well into the twentieth century.

Drumont did not invent anti-Jewish hostility in France. He gave it a powerful voice and modernized this form of political and religious animosity throughout many sectors of society. He proclaimed himself a racist and asserted that the millennial conflict between Jew and Gentile was essentially a struggle between races and that this struggle would have come to a head in the next generation. In this regard his program was dangerously modern, bearing within itself the dynamism for the massive persecutions which were to become the hallmark of our century.

Because of the focus of this book it is important to maintain a balance view of the times and society in which Drumont functioned. It must not be thought that France is an anti-semitic country. It is perhaps no more antisemitic than any other major traditional Western democracy. What lends credence to the negative opposing view are phenomena like the Dreyfus affair and the Vichy period. It is necessary to keep in mind that most of the country did not subscribe to Drumont's world vision. The disadvantages of the Jews as Jews stem from the observation made by Sartre to the effect that their friends are not nearly as committed as their enemies while the general public remains largely indifferent to their fate in times of danger. Having observed this, a general balance of Drumont's influence and impact can be established.

In the last quarter of the twentieth century Drumont's name is not always recognizable among his countrymen. Although fresh flowers are still placed by admirers on his tomb in the Père Lachaise cemetery, it is doubtful that most visitors would be aware of his activities were it not for the inscription in the crypt identifying him as the author of *La France juive.* One measure of his success, however, can be gauged by the degree of sympathy which his social ideas gain beyond the immediate small circle of admirers whenever his land perceives itself to be threatened.

In the elections of 1984 the radical right Front National led by the eloquent Jean-Marie Le Pen received two million votes on a campaign platform mainly aimed at the third-world foreigners residing in France. While Le Pen publicly disavowed any taint of antisemitism he bluntly declared that he was not obliged to admire what some considered the contributions made by Jews in France. Furthermore his slogan "Les Français d'abord" is quite similar to "La France aux Français" of Drumont. Jews may not be the principal targets of his denunciations of France's ills, but many of his arguments stem from the same ideological source which animated the success of Drumont.

Since the last world war French public opinion polls do record a relative decline in the expression of antisemitic sentiment. But as Paula Hyman demonstrates in her study *From Dreyfus to Vichy*, a pervasive sense of xenophobia in times of crisis can lend strength to the forces of antisemitism. Because of Drumont's activities animosity towards Jews did intensify over the past century in France. From the political controversies of the early Third Republic till the rumors of Orléans the legacy of Edouard Drumont demonstrates its durability in times of trouble.

## Notes

[1] Raymond Aron, *De Gaulle, Israel and the Jews* (New York: Praeger, 1968), p.24. See also Sylvia Kowitt Crosbie, *A Tacit Alliance: France and Israel after Suez and the Six Day War* (Princeton: Princeton University Press, 1974).

[2] See Sternhell, *La Droite révolutionnaire,* p. 317.

[3] See Léon Poliakov, *De l'antisionisme à l'antisémitisme* (Paris: Calmann-Lévy, 1969). According to Poliakov it is instructive to note that as Joseph Pozzo di Borgo, a backer of *La Libre Parole,* had denounced Jews in the 1930s, his relative, Olivier Pozzo di Borgo, was supporting anti-Zionism in the 1960s.

[4] See Edgar Morin, *La Rumeur d'Orléans* (Paris: Seuil, 1969). Concerning accusations of Jewish control of white slave trade in Orléans around the time of the Dreyfus affair, see Le Chanoine Cochard, *La Juiverie d'Orléans* (Orléans: Herluison, 1895), p.9.

[5] On antisemites' use of Marx's anti-Jewish writings, see Julius Carlebach, *Karl Marx and the Radical Critique of Judaism* (London: Routledge and Kegan Paul, 1978), pp.344-358. On leftist exploitation of antisemitism in France, see Grigory Svirsky, *Hostages: The Personal Testimony of a Soviet Jew* (New York: Knopf, 1976), pp.302-305.

Quoted by H.A. Deivies, *An Outline History of the World* (London: Oxford University Press, 1937), p. 479. Regarding the Jewish state, Coston's periodical, *Lectures Françaises,* in September 1967 wrote that its editorial policy had never agreed with that of this progressive journal: "having said this, we are more than happy to point out to our readers a brochure which *Témoignage Chrétien* just published on the Arab-Israeli war...damaging for the Israelis...buy it and spread the word..." On this Catholic journal, see the comments of Georges Coston, *Infiltrations ennemies dans l'église* (Paris: La Librairie Française, 1970), pp. 168-178. On the condition of Jews in modern France, see Andre Harris and Alain de Sedouy, *Juifs et Français* (Paris: Bernard Grasset, 1979). For a denial of the link between socialist and antisemitic demonology, see Sartre, *Antisemite and Jew* (New York: Schocken, 1948). p. 37.

7  Louis Bernard, *L'Antisémitisme démasqué: étude sociale, politique, et économique par un catholique* (Paris: A. Charles Librairie, 1894), p.136. Bernard does recognize that Drumont is correct in condemning the injustices of contemporary French society which both feel doomed to pass away, but "his furious hatred stirs it up and leads it astray to the point of not allowing him to see the exaggeration of what he is writing." p. 119. and "....he appeals to the blind and brutal passions which swarm in the lower depths of a rabble aroused by the dissolute appetites begotten by an old society." p.125.

8  See Eugen Weber, *Varieties of Fascism* (New York: Van Nostrand Reinhold, 1964), pp.26-69.

9  Maurice Barrès was a great admirer of Drumont and a much more successful writer many of whose ideas dreived from these sources. See Robert Soucy, *Fascism in France: The Case of Maurice Barrès* (Berkeley: University of California Press, 1972)  and Zeev Sternhell, *Maurice Barrès et le nationalisme français* (Paris: Armand Colin, 1972).

10  Katz, *From Prejudice to Destruction*, op. cit., p. 296.

## Appendix: Drumont and the Police

The question of Drumont's possible connection with the police is long-standing although the evidence must remain inconclusive. His career was dogged from the early years by the accusation of his being a police informer. This type of charge was not uncommon during the nineteenth century, but given the absence of concrete proof it stands as conjecture. In his book, *Edouard Drumont et les jésuites,* (1902), Stéphane Arnoulin restates and elaborates the charge that Drumont was a police spy around the time of his association with Charles Marchal de Bussy during the late 1860s. Whatever secret police files that did exist they were destroyed by fire at the Prefecture of Police during the Paris Commune of 1871.

For a figure as controversial as Drumont it would be reasonable to expect his actions to have been monitored in turn by police informants. However, many of the dossiers on various public personalities assembled during the 1890s were destroyed according to the special catalogue established by J. Chaumié of the Correspondence de la Division criminelle du Ministère de la Justice, number BB18 1815-2176, which is to be found in the Grande Salle des Inventaires of the Archives Nationales, Paris. Apart from a few interesting references to the activities of members of Drumont's staff at the *Libre Parole* there exists little material of major significance indicated under the catalogue numbers found int he bibliography of this study. The most extensive part of these files pertaining to such activities and events is filed under BB18 2062, 1259 a97 and deals with antisemitic disturbances in Aleria at the time of the Dreyfus affair. Another large dossier, 2164 1434 A00, deals with anti-Jewish activities across France immediately after the turn of the century and testified to the post-Dreyfus decline of Drumont's type of political agitation. *Le Petit Rouennais*, for example, of 6 February 1901, reports: "nationalism or antisemitism--it's all the same--has hitherto been a fiasco in Rouen."

One curious report from this collection is revealing of government attitudes and is filed under BB18 2130 1525 A99. Here it is reported that in early August 1899 Drumont had ordered 300,000 tricolor cocards to be printed by the firm of Parisot. In the eyes of the Ministère de la Justice the fact that the cocards bore the cry "Down with the Jews" might have constituted a direct provocation against public order. "The distribution of this printed matter probably is not without danger from the viewpoint of public tranquility...this distribution could have constituted in former legislation...the offense foreseen by the article of 11 August 1848." On this occasion, however, neither court nor police could decide whether Drumont's anti-Jewish campaign truly represented a threat to civilian life in the eyes of the law despite the widespread riots provoked by Drumont's militant program.

Given the controversial scope and nature of Drumont's career it might be expected that his activities would have been closely and extensively monitored by the authorities. However, this was not the case. There does exist a file of sorts on Drumont numbered E A/96/8 to be found at the Archives de la Préfecture de Police de Paris. But this dossier only contains about six newspaper clippings, a poster and no police reports of the kind which are found in the dossiers of other prominent controversial public figures. In the opinion of Mme. Denise Monney and her assistants Drumont's dossier appears to have been possibly cleaned out presumably by someone sympathetic to his cause. In short, archival sources, particularly police reports, on Drumont afford the researcher little worthwhile material for study.

# Bibliography

## Primary Sources

### I. Archival Material

Archives Nationales, Paris
Catalogue de la Correspondance de la Division criminelle du Ministère de la Justice, established by J. Chaumie, BB18 18-2176, containing dossiers pertaining to the activities of Drumont's staff and associates.

Quesnay de Beaurepaire attacked by the *Libre Parole*,
BB18 1884 A92
Rothschild marriage assailed.                                BB18 1900 1659 A92
Fraud charges against J. B. Gérin               BB18 1936 1161 A93
*Libre Parole* articles on morals scandal at Prévost Orphanage at Cempuis.                                      BB18 1982 2786 A94
*Libre Parole* article defaming head of state       BB18 2022 129 A96
Drumont's participation in demonstrations at Lyon of Con gress for Démocratie chrétienne.           BB18 2026 496 A96

*Libre Parole* defamation of President of the Republic.
BB18 2051 129 A97
Antisemitic attacks in Algeria during Dreyfus Affair.
BB18 2062 1259 A97
*Libre Parole* article by J. Drault against Lutaud, the prefect of Algiers, 14 December 1898.          BB18 2107 2673 A98
Antisemitic demonstrations in France.         BB18 2110 129 A99
Drumont's order to have the Parisot firm print antisemitic pro paganda cocards.                              BB18 2130 1535 A99
Trial coverage concerning *Libre Parole* attacks against Rothschild during 1900-1901.                     BB18 2167 1669 A00
National anti-Jewish demonstrations 1900-1904 B18 2164 1434 A00
Archives de la Préfecture de Police de Paris
Drumont dossier E A/96 8

Bibliothèque Nationale, Paris, Département des Manuscrits

Correspondence from Edouard Drumont

To Maurice Septet, 15 April 1886, 14630
To Alexander Dumas fils, n.d. 14664 ff. 296-302
To the Abbe François Nau, 8 December 1892  14855 ff. 461-463
To Edouard Lockroy, n.d. 25161 f. 359
To Germain Bapst, n.d. 24529 f. 511

To Germain Bapst 28 January 1904 24866
To Jehan Rictus, 28 June 1895 24554 ff. 726-727
To Alexandre Dumas fils, 11 January 1874   24637 ff. 471-472
To Paul Nadar, 19 June 1883 24268 ff. 450-451
To Paul Nadar, 19 April 1888 24268 ff. 456
To Paul Nadar, 18 January 1896 24268 ff. 464
To François Veuillot, November 1913 24621 ff. 490
To Félix Nadar, 20 June 1892 22995 ff. 514

\*\*\*\*\*\*

From Félix Nadar, 15 April 1888 24988 ff. 255-256

Houghton Library, Harvard University
Lee Friedman Fund. *PFC9 D8262 Z898d 16.
Extraordinaire recueil composé à l'intention d'Edouard Drumont
pour lui être offert par ses électeurs et admirateurs d'Algérie.

## II. Newspapers and Reviews

L'Action Francaise
L'Almanach d'Action Francaise
Les Annales de Philosophie Catholique
L'Antijuif
L'Arche
Au Pilori
L'Aurore
L'Autorite
Der Berliner Tageblatt
Le Bien Public
Le Cahier Jaune
Les Cahiers de l'Ordre
La Chronique de Paris
La Chronique Illustrée
La Civiltà Cattolica
Combat
Le Contemporain
Le Cri
Le Cri du Peuple
La Croix
The Daily Chronicle
La Dépêche
Le Diable à Quatre
Les Documents Maçonniques
Le Droit de Vivre
L'Echo du Merveilleux
L'Eclair
L'Endehors

Esprit
L'Evénement
Evidences
L'Express du Midi
Le Figaro
La France
La France Européenne
La France Militaire
La France Nouvelle
La France au Travail
Le Gaulois
La Gazette de France
Gil Blas
L'Humanité
L'Humanité Nouvelle
The Illustrated London News
L'Illustration
L'Inflexible
L'Intransigeant
Je Suis Partout
Jewish Social Studies
Le Jour
Le Journal
Le Journal des Débats
Le Journal des Sciences Militaires
Judaism
La Juste Parole
La Justice
La Lanterne
Lectures Françaises
Le Libertaire
La Liberté
La Libre Parole
La Libre Parole Illustrée
Le Livre
La Lutte Anti-Juive et Anti-Maçonnique
La Mâchoire d'Ane
La Marseillaise
Le Matin
La Mère Duchêne
Minute
Le Monde
Le Moniteur du Bâtiment
Le Mouvement Socialiste
La Nation
Le National
Le National Bruxellois
Neue Freie Presse

The New York Times
L'Officiel
L'Oeuvre Française
Osservatore Romano
Paris-Soir
La Patrie
La Patrie Française
Le Petit Illustré
Le Petit Journal
Le Petit Parisien
La Petite Republique Française
Le Peuple Francais
Le Pilori
La Presse
La Presse Théâtrale
La Question Juive dans la France et dans le Monde
Le Quotidien
Le Radical
Le Rappel
La République Française
Le Réveil
Le Réveil de Royan
Le Réveil du Peuple
La Revendication
The Review of Reviews
La Revue Blanche
La Revue Bleue
La Revue des Deux Mondes
La Revue d'Histoire Moderne et Contemporaine
La Revue du Monde Catholique
La Revue de la Révolution
La Revue Graphologique
La Revue Indépendante
La Revue Universelle
Le Rire
The San Francisco Evening Bulletin
The San Francisco Examiner
Scribner's Monthly
La Semaine Financière
Le Siècle
La Sociale
Le Soir
Le Soleil
The South Wales Argus
Der Stürmer
La Tante Duchêne
Le Télégramme
Le Télégramme de Toulouse

Témoignage Chrètien
Le Temps
La Tribune Française
L'Univers
Le Vengeur
La Vérité
La Vie Illustrée
La Vieille France
The Wiener Library Bulletin

## III. Works by Drumont

*Richard Wagner, l'homme et le musicien, à propos de "Rienzi."*
Paris: Dentu, 1869.

*Je Déjeune à midi.* (with Aimé Dollfus) Paris: Lévy, 1875

*Mon vieux Paris.* Paris: Charpentier, 1878.

*Les Fêtes nationales à Paris.* Paris: Baschet, 1879.

*Le dernier des Trémolin.* Paris: Palme, 1879.

*La Mort de Louis XIV, journal des Anthoine,* published for the first
time with introduction by E. Drumont. Paris: Quantin, 1880.

Edition of Saint-Simon, *Papiers inédits* Paris: Quantin, 1880.

*Le Vol des diamants de la couronne au Garde-Meuble.* Paris:
Santon, 1885.

*La France juive, essai d'histoire contemporaine.* Paris: Marpon et
Flammarion, 1886, 2 vols.

*La France juive devant l'opinion.* Paris: Marpon et Flammarion,
1886.

*La Fin d'un monde, étude psychologique et sociale.* Paris: Savine,
1889.

*La Dernière bataille.* Paris: Dentu, 1890.

*Le Testament d'un antisémite.* Paris: Dentu, 1891.

*Le Secret de Fourmies.* Paris: Savine, 1892.

*Mon vieux Paris, hommes et choses.* second edition, Paris:
Flammarion, 1893.

*De l'or de la boue, du sang. Du Panama à l'anarchie.* Paris: Flammarion, 1896.

*Mon vieux Paris.* second series. Paris: Flammarion, 1897.

*Les Juifs contre la France, une nouvelle Pologne.* Paris: Librairie Antisémite, 1899.

*Nos Maîtres, la tyrannie maçonnique.* Paris: Librairie Antisémite, 1899.

*Le Peuple juif.* Paris: Libraire Antisémite, 1900.

*Les Trétaux du succès.* Paris: Flammarion, 1900. 2 vols.

    vol. I *Figures de bronze ou statues de neige.*
    vol. II *Les Héros et les pitres.*

*Vieux portraits, vieux cadres.* Paris: Flammarion, 1903.

*Contre les insulteurs de Jeanne d'Arc* Paris: Action Française, 1904.

*Sur le chemin de la vie, souvenirs.* Paris: Cres, 1914.

Anthologies of Drumont's works

Beau de Loménie, Emmanuel, *Edouard Drumont ou l'anti-capitalisme national.* Paris: Pauvert, 1967.

Rouault, Joseph-Marie. *La Vision de Drumont.* Paris; Mercure de France, 1944.

Prefaces by Drumont

(Anonymous) *Aux Electeurs. Combes et son fils Edgar, la chute de Combes, Jaures, trois satires.* Paris: Librairie Antisémite, n.d.

Anger, Henri-Rasme. *Trois ballades anti-juives.* Paris: 1902.

Billing, Robert de. *Le Baron de Billing.* Paris: Savine, 1895.

Brisecou, Jean. *La Grande conjuration organisée pour la ruine de la France, dénoncée par Jean Brisecou.* Autun: Coquegniot, 1887.

Desportes, Henri. *Le Mystère du sang chez les juifs de tous les temps.* Paris: Savine, 1889.

Desportes, Henri. *Tué par les juifs.* Paris: Savine, 1890.

Devaux, Paul. *Joseph et Mardochée, étude critique sur l'hégénomie sémitique.* Paris: Union des Bibliophiles, 1887.

Drault, Jean. *Ligue pour le refus de l'impôt.* Dijon: 1902.

Dupouy, Edmond. *Sciences occultes et physiologie psychique.* Paris: Flammarion, 1903.

Duruskam, Jean. *Est-ce un crime? opinions de docteur.* Paris: Chamuel, 1911.

Duval, Maurice. *Le Carnet d'un passant.* Paris: Bernard, 1904.

Fauriette, Léon. *Drumont.* Puteaux-sur-Seine: Prieur et Dubois, 1902.

Fleurance, Gustave de. *Expulseurs et expulsés.* Paris: Létouzey, 1888.

Fore-Fauré. *Face aux juifs! essais de psychologie sociale contemporaine.* Paris: Savine, 1891.

Garreau, Anna. *Aicha.* Paris: Carré, 1890.

Lamilot, Roger. *La Fille de la France juive, ou l'école sans Dieu.* Perpignan: Roque, 1887.

Lioubow, Genia. *L'Art divinatoire.* Paris: Flammarion, 1903.

Maurain, Joseph. *L'Elu du peuple, moeurs d'à-présent.* Paris: 1892.

Méry, Gaston. *La Voyante de la rue de Paradis.* Paris: Dentu, n.d.

Monniot, Albert. *Les Gouvernants contre la nation.* Paris: Librairie Antisémite, 1900.

*Le Crime rituel chez les juifs.* Paris: Tequi, 1914.

Ollivier, Le R. P. Marie-Joseph-Henri, O.P. *Après la terrible catastrophe du Bazar de la Charité.* Funeral sermons including an interpretation of Father Ollivier's speech by Drumont. Paris: Pierret, 1897.

Pascal, Le P. Georges de. *La Juiverie.* Paris: Gautier, 1887.

Reignier, Gabriel. *Les Faux dieux*. Paris: Charles, 1892.

Rohling, August. *Le Juif selon le talmud*. Paris: Savine, 1889.

Rouyer, Mme. Camille. *Les Chemins de la vie*. Tours: Mame, 1900.

Soleilhac, Paul. *Le Grand levier, ou de la presse et de son influence politique et sociale à notre époque*. Paris: Gautier, 1906.

Tauxier, Octave. *De l'inaptitude des Français à concevoir la question juive*. Paris: Bureaux de l'Action Française, 1900.

Trioullaire. *L'Antichrist*. Paris: Librairie Antisémite, 1900.

Viau, Raphaël. *Ces bons Juifs!* Paris: Peirret, 1898.

IV. Works and articles concerning Drumont

Ancelle, Dominique. "Drumont," *Ordre Français,* no. 134 (1969) 40-50, no. 135, 51-62; (1970), no. 137, 39-51, no. 138, 57-67.

Anderson, Thomas. "Edouard Drumont and the Origins of Modern Anti-Semitism," *Catholic Historical Review,* LIII (1967-1968), 28-42.

Anon. *Edouard Drumont et son oeuvre*. Paris: Dupont, 1898.

D'Alméras, Henri. *Avant la gloire, leurs débuts*. Paris: Société d'Imprimerie et de la Librairie, 1903.

L'Archiviste. *Drumont et Dreyfus. Etudes sur la Libre Parole de 1894 a 1895*. Paris: Stock, 1898.

Arnoulin, Stéphane. *Edouard Drumont et les jésuites*. Paris: Librairie des Deux Mondes, 1902.

Aron, Joseph. *Mon pauvre Drumont*. Paris: Paul Schmidt, n.d.

Audiffrent, Georges. *A M. Drumont, auteur de la France Juive et de la Fin d'un monde*. Paris: Welter, 1889.

*La Seconde à M. Drumont*. Marseille: Librairie Marseillaise, 1892.

Baron, Edgar. *Lettre ouverte à Edouard Drumont*. Niort: Lemercier et Alliot, 1895.

*Suite aux lettres ouvertes a Edouard Drumont.*
Fontenay-le-Comte, l'auteur, 1897.

*Suite aux lettres ouvertes à Drumont et à l'abbé XXX.*
Fontenay-le-Comte, l'auteur, 1898.

Bastaire, jean. "Drumont et l'antisémitisme," *Esprit,* March,
1964).

Barrucaud, Victor. *M. Drumont et l'Algérie.* Moustapha: Imprimerie Algérienne, 1902.

Beau de Loménie, Emmanuel. *Edouard Drumont ou l'anti-capitalisme national.* Paris: Pauvert, 1967.

Bernanos, Georges. "Edouard Drumont," *Cours et conférences
d'Action Francaise.* (October 19290, 136.

"Le Temps d'Edouard Drumont," *Revue Universelle,* (1930),
tome 43, 641-662.

*La Grande peur des bien-pensants.* Paris: Grasset, 1931.

Berr, Emmanuel. "Edouard Drumont," *La Revue Bleue,* tome
LXXV (1890), 458-462.

Bertaut, Jules. *Figures contemporaines. Chroniqueurs et polémistes.* Paris: Sansot, 1906.

Biez, Jacques de. *La Question juive: La France ne peut pas être
leur terre promise.* Paris: Marpon et Flammarion, 1886.

Biucchi, Hubert. "Drumont, roi d'Alger," *Le Soleil,* no. 3,
(April 1966), 7-8.

Bloy, Leon. *Le Salut par les Juifs. Paris: Demay, 1892.*

Braisne, H. de. "J. Lemaitre, J. Jullien et Ed. Drumont chez
eux," *La Nouvelle Revue,* CXVI, (1899), 124-126.

Brisson, Adolphe. *Les Prophètes...* Paris: Taillandier, 1903.

Brunetière, Ferdinand. "Revue littéraire," *La Revue des Deux
Mondes,* LXXV (1886), 693-704.

Busi, Frederick. "The Legacy of Edouard Drumont as an écrivain de combat," *Nineteenth Century French Studies,* IV, no. 3, (Spring 1976), 385-393.

"The Balzacian Imagination in the Dreyfus Affair: Edouard Drumont as a reader of Balzac," *Nineteenth Century French Studies.* VI, nos. 3 & 4 (Spring-Summer 1978), 174-188.

"Anti-Semites on Zionism: The Case of Herzl and Drumont," *Midstream,* vol. XXV, no. 2, February 1979, 18-27.

Clary, N. "French Anti-Semitism during the Years of Drumont and Dreyfus," Dissertation Abstracts International (Ann Arbor) 31, 1971, no. 7, 3462.

Cornilleau, Robert. *Types et silhouetttes: Edouard Drumont, peintre d'histoire.* Paris: S.M. n.d.

Coston, Henry. "Edouard -Adolphe Drumont," *Dictionnaire de la politique française.* Paris: Publications Henry Coston, 1967. pp. 386-389.

Croquez, Albert. *Figures françaises d'aujourd'hui. Edouard Drumont.* Paris: Nouvelle Librairie Nationale, 1909.

Daudet, Leon. *Le Pays des parlementaires.* Paris: Flammarion, 1901.

*La France en alarme.* Paris: Flammarion, 1904.

"Edouard Drumont ou le sens de la race," *La Revue Universelle,* IV, (1921), 1-31.

*Les Oeuvres dans les hommes.* Paris: Nouvelle Librairie Nationale, 1922. pp. 143-196.

*Souvenirs.* Paris: Nouvelle Librairie Nationale, 1922.

*Etudes et milieux littéraires.* Paris: Grasset, 1927.

Dissaux, Philippe, "Les Débuts de *la Libre Parole,* 1892-1894." (D.E.S., Paris 1965), unpublished dissertation.

Dominique, Pierre. *Les Polémistes français depuis 1789.* Paris: La Colombe, 1962. pp. 265-280.

"Edouard Drumont et la Commune," *Le Soleil,* no. 7 (February 1966), 8.

Drault, Jean. Drumont, *la France et la Libre Parole*. Paris: Malfère, 1935.

Drumont, Madame Edouard. *A French Mother in War Time*. Translated by Grace Bevir. New York: Longmans Green, 1916.

Duclos, Paul. "Catholiques et juifs autour de l'affaire Dreyfus," *Revue d'Histoire de l'Eglise de France*, LXIV, no. 172. January-February 1978. 39-53.

Fauriette, Léon. *Drumont*. Paris-Puteaux-sur-Seine: Prieur et Dubois, 1902.

Garredi, Marius. *Catholicisme et Judaïsme: Réponse à la France juive de Drumont.* Paris: Dentu, 1888.

Gohier, Urbain. "Drumont nous manque," *Le Réveil du Peuple*. no. 82 (10 May 1944), 1.

Gribayedoff, Valerian. "M. Drumont, Who Rings the Tocsin?" *Review of Reviews*, XVII (1898), 311-315.

Guérin, Arsène. *A Propos de la France juive*. Paris: Librairie Internationale de l'oeuvre de Saint-Paul, 1886.

"Sur *la France juive*," *La Revue du Monde Catholique*, no. 86, (1886), 405-419.

Guérin, Jules-Napoleon. *Les Trafiquants de l'antisémitisme*. Paris: Juven, 1905.

Guerlac, Othon. *Trois Apôtres: Drumont, Rochefort, Séverine*. *Paris: Alcan Lévy, 1896.*

Havard, Oscar. *M. Edouard Drumont et la France juive*. Paris: Levé, 1886.

Jacquet, l'Abbe A.-J. *Opportunisme, orléanisme, impérialisme... tout ça se vaut. L'antisémitisme et les vieux partis.* *Lettres d'un curé antisémitisme à M.E. Drumont*. Paris: Librairie de la Croisade française, 1898.

Jolly, Jean. ed. *Dictionnaire des parlementaires français, 1889-1940*. Paris: Presses Universitaires de France, 1966, vol. IV, pp. 1497-1498.

Kahn, Gustave. "Drumont littérateur," *La Revue Blanche* (15 March 1901), 441-445.

196

Labroue, Henri. Professeur d'histoire du judaïsme à la Sorbonne. "L'Antijudaïsme en France de 1870 a 1914," *Pariser Zeitung* (21 July 1943), 2.

Lauzel, Maurice. *La Robe courte, M. Edouard Drumont*. Paris: Librairie de la Revue Socialiste, 1898.

Lefas, Alex. "Edouard Drumont," *Le Correspondant*, tome 266, (1917), 553-557.

Lenornand, J. *Questions algériennes: le péril étranger*. Paris: Librairie Africaine et Coloniale, 1899.

Ligneau, Jean de. *Juifs et antisémites en Europe*. Paris: Toira:, 1891, pp. 36-45.

Manouvriez, Abel. "Edouard Drumont et son oeuvre," *Libertés Françaises* (1957), no. 17, 72-83, no 18. 3-12, no. 19. 44-59, no. 20. 68-82, no. 21. 90-102. -

Marin, Paul. *Drumont*. Paris: Stock, 1899.

Maurras, Charles. "Drumont," *Dictionnaire politique et critique*, Pierre Chardon, ed. Paris: A La Cité des Livres, tome I, pp. 393-395.

McCully, William C. "Drumont and Dreyfus: a French Chauvinist Editor and his Newspaper," Diss. Notre Dame University, 1973.

Mermeix. *Les Antisémites en France*. Paris: Dentu, 1892.

Méry, Madame Gaston. "A Edouard Drumont," *L'Echo du Merveilleux*, no. 336. (1 January 1911), 1-2.

Millot, J.-E. *Aux Prolétaires de France*. Asnières: Imprimérie du Progrès, 1889.

Missoffe, Michel. *Gyp et ses amis*. Paris: Flammarion, 1932.

Mitchell, Alan. "La Mentalité xénophobe: contre-espionnage et racines de l'affaire Dreyfus," *Revue d'histoire moderne et contemporaine* 29 (July 1982): 489-99.

Morienval, J. "Edouard Drumont," *Catholicisme: hier, aujourd' hui, demain*. G. Jacquemet, ed. Paris: Létouzey et Ané, 1947-1957, III, p. 1130.

Mourre, Michel. "Edouard Drumont," *Dictionnaire d'Histoire Universelle*. Paris: Editions Universitaires, 1968, vol. I, p. 580.

Penboch, J. de. *Réponse à la Fin d'un monde d'Edouard Drumont*. Paris: Létouzey, 1889.

Plantivaux, Raphaël. *Tartuffe*. Paris: Editions de l'Anthologie, 1900.

Ploncard d'Assac, Jacques. *Edouard Drumont*. Lisbon: Silvas, Lda, 1973. La Lettre Politique, LXVII.

Poulain, Henri. "Présences d'Edouard Drumont," *La Chronique de Paris*. no. 7 (May 1944), 24-36.

Rabi, W. "L'Antisémitisme francais au XIXe siecle. 1. De l'antisemitisme traditionnel a l'antisemitisme 'revolutionnaire' de Toussenel," *L'Arche*, no. 52, (May 1961), 30-35; 2. "Drumont, l'apôtre myope," *L'Arche*, no. 53, (June 1961), 36-39.

Reinach, Joseph. *Drumont et Dreyfus: études sur la Libre Parole de 1894 à 1895*. Paris: Stock, 1898. (This book was published under the pseudonym "l'Archiviste").

Renaut, l'Abbé Charles. *L'Israélite Edouard Drumont et les sociétés secrètes actuellement*. Paris: chez l'auteur, 1896.

Reynaud, Leonce. *La France n'est pas juive*. Paris: Morot et Chuit, 1886.

*Les Juifs français devant l'opinion*. Paris: Lahure, 1887.

*Les Français Israélites*. Paris: Lahure, 1901.

Rochetal, Albert de. "Edouard Drumont," *la Revue Graphologique*. XXIII (1906), 301-305.

Saillefest, Jean. "Drumont notre maître," *Je Suis Partout*. no. 668. (28 April 1944), 1.

Schapira, Israel. *Der Antisemitismus in der französischen Literatur: Edouard Drumont und seine Quellen*. Berlin: Philo-Verlag, 1927.

Talmeyr, Maurice. "Souvenirs de la Comédie Humaine," *Le Correspondant*, tome 309, (1927), 684-687.

*Souvenirs de la comédie humaine*. Paris: Perrin, 1929.

Taxil, Léo. *M. Drumont, étude psychologique.* Paris: Létouzey et Ané, 1890.

Temerson, H. "Edouard-Adolphe Drumont," *Dictionnaire de biographie française.* Paris: Létouzey et Ané, 1967, vol. XI, pp. 852-854.

Thieme, Hugo P. *Bibliographie de la littérature française de 1800 à 1930.* Paris: Droz, 1933. vol. I, pp. 616-617.

Vanikoff, Maurice. "Documents sur les débuts d'Edouard Drumont," *Evidences,* no. 3 (1949), 15-18.

Viau, Raphaël. *Vingt ans d'antisémitisme. 1889-1909.* Paris: Fasquelle, 1910.

Weill, Alexandre. *La France catholique et athée.* Paris: Dentu, 1886.

*Epîtres cinglantes à M. Drumont.* Paris: Dentu, 1888.

Winock, Michel. "Edouard Drumont et l'antisémitisme en France avant l'affaire Dreyfus," *Esprit,* no. 403, (May 1971), 1085-1106.

*Edouard Drumont et Cie: antisémitisme et fascisme en France* Paris: Seuil, 1982.

"Le Cinquantenaire de *'La Libre Parole',*" *France Européenne,* special edition (20 April 1942), 1-18.

V. Works on the Dreyfus Affair with frequent references to Drumont

Arendt, Hannah. "From the Dreyfus Affair to France Today," *Essays on Antisemitism.* Koppel Pinson, ed. New York: Conference of Jewish Relations, 1946.

*The Origins of Totalitarianism.* New York: Meridian Books, 1958.

*The Jewish as Pariah.* Ron Feldman, ed. New York: Grove Press, 1978.

Barrès, Maurice. *Scènes et doctrines du nationalisme.* Paris: Plon, 1925.

Baumont, Maurice. *Aux Sources de l'affaire: l'affaire Dreyfus d'après les archives diplomatiques.* Paris: Les Productions de Paris, 1959.

Baylen, Joseph. "Dreyfus and the Foreign Press: the Syndicate and the *Daily News*, February-March 1898," *French Historical Studies*, VII, (1972), 332-348.

Boussel, Patrice. *L'Affaire Dreyfus et la presse*. Pris: Colin, 1960.

Bredin, Jean-Denis. *The Affair: The Case of Alfred Dreyfus*. New York: Braziller, 1985.

Brombert, Victor. "Toward a Portrait of the French Intellectual," *The Partisan Review*, XXVII (1960), 480-502.

Bruguerette, Abbé J. *L'Affaire Dreyfus et la mentalité catholique en France*. Paris: 1904.

Burns, Michael. *Rural Society and French Politics: Boulangism and the Dreyfus Affair*. Princeton: Princeton University Press, 1984.

Busi, Frederick. "The Dreyfus Affair and the French Cinema," *The Wiener Library Bulletin*, XXIX, nos. 39/40 (1976), 56-59.

"The Dreyfus Case: An Affair without End," *Judaism*, vol. XXV, no. 1, (Winter 1976), 8-19.

"The First Dreyfus Affair," *Judaism*, vol. xxvii, no. 4. (Fall 1978), 468-475.

"A Bibliographical Overview of the Dreyfus Affair," *Jewish Social Studies*, vol. XL, no. 1, (Winter 1978), 25-40.

Capéran, Louis. *L'Anticléricalisme et l'affaire Dreyfus*, 1897-1899, Toulouse: Imprimérie Régionale, 1948.

Chapman, Guy. *The Dreyfus Case: A Reassessment*. London: Rupert Hart-Davis, 1955.

*The Dreyfus Trials*. New York: Stein and Day, 1972.

Charensol, G. *L'Affaire Dreyfus et la Troisième République*. Paris: Kra, 1930.

Charpentier, Armand. *Historique de l'affaire Dreyfus*. Paris: Fasquelle, 1933.

Chérasse, Jean and Patrice Boussel. *Dreyfus ou l'intolérable vérité*. Paris: Pygmalion, 1975.

Czempiel, Ernest-Otto. *Das Deutsche Dreyfus-Geheimnis*. Munich: Scherz, 1966.

Dardenne, Henriette. *Lumières sur l'affaire Dreyfus*. Paris: Nouvelles Editions Latines, 1964.

Delhorbe, Cecile. *L'Affaire Dreyfus et les ecrivains français*. Paris: Attinger, 1932.

Derfler, Leslie. *The Dreyfus Affair: Tragedy of Errors?* Problems in European Civilization. Lexington, Mass. Heath, 1963.

Dreyfus, Alfred. *Five Years of My Life. 1894-1899*. New York: McClure, Phillips, 1901.

and Pierre Dreyfus. *The Dreyfus Case*. Translated by Donald McKay. New Haven: Yale University Press, 1937.

Dutrait-Crozon, Henri. *Joseph Reinach, historien*. Paris: Savaété, 1905.

*Précis de l'affaire Dreyfus*. Paris: Nouvelle Librairie Nationale, 1909.

Gauthier, Robert. ed. *"Dreyfusards!" Souvenirs de Mathieu Dreyfus et autres inédits*. Paris: Julliard, 1965.

Giscard d'Estaing, Henri. *D'Esterhazy a Dreyfus*. Paris: Plon, 1960

Grand-Carteret, John. *L'Affaire Dreyfus et l'image*. Paris: Flammarion, 1898.

Guillemin, Henri. *L'Enigme Esterhazy*. Paris: Gallimard, 1962.

Halasz, Nicholas. *Captain Dreyfus: The Story of a Mass Hysteria*. New York: Simon and Schuster, 1955.

Iliams, Thomas M. *Dreyfus, Diplomatists, and the Dual Alliance: Gabriel Hanotaux at the Quai d'Orsay. (1894-1898)*. Etudes d'Histoires Economique, Politique et Sociale. Geneva: Droz, 1962.

Jaurès, Jean. *Les Preuves: Affaire Dreyfus.* Paris: La Petite République, 1898.

Johnson, Douglas. *France and the Dreyfus Affair.* New York: Walker, 1966.

Kayser, Jacques. *The Dreyfus Affair.* New York: Covici Friede, 1931.

Kedward, H. R. *The Dreyfus Affair: Catalyst for Tensions in French Society.* London: Longmans, Green, 1965.

Larkin, Maurice. *Church and State after the Dreyfus Affair: The Separation Issue in France.* New York: Barnes and Noble, 1974.

Leblois, Louis. *L'Affaire Dreyfus.* Paris: Quillet, 1929.

Lewis, David. *Prisoners of Honor: the Dreyfus Affair.* New York: William Morrow, 1973.

Lipschutz, Leon. *Bibliographie thématique et analytique de l'affaire Dreyfus.* Paris: Editions Fasquelle, 1970.

Lombarès, Michel de. *L'Affaire Dreyfus: la clef du mystère.* Paris: Laffont, 1972.

Mazel, Henri. *Histoire et psychologique de l'affaire Dreyfus.* Paris: Boivin, 1934.

Miquel, Pierre. *L'Affaire Dreyfus.* Que Sais-Je? Paris: Presses Universitaires de France, 1964.

*Une Enigme? l'Affaire Dreyfus.* Dossier Clio. Paris: Presses Universitaires de France, 1972.

Paléologue, Maurice. *An Intimate Journal of the Dreyfus Case.* New York: Criterion Books, 1957.

Quillard, Pierre. *Le Monument Henry.* Paris: Stock, 1899.

Reinach, Joseph. *Histoire de l'affaire Dreyfus.* 7 vols. Paris: Fasquelle, 1903-1911.

Reinach, Theodore. *Histoire sommaire de l'affaire Dreyfus.* Paris: Ligue des Droits de l'homme, 1924.

Roux, Georges. *L'Affaire Dreyfus.* Paris: Perrin, 1972.

Thomas, Marcel. *L'Affaire sans Dreyfus*. Paris: Fayard, 1961.

Weil, Bruno. *L'Affaire Dreyfus*. Paris: Gallimard, 1930.

"Zola, the Dreyfus Case, and the Anti-Jewish Crusade in France," *Review of Reviews,* XVII, (1898), 309-311, 315-320.

## VI. Additional secondary sources

Ageron, Charles-Robert. *Les Algériens musulmans et la France (1871-1919)* Paris: Presses Universitaires de France, 1968. 2 vols.

Albajat, Antoine. *La Vie de Jesus d'Ernest Renan*. Paris: Malfère, 1933.

Albert, Phyllis Cohen. *The Modernization of French Jewry: Consistory and Community in the Nineteenth Century*. Waltham, Mass. Brandeis University Press, 1977.

Ambès, Baron d'. *Intimate Memoirs of Napoleon III*. Boston: Little, Brown, 1912. vol. II

Angebert, Jean-Michel. *The Occult and the Third Reich*. New York: MacMillan, 1974.

Ansky, Michel. *Les Juifs d'Algérie: du décret Crémieux à la libération*. Paris: Editions du Centre, 1950.

Arnold, Matthew. "Hebraism and Hellenism," *Culture and Anarchy*. Cambridge: Cambridge University Press, 1957.

Aron, Raymond. *De Gaulle, Israel, and the Jews*. New York: Praeger, 1968.

Aubéry, Pierre. *Milieux juifs de la France contemporaine*. Paris: Plon, 1957.

Barrès, Maurice. *Leurs figures*. Paris: Emile Paul, 1911.

and Charles Maurras. *La République ou le roi*. Correspondence, Paris: Plon, 1970.

Baum, Gregory. *Is the New Testament Anti-Semitic?* Glen Rock: Paulist Press, 1960.

Beau de Loménie, Emmanuel. *Les Responsabilités des dynasties bourgeoises.* 5 vols. Paris: Denoel, 1943-1973

Bell, Ernest. *Fighting the Traffic in Young Girls.* New York: Ball and Walter, 1910.

Bellanger, Claude, et al. *Histoire générale de la presse française.* Paris: Presses Universitaires de France, 1969, vol. II.

Belloc, Hilaire. *The Jews.* Boston: Houghton, Mifflin, 1922.

Bernstein, Samuel. *Auguste Blanqui and the Art of Insurrection.* London: Lawrence and Wishart, 1971.

Bessede, Robert. *La Crise de la conscience catholique.* Paris: Klincksieck, 1975.

Biddiss, Michael. *Father of Racist Ideology: The Social and Political Thought of Count Gobineau.* New York: Weybright and Talley, 1970.

Billig, Joseph. *Le Commissariat général aux questions juives.* 3 vols. *(1941-1944)* Paris: Editions du Centre, 1955-1960.

Billy, André. *Les Ecrivains de combat.* Paris: Les Oeuvres Représentatives, 1931.

Blum, Ernest. *Biographie complète de Henri Rochefort.* Bruxelles: Rozez, 1868.

Blum, Léon. *Souvenirs de l'affaire Dreyfus.* Paris: Gallimard, 1935.

Blumenkrantz, Bernhard. *Bibliographie des juifs en France.* Toulouse: Privat, 1974.

*Histoire des Juifs en France.* Toulouse: Privat, 1972.

Blumenthal, Henry. *A Reappraisal of Franco-American Relations. (1830-1871).* Chapel Hill: University of North Carolina, 1959.

Bohlen, Charles. *The Transformation of American Foreign Policy.* New York: Norton, 1969.

Golléry, Joseph. *Léon Bloy.* vol. III. Paris: Albin-Michel, 1954.

Bondy, Louis. *Racketeers of Hatred: Julius Streicher and the Jew Baiters' International.* London: Newman Wolsey, 1946.

Bonnery, Laurent. *Les Journées sanglantes de fevrier 1934.* Paris: Flammarion, 1935.

Bontoux, G. *Louis Veuillot et les mauvais maîtres.* Paris: Perrin, 1911.

Bornecque, Jacques-Henry. *Les Années d'apprentissage d'Alphonse Daudet.* Paris: Nizet, 1951.

Bournand, François. *Les Juifs et nos contemporains.* Paris: Pierret, 1898.

Brabant, Frank. *The Beginnings of the Third Republic in France.* London: MacMillan, 1940.

Bramsted, Ernest. *Aristocracy and the Middle Class in Germany.* Chicago: University of Chicago, 1964.

Brazill, William. *The Young Hegelians.* New Haven: Yale University Press, 1970.

Bouvier, Jean. *Les Deux scandales de Panama.* Paris: Julliard, 1964.

*Le Krach de l'Union Generale.* Paris: Presses Universitaires de France, 1960.

*Les Rothschilds.* Paris: Fayard, 1967.

Britton, J. *A Narrative of Memorable Events in Paris in 1814.* London: Printed for the editor, 1828.

Bury, J.P.T. *Gambetta and the National Defence.* London: Longmans, Green and Co. 1936.

Busi, Frederick. "In the Lair of the Fascist Beast," *Midstream,* vol. XIX, no. 2. (February 1973), 14-24.

Byrnes, Robert. *Antisemitism in Modern France: The Prologue to the Dreyfus Affair.* New Brunswick: Rutgers University Press, 1950.

Cahm, Eric. *Péguy et le nationalisme français.* Paris: Cahiers de l'Amitié Charles Péguy, 1972.

Cambell, Thomas S. J. *The Jesuits.* 2 vols. New York: The Encyclopedia Press, 1921.

Cameron, Ian. *The Impossible Dream: Panama*. London: Hodden and Stoughton, 1971.

Carlebach, Julius. *Karl Marx and the Radical Critique of Judaism*. London: Routledge and Kegan Paul, 1978.

Carter, A. E. *The Idea of Decadence in French Literature*. Toronto: University of Toronto Press, 1958.

Cecil, Robert. *The Myth of the Master Race*. New York: Dodd, Mead, 1972.

Céline, Louis-Ferdinand. *Bagatelles pour un massacre*. Paris: Denoël, 1937.

*L'Ecole des cadavres*. Paris: Denoël, 1938.

Cesare, R. de. *The Last Days of Papal Rome*. Boston; Houghton Mifflin, 1909.

Charles, l'abbé. *Solution de la question juive*. Paris: La Renaissance Française, n.d.

Chastenet, Jacques. *Histoire de la Troisième République*. vols. II and III. Paris: Hachette, 1954, 1955.

Chavardès, Maurice. *Le 6 décembre: la république en danger*. Paris: Calmann-Lévy, 1966.

Chirac, Auguste. *Les Rois de la république: histoire des juiveries*. 2 vols. Paris: Dentu, 1888, 1889.

Chouraqui, Andre. *La Saga des juifs en Afrique du nord*. Paris: Hachette, 1972.

*L'Alliance Israélite Universelle et la renaissance juive contemporaine*. Paris: Presses Universitaires de France, 1965.

Christophe, Lucien. *Louis Veuillot*. Paris: Wesmael-Charlier, 1967.

Cochard, le Chanoine. *La Juiverie d'Orléans*. Orléans: Herluison, 1895.

Cohn, Norman. *Europe's Inner Demons: an Enquiry Inspired by the Great Witch-Hunt*. New York: Basic Books, 1975.

*Warrant for Genocide: the Myth of the Jewish World-Conspiracy and the Protocols of the Elders of Zion*. New York: Harper

206

and Row, 1967.

Corpechot, Louis. *Souvenirs d'un journaliste.* vol. I, Paris: Plon, 1936.

Coston, Henry. *La République de Grand Orient.* Paris: Lectures Françaises, *special number (January 1964).*

Cotta, Michèle. *La Collaboration 1940-1944.* Paris: Colin, 1964.

Crémieux-Foa, Ernest. *La Campagne antisémitique. Les duels. Les responsabilités.* Paris: 1892.

Crosbie, Sylvia Kowitt. *A Tacit Alliance: France and Israel after Suez and the Six Day War.* Princeton: Princeton University Press, 1974.

Cuddihy, John Murray. *The Ordeal of Civility.* New York: Basic Books, 1974.

Cunliffe, Margaret. *The Martyrdom of an Empress.* New York: Harper and Brothers, 1901.

Curtis, Michael. *Three against the Republic: Sorel, Barrès, and Maurras.* Princeton: Princeton University Press, 1959.

Dagan, Henri. *Enquête sur l'antisémitisme.* Paris: Stock, 1899.

Dansette, Adrien. *Les Affaires de Panama.* Paris: Perrin, 1934.

*Histoire religieuse de la France contemporaine.* Paris: Flammarion, 1965.

Daudet, Alphonse. *Les Rois en exil.* Paris: Flammarion, 1879.

Daudet, Léon. *Quand vivait mon père.* Paris: Grasset, 1940.

Davies, Alan. *Anti-Semitism and the Christian Mind.* New York: Herder and Herder, 1969.

Dawidowicz, Lucy. *The War on the Jews. 1933-1945.* New York: Holt Rinehart Winston, 1975.

*The Jewish Presence: Essays on Identity and History.* New York: Holt, Rinehart and Winston, 1977.

Debré, Moses. *The Image of the Jew in French Literature.* New York: Ktav, 1970.

Del Bo, Giuseppe. *La Comune di Parigi.* Milan: Feltrinelli, 1957.

Delamare, Edith, et al. *Infiltrations ennemies dans l'église.* Paris: La Librairie Française, 1970.

Delaporte, Jean. *Connaissance de Peguy.* 2 vols. Paris: Plon, 1944.

Desachy, Paul. *Louis Leblois.* Paris: Rieder, 1934.

Dimier, L. *Les Maîtres de la contre-révolution au dix-neuvieme siecle.* Paris: Nouvelle Librairie Nationale, 1907.

Disraeli, Benjamin. *Coningsby.* New York: The Century Company, 1894.

Dommaget, Maurice. *Histoire du drapeau rouge.* Paris: Edition Libre de l'Etoile, 1967.

Drault, Jean. *Histoire de l'antisémitisme.* Paris: Edition C.-L., 1942.

Dresden, Donald. *The Marquis de Morès.* Norman: University of Oklahoma Press, 1970.

Dubnow, Simon. *History of the Jews in Russia and Poland.* vol. II, Philadelphia: Jewish Publication Society, 1918.

Duprat, François. *Les Mouvements d'extrême droite en France depuis 1944.* Paris: Editions Albatros, 1972.

Dupuy, Aimé. *1870-1871, la guerre, la commune et la presse.* Paris: Colin, 1959.

Duquesne, Jacques. *Les Catholiques français sous l'occupation.* Paris: Grasset, 1966.

Edinger, Edward. *Ego and Archetype.* New York: Putnam, 1972.

Elon, Amos. *Herzl.* New York: Holt, Rinehart and Winston, 1975.

Ettinger, S. "New Trends in the Development of the Jewish People after the First World War," *A History of the Jewish People.* H.H. Ben-Sasson, ed. Cambridge: Harvard University Press, 1976.

Fernand-Laurent, J. C. *Gallic Charter.* Boston: Little Brown, 1944.

Fest, Joachim. *Hitler.* New York: Harcourt Brace Jovanovich,

1973.

Feuerwerker, David. *L'Emancipation des Juifs en France: de l'Ancien Régime a la fin du Second Empire*. Paris: Albin-Michel, 1976.

Flannery, Edward. *The Anguish of the Jews*. New York: Mac-Millan, 1965.

*France de l'affaire Dreyfus a nos jours*. Catalogue no. 1. Paris: Bibliothèque du Centre de Documentation Juive Contemporaine, 1964.

*France, le troisieme Reich, Israel.* Catalogue no. 2. Paris: Bibliothèque du Centre Documentation Juive Contemporaine, 1968.

*France during the German Occupation.* 3 vols. Stanford: The Hoover Institute, 1957.

Frank, Walter. *Nationalismus und Demokratie im Frankreich der dritten Republik*. Hamburg: Hanseatische Verlaganstalt, 1933.

Friedman, Lee. *Zola and the Dreyfus Case*. New York: Haskell House, 1966.

Gaiglas, Vytas. *Ernest Renan and his French Catholic Critics*. North Quincy, Mass. Christopher House, 1972.

Gallo, Max. *Cinquieme colonne: 1930-1940*. Paris: Plon, 1970.

Gautherot, Gustave. *Thiers et Mgr Darboy*. Paris: Plon, 1910.

Gayraud, l'abbé Hippolyte. *L'Antisemitisme de Saint-Thomas d'Aquin*. Paris: Dentu, 1896.

Girard, Patrick. *Les Juifs de France de 1789 a 1860, de l'emancipation a l'egalite*. Paris: Calmann-Levy, 1976.

Girard, Rene. *La Violence et le sacré*. Paris: Grasset, 1972.

Girardet, Raoul. *Le Nationalisme français 1871-1914*. Paris: Colin, 1966.

Giraudoux, Jean. *Pleins pouvoirs*. Paris: Gallimard, 1939.

Glock, Charles and Rodney Stark. *Christian Beliefs and Anti-Semitism*. New York: Harper and Row, 1966.

Goncourt, Edmond and Jules. *Paris and the Arts: from the Goncourt Journal.* George Becker and Edith Philips, ed. Ithaca: Cornell University Press, 1971.

Gordon, Bertram M. *Collaborationism in France during the Second World War.* Ithaca: Cornell University Press, 1980.

Gougenot des Mousseaux, Henri. *Emancipation aux Antilles.* Paris: Darvoir et Fontain, 1844.

*Les Hauts phénomènes de la magie.* Paris: Plon, 1865.

*Les Juifs, le judaïsme et la judaïsation des peuples chrétiens.* Paris: Plon, 1869.

*Des Prolétaires.* Paris: Mellier, 1846.

Griffiths, Richard. *The Reactionary Revolution: The Catholic Revival in French Literature. 1870-1914.* New York: Frederick Ungar, 1965.

Guerard, Albert Leon. *French Civilization in the Nineteenth Century.* New York: The Century Company, 1914.

Guichard, Max. *La Musique et les lettres en France au temps du wagnérisme.* PAris: Presses Universitaires de France, 1963.

Gutman, Robert. *Richard Wagner: the Man, his Mind, and his Music.* New York: Harcourt, Brace and World, 1968.

Halévy, Daniel. *The End of the Notables.* Middletown, Conn. Wesleyan University Pess, 1974.

*My Friend Degas.* Middletown, Conn. Wesleyan University Press. 1964.

Hanotaux, Gabriel. *Histoire de la France contemporaine.* 4 vols. Paris: Ancienne Librairie Furne, n.d.

Harkabi, Yehoshafat. *Arab Attitudes to Israel.* Jerusalem: Israeli Universities Press, 1972.

Harris, Joseph. *The Tallest Tower.* Boston: Houghton Mifflin, 1975.

Haslip, Joan. *The Sultan: the Life of Abdul Hamid II.* New York: Holt, Rinehart and Winston, 1973.

210

Hay, Malcolm. *Europe and the Jews.* Boston: Beacon Press, 1961.

Hayes, Carlton. *A Generation of Materialism 1871-1900.* New York: Harper and Row, 1941.

Hausser, Elizabeth. *Paris au jour le jour. Les Evénements vus par la presse, 1900-1919.* Paris: Editions de Minuit, 1968.

Heer, Friedrich. *God's First Love: Christians and Jews over Two Thousand Years.* London: Weidenfeld and Nicolson, 1967.

Heine, Heinrich. *Lutezia.* Leipzig: Insel, 1959.

Hemmings, F.W.J. *Culture and Society in France 1848-1898: Dissidents and Philistines.* London: B.T. Batsford Ltd., 1971.

Herriot, Edouard. *In Those Days.* New York: Old and New World Press, n.d.

Hertzberg, Arthur. *The French Enlightenment and the Jews.* New York: Columbia University Press, 1968.

Herzog, Wilhelm. *From Dreyfus to Pétain: The Struggle of a Republic.* New York: Creative Arts Press, 1947.

Huysmans, Joris-Karl. *La Cathédrale.* Paris: Stock, 1899.

Hyman, Paula. *From Dreyfus to Vichy: The Remaking of French Jewry, 1906-1939.* New York: Columbia University Press, 1979.

Israël, Alexandre. *L'Ecole de la République: la grande oeuvre de Jules Ferry.* Paris: Hachette, 1931.

Jab. *Le Sang chrétien dans les rites de la synagogue moderne.* Paris: Gautier, 1889.

Jacquet, A. J. *République plébiscitaire: mémoire sur les pratiques d'arriver à l'anéantissement de la patrimoine juives en France.* Paris: Nouvelle Bibliothèque Nationale, 1897.

Jahoda, Gustav. *The Psychology of Superstition.* Harmondsworth: Peguin Books, 1969.

Jehouda, Joshé. *Les Cinq étapes du judaïsme émancipé.* Geneva: Editions Synthésis, 1942.

Juin, Hubert. *Ecrivains de l'avant-siecle.* Paris: Seghers, 1972.

Jurt, Joseph. *Les Attitudes politiques de Georges Bernanos.* Fribourg: Editions Universitaires, 1968.

Katz, Jacob. *From Prejudice to Destruction: Antisemitism, 1700-1933.* Cambridge, Mass. Harvard University Press, 1980.

Knapp, Bettina. *Céline: Man of Hate.* University: University of Alabama Press, 1974.

Kropotkin, Peter. *Memoirs of a Revolutionist.* Cambridge, Mass.: Houghton Mifflin, 1899.

Kubizek, August. *The Young Hitler I Knew.* New York: Tower, 1955.

Labroue, Henri. *Voltaire antijuif.* Paris: Les Documents Contemporains, 1942.

Laloum, Jean. *La France antisémite de Darquier de Pellepoix.* Paris: Editions Syros, 1979.

Lawton, Frederick. *The Third French Republic.* Philadelphia: Lippincott, 1909.

Lazare, Bernard. *Antisemitism: Its History and Causes.* New York: International Library Press, 1903.

*Une Erreur judiciaire.* Bruxelles: Monnom, 1896.

Lecache, Bernard. *Séverine.* Paris: Gallimard, 1930.

Lecanuet, R. P. *L'Eglise de France sous la Troisième République.* 4 vols. Paris: Felix-Alcan, 1930-1931.

Lehrmann, Charles. *The Jewish Element in French Literature.* Rutherford: Fairleigh Dickenson University Press, 1971.

Leroy-Beaulieu, Anatole. *L'Antisémitisme.* Paris: Calmann-Lévy, 1897.

Lewy, Guenther. *The Catholic Church and Nazi Germany.* New York: McGraw-Hill, 1964.

Lidsky, Paul. *Les Ecrivains contre la Commune.* Paris: Maspéro, 1970.

Littel, Franklin H. *The Crucifixion of the Jews: The Failure of Christians to understand the Jewish Experience.* New York:

212

Harper and Row, 1975.

Livi, Francois. *J.-K. Huysmans, A Rebours et l'esprit décadent.* Paris: La Renaissance du Livre, 1972.

Livois, René. *Histoire de la presse française.* vol. II, Lausanne: Editions Seps, 1965.

Lolié, Frédéric. *Frère de l'empéreur, le duc de Morny.* Paris: Emile-Paul, 1909.

Lougée, Robert. *Paul de Lagarde 1827-1891: A Study of Radical Conservatism in Germany.* Cambridge, Mass. Harvard University Press, 1962.

Lovsky, F. *Antisémitisme et mystère d'Israël.* Paris: Albin-M-Michel, 1955.

Lubetzki, J. *La Condition des juifs en France sous l'occupation allemande.* Paris: Editions du Centre, 1954.

Magalaner, Marvin. *Time of Apprenticeship: The Fiction of Young James Joyce.* New York: Abelard: Schuman, 1959.

Maillard, Firmin. *Histoire des journaux publiés à Paris pendant le siège.* Paris: Dentu, 1871.

Mann, Thomas. "Richard Wagner and the Ring," *Essays of Three Decades.* Trans. H. T. Lowe-Porter. New York: Knopf, 1947.

Manévy, Raymond. *La Presse française.* Paris: Foret, 1950.

Marchal de Bussy, Charles. *Les Apôtres de Renan.* Paris: Beaufour, 1866.

*Dictionnaire amusant.* Paris: Delahaye, 1859.

*Vie de Judas.* Paris: Publications Populaires, 1866.

Marx, Karl. *Critique of Hegel's Philosophy of Right.* Trans. Annette Jolin and Joseph O'Malley. Cambridge: Cambridge Univeristy Press, 1970.

*On the Jewish Question. Collected Works.* vol. 4, New York: International Publishers, 1975.

Marrus, Michael. *The Politics of Assimilation: A Study of the French Jewish Community at the Time of the Dreyfus Affair.*

Oxford: Clarendon, 1971.

and Robert O. Paxton. *Vichy et les juifs*. Paris: Calmann-Lévy, 1981.

Martin, Benjamin F. *Count Albert de Mun: Paladin of the Third Republic*. Chapel Hill: The University of North Carolina Press, 1978.

Mayeur, Jean-Marie. "Les Congrés nationaux de la Démocratie chrétienne à Lyons 1896-1898," *Revue d'Histoire moderne et contemporaine*. (July-September) 1962. 171-206.

Memmi, Albert. *Portrait of a Jew*. Trans. Elisabeth Abbot. New York: Orion, 1962.

Méry, Gaston. *Les Apparitions de Tilly*. Paris: Fayard, n.d.

*La Voyante de la rue de Paradis*. Paris: Dentu, n.d.

Meyer, Arthur. *Ce que mes yeux ont vu*. Paris: Plon, 1911.

*Ce que je peux dire*. Paris: Plon, 1912.

Meynie, Georges. *L'Algérie juive*. Paris: Nouvelle Librairie Parisienne, 1887.

Micaud, Charles. *The French Right and Nazi Germany*. Durham: Duke University Press, 1943.

Michaelis, Meir. *Mussolini and the Jews: German-Italian Relations, and the Jewish Question in Italy 1922-1945*. Oxford: The Clarendon Press, 1979.

Milner, Max. *Le Diable dans la littérature française*. 2 vols. Paris: Corti, 1960.

Misrahi, Robert. *Marx et la question juive*. Paris: Gallimard, 1972.

Mitchell, Alan. "La Mentalité xénophobe: contre-espionnage et racines de l'affaire Dreyfus," *Revue d'histoire moderne et contemporaine* 29 (July 1982): 489-99.

Molnar, Thomas. *The Decline of the Intellectual*. New York: Meriden, 1961.

Montefiore, C. G. *The Synoptic Gospels*. London: MacMillan, 1927.

214

Morain, Alfred. *The Underworld of Paris.* New York: Blue Ribbon, 1931.

Morin, Edgar. *La Rumeur d'Orléans.* Paris: Seuil, 1969.

Mosse, George L. *Toward the Final Solution: A History of European Racism.* London: Dent & Sons, 1978.

Newman, Ernest. *The Life of Richard Wagner,* vol. II. New York: Knopf, 1965.

Newman, Louis Israel. *Jewish Influences on Christian Reform Movements.* New York: Columbia University Press, 1925.

Nitti, Francesco. *Catholic Socialism.* London: George Allen, 1911.

Noland, Aaron. *The Founding of the French Socialist Party.* Cambridge, Mass. Harvard University Press, 1956.

Nolte, Ernst. *Three Faces of Fascism: Action Française Italian Fascism, National Socialism.* Trans. Leila Vennewitz. New York: Holt,Rinehart Winston, 1966.

Osgood, Samuel. *French Royalism since 1870.* The Hague: Martinus Nijhoff, 1970.

Pagés, Léon."Le Chevalier Gougenot des Mousseaux et ses travaux sur la magie contemporaine," *Annales de Philosophie chrétienne.* no. 82 (October 1977), 306.

Parkes, James. *The Emergence of the Jewish Problem 1878-1939.* London: Oxford University Press, 1948.

Partin, Malcolm. *Waldeck-Rousseau, Combes and the Church.* Durham: Duke University Press, 1969.

Parthurier, Maurice. *Morny et son temps.* Paris: Hachette, 1969.

Paxton, Robert. *Parades and Politics at Vichy: French Officer Corps under Marshall Pétain.* Princeton: Princeton University Press, 1966.

*Vichy France: Old Guard and New Order 1940-1944.* New York: Knopf, 1972.

Petit, Jacques. *Bernanos, Bloy, Claudel, Péguy: quatre écrivains catholiques face à Israël.* Paris: Calmann-Lévy, 1972.

Peyre, Henri. *Qu'est-ce que le symbolisme?* Paris: Presses Universitaires de France, 1974.

Philips, C. S. *The Church in France.* vol. I. London: Mowbray, 1929.

Picard, Edmond. *L'Aryano-sémitisme.* Bruxelles: Lacomblez, 1898.

Pierrard, Pierre. *Juifs et catholiques français.* Paris: Fayard, 1970.

Ploncard d'Assac, Jacques. *Doctrines du nationalisme.* Paris: Librairie Française, 1958.

Poliakov, Léon. *De l'antisionisme à l'antisémitisme.* Paris: Calmann-Levy, 1969.

*Histoire de l'antisémitisme.* 4 vols. Paris: Calmann-Levy, 1955-1977.

and Jacques Sabille. *Jews under the Italian Occupation.* Paris: Editions du Centre, 1955.

*The Aryan Myth: A History of Racist and Nationalist Ideas in Europe.* Trans. Edmund Howard. New York: Basic Books, 1974.

Polonski, Jacques. *La Presse et la propaganda et l'opinion publique sous l'occupation.* Paris: Editions du Centre, 1946.

Power, Thomas. *Jules Ferry and the Renaissance of French Imperialism.* New York: King's Crown Press, 1944.

Plumyène, J. amd R. Lasierra. *Les Fascismes français 1923-1963.* Paris: Seuil, 1963.

Prajs, Lazare. *La Fallacité de l'oeuvre romanesque des freres Goncourt.* Paris: Nizet, 1974.

Praz, Mario. *The Romantic Agony.* Trans. Angus Davidson, London: Oxford University Press, 1954.

216

Pulzer, P.G.J. *The Rise of Political Anti-Semitism in Germany and Austria.* New York: John Wiley: 1964.

Rabi, W. *Anatomie du judaïsme francais.* Paris: Editions de Minuit, 1962.

Raffalovitch, Arthur. *L'Abominable vénalité de la presse.* Paris: Librairie du Travail, 1931.

Raitt, A. W. *Villiers de l'Isle-Adam et le mouvement symboliste.* Paris: Corti, 1965.

Ramsay, W. M. *Impressions of Turkey.* New York: Putnam, 1967.

Rebatet, Lucien. *Les Décombres.* Paris: Denoël, 1942.

Reinharz, Jehuda. *Fatherland or Promised Land: The Dilemma of the German Jew 1893-1914.* Ann Arbor: University of Michigan Press, 1975.

Rémond, René. *The Right Wing in France: From 1815 to de Gaulle.* Trans. James M. Vaux. Philadelphia: University of Pennsylvania Press, 1966.

Reynaud, Léonce. *Les Français Israélites.* Paris: Lahure, 1901.

Ridge, George Ross. *The Hero in French Decadent Literature.* Athens: University of Georgia Press, 1961.

Robertson, Priscilla. *Revolutions of 1848: A Social History.* New York: Harper and Row, 1960.

Rochefort, Henri. *The Adventures of My Life.* Trans. Ernest W. Smith. 2 vols. London: Arnold, 1896.

Rollet, Henri. *L'Action sociale des catholiques en France.* Paris: Editions Contemporaines, Boivin, n.d.

Ruether, Rosemary. *Faith and Fratricide: The Theological Roots of Anti-Semitism.* New York: Seabury Press, 1974.

Sachar, Abram Leon. *A History of the Jews.* New York: Knopf, 1955.

Sachs, Murray. *The Career of Alphonse Daudet.* Cambridge, Mass. Harvard University Press, 1965.

Sans, Edouard. *Richard Wagner et la pensée schopenhauerienne.*

Paris; Klincksieck, 1969.

Saint-André, C. C. de. *Francs-Maçons et juifs: sixième âge de l'église d'après l'apocalypse.* Paris: Société Générale de Librairie Catholique, 1881.

Saint-Paulien, Maurice-Ivan. *Histoire de la collaboration.* Paris: L'Esprit Nouveau, 1964.

Sartre, Jean-Paul. *Portrait of an Antisemite.* Trans. Eric de Mauny. London: Secker and Warburg, 1948.

Schorsch, Ismar. *Jewish Reactions to German Anti-Semitism, 1870-1914.* New York: Columbia University Press, 1972.

Sedwick, Alexander. *The Ralliement in French Politics, 1890-1898.* Cambridge, Mass. Harvard University Press, 1967.

Serant, Paul. *Le Romantisme fasciste: étude sur l'oeuvre politique de quelques écrivains français.* Paris: Fasquelle, 1959.

Servières, Georges. *Richard Wagner juge en France.* Paris: Librairie Illustrée, 1887.

*Tannhauser à l'opéra en 1895.* Paris: Fischbacher, 1895.

Shaw, George Bernard.  *The Perfect Wagnerite.* New York: Dover, 1967.

Sicard, Maurice-Ivan. *La Commune de Paris contre le communisme.* Paris: Etudes et Documents, 1944.

Siegfried, André. *Suez and Panama.* New York: Harcourt Brace, 1940.

Simon, Maron. *The Panama Affair.* New York: Scribner's 1971.

Soderini, Eduardo. *The Pontificate of Leo XIII.* Trans. Barbara Barclay Carter. vol. I, London: Burns, Oates and Washburne, 1934.

Sokoloff, Alice Hunt. *Cosima Wagner.* New York: Dodd, Mead, 1969.

Soltau, Roger. *French Political Thought in the 19th Century.* New York: Russell and Russell, 1959.

Sombart, Werner. *The Jews and Modern Capitalism.* London:

T. Fischer Unwin, 1913.

Sorlin, Pierre. *La Croix et les juifs (1880-1899).* Paris: Grasset, 1967.

Soucy, Robert. *Fascism in France: The Case of Maurice Barrès.* Berkley: University of California Press, 1972.

Southern, R. W. *Western Views of Islam in the Middle Ages.* Cambridge, Mass. Harvard University Press, 1954.

Spencer, Philip. *Politics of Belief in 19th Century France: Lacordaire, Michon, Veuillot.* New York: Grove Press, 1954.

Spire, André. *Souvenirs a batons rompus.* Paris: Albin-Michel, 1962.

Starkie, Enid. *Petrus Borel: The Lycanthrope.* New York: New Directions, 1954.

Stern, Fritz. *Gold and Iron: Bismarck, Bleichröder, and the Building of the German Empire.* New York: Knopf, 1977.

Stern, Leon. *The Racial Thinking of Richard Wagner.* New York: Philopsophical Library, 1950.

Sternhell, Zeev. *Maurice Barres et le nationalisme français.* Paris: Colin, 1972.

*La Droite révolutionnaire 1885-1914: les origines françaises du fascisme.* Paris: Seuil, 1978.

Stewart, Desmond. *The Middle East: Temple of Janus.* New York: Doubleday, 1971.

Strack, Hermann. *The Jews and Human Sacrifice: Human Blood in Jewish Ritual.* Trans. H.F.E. Blanchamp. New York: Benjamin Bloom, 1971.

Svirsky, Grigory. *Hostages: The Personal Testimony of a Soviet Jew.* Trans. Gordon Clough. New York: Knopf, 1976.

Szajowksi, Zosa. *Jews and the French Revolutions.* New York: Ktav, 1970.

"Di Yidn in der Pariser Komune," *Yidn in Frankraikh.* (in Yiddish), New York: YIVO, 1942.

Taxil, Leo. *Confessions d'un ex-libre penseur.* Paris: Létouzey et Ané, n.d.

Tharaud, Jérôme and Jean. *Pour les fidèles de Péguy.* Paris: Cahiers de la Quinzaine, 1927.

Thierry, Augustin. *Les Grandes mystifications littéraires.* vol. II, Paris: Plon, 1913.

Tilloy, A. *Le Péril Judéo-Maçonnique--le Mal--le Remède.* Paris: Librairie Antisémite, 1897.

Tison-Braun, Micheline. *La Crise de l'humanisme.* 2 vols. Paris: Nizet, 1958, 1968.

Toussenel, Alphonse. *Les Juifs, rois de l'époque.* 2 vols. Paris: Marpon, 1886.

Trachtenberg, Joshua. *The Devil and the Jews: The Medieval Conception of the Jew and its Relation to Modern Anti-Semitism.* New Haven: Yale University Press, 1943.

Trocase, F. *L'Autriche juive.* Paris: Pierret, 1899.

Vandam, Albert. *Men and Manners of the Third Republic.* New York: Pott and Co., 1904.

Viau, Raphaël and François Bournand. *Les Femmes d'Israël.* Paris: Pierret, 1890.

Viereck, Peter. *Meta-Politics: The Roots of the Nazi Mind.* New York: Capricorn, 1960.

Villemessant, Hippolyte. *Le Diable a Quatre.* 1868.

*Mémoires d'un journaliste.* 6 vols. Paris: Dentu, 1878-1884.

Verdes-Leroux, Jeannine. *Scandale financier et l'antisémitisme catholique.* Paris: Le Centurion, 1969.

Vogüé, Charles-Jean Melchior de. *Notes sue le temple de Jérusalem.* Paris: Didier, 1863.

*Le Temple de Jérusalem.* Paris: Noblet et Baudry, 1864.

Wagner, Richard. "Judaism in Music," *Stories and Essays.* Charles Osborne, ed. New York: The Library Press, 1973.

Washburn, Elihu. *Recollections of a Minister to France.* vol. I. New York: Scribner's, 1887.

Weber, Eugen. *Action Française.* Stanford: Stanford University zess, 1962.

*The Nationalist Revival in France 1905-1914.* Berkeley: University of California Press, 1959.

*Satan franc-maçon: la mystification de Léo Taxil.* Paris: Julliard, 1964.

*Varieties of Fascism: Doctrines of Revolution in the Twentieth Century.* New York: Van Nostrand Reinhold, 1964.

Whiteside, Andrew G. *The Socialism of Fools: Georg Ritter von Schonerer and Austrian Pan-Germanism.* Berkeley: University of California Press, 1975.

Willard, Claude. *Les Guesdistes: le mouvement socialiste en France (1893-1905).* Paris: Editions Sociales, 1965.

Williams, Rogers. *The French Revolution of 1870-1871.* New York: Norton, 1969.

*Henri Rochefort: Prince of the Gutter Press.* New York: Scribner's, 1966.

Wilson, Nelly. *Bernard-Lazare: Antisemitism and the problem of Jewish Identity in Late Nineteenth Century France.* Cambridge: Cambridge University Press, 1978.

Wilson, Steven. "The Antisemitic Riots of 1898 in France," *Historical Journal,* vol. XVI, (1973), 789-806.

"Antisemitism and Jewish Responses in France during the Dreyfus Affair," *European Studies Review.* vol. VI (1976).

"Antisemitism in France during La Belle Epoque,"*Wiener Library Bulletin,* vol. XXIX (1976), 2-8.

"Catholic Populism in France at the Time of the Dreyfus Affair: *The Union Nationale,"* *Journal of Contemporary History,* vol. 10, no. 4 (October 1975), 667-705.

*Ideology and Experience: Antisemitism in France at the Time of the Dreyfus Affair.* Rutherford, New Jersey: Fairleigh Dickinson University Press, 1982.

Winock, Michel and Jean-Pierre Azéma. *La III<sup>e</sup> Republique (1870-1940)*. Paris: Calmann-Lévy, 1970.

Wistrich, Robert. "French Socialists and the Dreyfus Affair," *Wiener Library Bulletin*. vol. XXVIII (1975), 9-20.

*Revolutionary Jews from Marx to Trotsky*. New York: Barnes and Noble, 1976.

Wolitz, Seth. *The Proustian Community*. New York: New York University Press, 1971.

Wright, Gordon. *France in Modern Times*. Chicago: Rand Mc Nally, 1960.

Zeldin, Theodore. *The Political System of Napoleon III*. New York: Norton and Company, 1971.

*France 1848-1945*. vol. I, *Ambition, Love and Politics*. vol. II, *Intellect, Taste and Anxiety*. Oxford: Clarendon Press, 1973, 1977.

Zévaès, Alexandre. *Au Temps du Boulangisme*. Paris: Gallimard, 1930.

Zola, Emile. *La Vérité en marche*. Paris: Fasquelle, 1929.

# Index